T0312131

Buen Vivir as an Alternative to Sustainable Development

Until recently, the concept of Buen Vivir has only been loosely articulated by practising communities and in progressive policy in countries like Ecuador. What it actually means has been unclear, and in the case of policy, contradictory. As such there has been a lack of understanding about exactly what Buen Vivir entails, its core principles, and how to put it into practice. This book, based on extensive theoretical and field research of Buen Vivir as an alternative to sustainable development, fills that gap and offers a concrete way forward. It uses an ethnographic study in Cotacachi County, in Ecuador's highland communities, to explore how communities understand and practice Buen Vivir. Combining this with what we already know about the concept theoretically, the book then develops a framework for Buen Vivir with 17 principles for practice.

Exploring Buen Vivir's evolution from its indigenous origins, academic interpretations, and implications for development policy, to its role in endogenous, community-led change, this book will be of interest to policy-makers and development professionals. It will also be of great value to activists, students, and scholars of sustainability and development seeking grassroots social and environmental change.

Natasha Chassagne is an Adjunct Research Fellow at Swinburne University of Technology's Centre for Social Impact, Australia. Natasha's doctoral research looked at the viability of Buen Vivir as an alternative to Sustainable Development. Natasha is a political scientist by training in international law and international relations, specialising in human rights and environmental law. She has worked as a Sustainability Consultant, and writes and researches on sustainability, wellbeing, and climate change issues.

Routledge Studies in Sustainable Development

This series uniquely brings together original and cutting-edge research on sustainable development. The books in this series tackle difficult and important issues in sustainable development including: values and ethics; sustainability in higher education; climate compatible development; resilience; capitalism and de-growth; sustainable urban development; gender and participation; and well-being.

Drawing on a wide range of disciplines, the series promotes interdisciplinary research for an international readership. The series was recommended in the *Guardian*'s suggested reads on development and the environment.

Buen Vivir as an Alternative to Sustainable Development

Lessons from Ecuador

Natasha Chassagne

Routledge
Taylor & Francis Group

LONDON AND NEW YORK

First published 2021
by Routledge
2 Park Square, Milton Park, Abingdon, Oxon OX14 4RN

and by Routledge
52 Vanderbilt Avenue, New York, NY 10017

Routledge is an imprint of the Taylor & Francis Group, an informa business

© 2021 Natasha Chassagne

The right of Natasha Chassagne to be identified as author of this work
has been asserted by her in accordance with sections 77 and 78 of the
Copyright, Designs and Patents Act 1988.

All rights reserved. No part of this book may be reprinted or reproduced or
utilised in any form or by any electronic, mechanical, or other means, now
known or hereafter invented, including photocopying and recording, or in
any information storage or retrieval system, without permission in writing
from the publishers.

Trademark notice: Product or corporate names may be trademarks or
registered trademarks, and are used only for identification and explanation
without intent to infringe.

British Library Cataloguing-in-Publication Data
A catalogue record for this book is available from the British Library

Library of Congress Cataloging-in-Publication Data
A catalog record has been requested for this book

ISBN: 978-0-367-90143-1 (hbk)
ISBN: 978-1-003-02307-4 (ebk)

Typeset in Times New Roman
by Deanta Global Publishing Services, Chennai, India

To my children Alexandre and Zara, for whom I am fighting for a better world. And for Antoine, for his unending, unfaltering support and patience along the way.

Contents

Tables

Preface

The world is in peril. Sustainable Development has failed to achieve its social and environmental goals to end poverty and social injustice and to protect the environment and its peoples against the impacts of climate change. As an alternative but derivative model to traditional development, it was mandated with cleaning up the mess that its parent concept left behind. What we need now is to look towards alternatives to Sustainable Development, rather than another reformulation of the status quo.

It is in this predicament that I propose Buen Vivir as a practical and viable alternative to mainstream, neoliberal Sustainable Development – and one that can provide a concrete course of action, driven by communities for local needs.

By practical and viable, I mean a practical alternative that has political implications which change the present structure of economic and social relations; but also, one that is an endogenous, community-led process for change that goes beyond policy, discourse, and government rhetoric to improve social and environmental wellbeing, and that is biocentric in its approach.

Let me start by explaining a little bit about how I came to discover Buen Vivir. I was previously employed by a sustainability consulting company working with clients in various sectors. Of these clients, I often worked with major multinational resource extraction companies who would employ us to work with the communities in which they operate to understand the material environmental and social issues directly affecting and being affected by the communities. When working with these communities, I started to notice a coherent dialogue coming through: "Our real needs are not being met." Additionally, I could not turn my back to the environmental consequences of the actions of the companies who were instituting programs and projects under the guise of Sustainable Development. At the same time congruent discussions about the contradictions underlying the terminology of sustainability or Sustainable Development started emerging amongst professionals in this area.

Late 2011 to early 2012, I volunteered independently with seven different communities which make up the Cuellaje Parish in Cotacachi County in Ecuador, under guidance from a local advisor to the council. The aim of my volunteer project was to use my knowledge and experience in sustainability to help build local capacity for Sustainable Development; though these communities had already established perspectives and practices rooted in culture and tradition that seemed to me to address some of the issues around Sustainable Development, supported by the worldview of Buen Vivir. The people I met during this time epitomised Buen Vivir. They talked to me about Buen Vivir, and how they wish for an alternative way of doing things. I strongly felt that we could learn valuable lessons from them about wellbeing and sustainability.

I found that one of the most vital aspects of Buen Vivir is the nature of the relationship between society and the environment that supports it. In Western development language we may refer to the earth or land by the generic term "environment" but the Spanish word "*medio-ambiente*" has limited meaning as I was told on several occasions by my informants, both Indigenous and non-Indigenous. When I asked what the environment means to them, many replied that the term is incomplete. *Medio* meaning "half" and *ambiente* meaning "environment" – for them it implied a break with the environment, a disconnection to their earth. This is demonstrated by a deep and reciprocal connection to the land, supported by culture and language.

This reciprocity underlines livelihoods. There is a high dependence on small-scale agriculture to sustain livelihoods, and these traditional ways of life are vulnerable to environmental changes brought on by the effects of climate change, a history of heavy deforestation, and the threats like water and soil contamination that large-scale extractive projects pose in the region. Alternate and more sustainable options are continually discussed as more desirable methods.

During the project, community members broached several challenges to me, but the most significant was defining what sustainability meant for the parish in the wider context of an extractive economy. Community members were concerned about having large-scale extractive projects within their parish and, similarly, were uninterested in Western-style development. They saw a need to develop alternatives – in particular Buen Vivir – as a means of promoting and encouraging protection of their culture, society, and region's rich biodiversity. I wanted to delve deeper into its understanding, and so I spent the next few years researching it as part of my doctoral thesis.

This is an appropriate juncture to briefly explain a little about the methodology behind this research. My research is both theoretical and empirical and draws on a multidisciplinary approach that includes social science, anthropology, development studies, and political science. It is a qualitative study based on original fieldwork, the aim of which was to understand the nature of Buen Vivir as a concept, and how it is understood and practiced on the ground by examining experiences and knowledge. I did this through an ethnographic study, returning to Cotacachi County in Ecuador. The study included a series of semi-structured interviews with key informants, fieldwork observation, and discourse analysis.

Additionally, I had many informal conversations with community members in Cotacachi County about these issues, pertinent to Buen Vivir. These conversations constituted part of my data in the form of observations and "field notes." I generally carried either a notebook and/or my tablet everywhere I went to record key aspects of these observations, which I would later fill in with richer detail.

On other occasions I profited from the knowledge and contacts of my research assistant to be able to attend community meetings as a non-participant observer. This allowed me to observe the issues that were unfolding in the community without having any biased influence on the events. I had the opportunity to attend such meetings on several occasions, and for reasons for protecting the privacy of those attending, I will not specifically name which events they were, but they included meetings held for economic, social, and environmental purposes. More publicly, I was fortunate to attend a meeting as part of the local government's participatory budgeting processes. These meetings provided rich insights into local practices and ways of thinking and doing development.

Through my observations and interviews (participant and non-participant) I was able to gather many documents relevant to the topic. Additionally, I kept an eye on the local and national newspapers daily, both online and in public spaces, and collected articles relevant to the themes emerging on Buen Vivir. Daily media played a central role in my data collection, where I would collect, gather, and take notes from relevant sources. The National Dialogue by former President Correa, "Enlace Cuidadano," was broadcast on the radio weekly on Saturdays from the television show of the same name.

When I was not out in the field, I would listen to the broadcast to give me an idea of the policy direction from the Correa government. Sunday evenings I would watch a television show called "Buen Vivir – Ama la Vida," which discussed issues and questions around the government's interpretation of Buen Vivir. All these analyses have formed part of the co-construction of a practical pathway for Buen Vivir outlined in this book. It is my hope that this book provides you, the reader, with a practical way forward.

On a final note, I feel it crucial to the legitimacy of Buen Vivir in practice to note the inherent problems with terminology around Sustainable Development and sustainability, which have been discussed in both academia and development practice. The aim of this research has been not to replicate the same errors with Buen Vivir. However, everything must start with a term, and it is in the ways in which it is used that will more likely dictate its co-option, or not.

I am mindful of the issues involved in taking a Spanish term that has already lost a great deal of its substantive meaning after being translated from Kichwa, and subsequently translating it into English. I am also cognizant of the need to respect the Indigenous origins of the concept to avoid its co-optation by the dominant ideology, and dominant language (English). I argue, however, that if we are to decolonise "development" to seriously consider different ways of knowing and doing for wide-scale change, then we need to step outside of the core–periphery binary and vocalise these alternatives within the dominant structures; otherwise we are "preaching to the converted." Therefore, on occasion there may be a need to translate the term into the relevant working language, in this case English, and in a way that reflects the nature of the concept and its aims. This is the case in developing a framework for implementation. For this reason, I have occasionally interchangeably used the terms "Buen Vivir," "Good Life," and "Sumak Kawsay"; and "Vivir Bien", "Good Living" and "Suma Qamaña" respectively.

However, throughout this research I have primarily opted to keep use of the Spanish term.

I am also mindful of the possible of co-optation of these other voices that originate from Indigenous beliefs, as has been done in the past. The way Buen Vivir has evolved in recent years, and certainly the way it has been analysed in this research looks to its co-construction – an important way of approaching such a plural concept. It is about letting other voices be heard. We have so much to learn from decolonising the discussions about sustainability and wellbeing, and it is the only feasible and viable way that we can depart from the status quo. At this desperate point in our world's history, with climate change increasing its impacts and wellbeing rapidly declining, we need to change the way the world works, and the way we think, and this means empowering these other voices for solutions.

Before I go on, I would like to acknowledge the many things and people for which I am deeply grateful in this research, and that I hold close to my heart. The first is to the people of Cotacachi County in Ecuador, who inspired this project on the first place, by sharing with me their beliefs and values and their quest for Buen Vivir, the Good Life. My PhD supervisors Prof. Robyn Eversole and A/ Prof. Fred Gale provided such invaluable guidance and I am forever grateful. A special thanks – muchísimas gracias – to my local research assistant Carolina Carrión, without whom the fieldwork component of this research might not have been possible. Last but certainly not least is my family, especially my very supporting and patient husband Antoine, who has been both a rock and a sounding board throughout, and of course my beautiful children Alexandre and Zara, who were both born during the research journey.

Introduction

Neoliberal development has not worked and is not working. Development introduced colonialism, the industrial revolution, and capitalism, all of which have contributed to climate change and the social and ecological collapse we are now living in (IPCC 2015). This acknowledgement at the global policy level was a key driver behind Sustainable Development, which aims for intergenerational ecological sustainability while paradoxically continuing an economic growth trajectory.

Environmentally, climate change is the greatest challenge to our planet and its people, and science dictates that we must limit global temperature rise below two percent, but to do so society must act now, both globally and locally, to ensure not just ecological sustainability but social and environmental wellbeing – now and for the future. On its current trajectory, climate change is predicted to have direct effects on food security and human health, to increase the displacement of people, and to increase the risk of heat stress, storms, extreme precipitation, inland and coastal flooding, landslides, air pollution, drought, water scarcity, sea level rise, and storm surges (IPCC 2015). It is and will continue to affect human populations. We can no longer decouple the environment from human wellbeing or pretend that it is acceptable to do so.

Socially, disparity between the core and the periphery has been growing rapidly since the introduction of capitalism. The core refers to those dominantly wealthy countries, mainly in the West, and the periphery of countries around them. Countries in the core have exploited the natural resources in the periphery for decades in the name of Western neoliberal development, and one can almost visualise the flow of wealth and resources from the periphery to the core. This has had a raft of flow-on effects from extreme poverty to social dislocation. Both social and ecological sustainability have been a core focus globally since the Rio Conference of the Environment and Development in 1992. Yet, the situation is not improving.

A key outcome of the Rio Conference was the Brundtland Commission Report, which defined Sustainable Development as "development that meets the needs of the present without compromising the ability of future generations to meet their own needs" (*Our Common Future* 1987). How we go about satisfying needs and who defines them is a much-contested debate, as the definition provided no context, nor any strategies for change. In the neoliberal context, needs have often become equated to consumerist wants or desires, fuelling the search for more economic growth and thus concretising the cycle of social disparity and climate change perpetuated by the failure of development.

Latin America at a crossroads

Latin America is one continent highly affected by these failures of development, where inequality, social fractures, environmental destruction, and economic disparity are rife. Socially, Latin America is also one of the most unequal regions in the world – according to the United Nations Development Programme (UNDP) – where the disparity between rich and poor is only widening. In terms of environmental sustainability, it is one of the world's most important regions for its biodiversity. It contains over one third of the world's tropical rainforests, with the Amazon rainforest being described as "the lungs of the world" (Mische 1993).

Latin America, however, is at a crossroads (Escobar 2010). The continent has achieved much of its economic growth and development through large-scale resource extraction. The neoliberal economic growth argument underlines the type of development dependent on extractive projects. Many argue that this approach is contrary to the original needs' objectives of Sustainable Development, and that it only hinders social wellbeing and environmental conservation, failing to decrease the inequality at the root of many environmental and social problems. Moreover, traditional ways of life and social stability are vulnerable to environmental changes brought on by the effects of climate change, a history of heavy deforestation, and the threats that large-scale resource extraction projects pose in the region.

Human wellbeing and environmental sustainability are not only interdependent, but are both hanging in the balance. Make no mistake: It is not a regional problem, it is a global one. We are all affected. In response, there has been an impetus towards alternatives to development new techniques of development to ensure sustainability, rather than another alternative approach like Sustainable Development as it exists under the current neoliberal model. One such alternative is the Andean concept of "Buen Vivir."

Buen Vivir is a biocentric, holistic approach to wellbeing and sustainability which is as much ecological as it is social. In that respect, it is more appropriate to regard it as an alternative to Sustainable Development. It is a plural concept arising from traditional Indigenous cosmology and influenced by political discourse intended on emphasising the importance of traditional Indigenous knowledge. Endogenous by nature, Buen Vivir is entrenched in culture and ways of thinking in Latin America. But, beyond being an Andean cultural perspective of development, it can have real applicability in other community contexts. As an alternative to Sustainable Development, "meeting the needs of present and future generations" under Buen Vivir's biocentric focus means that it would not only consider human needs but environmental needs too, so the world may keep functioning in its society–nature continuum – a relationship in which each one supports the other.

On the other hand, current neoliberal conceptions of development are unapologetically anthropocentric, placing emphasis on economic growth and individual needs for human wellbeing, and often taking a "one-size-fits-all" approach, ignoring culture and context. A concept such as Buen Vivir puts "development" processes back into the hands of the people, satisfying what communities identify as their real needs from the bottom-up, rather than perceived needs from the top-down. It rejects economic growth as an indicator of wellbeing and focuses on holistic social and environmental wellbeing and the satisfaction of needs.

In that respect, Buen Vivir's holistic approach to social and environmental wellbeing necessitates new terminology to convey its aims, ethos, and projected outcomes. I refer to this as "Socio-Eco Wellbeing," which I define as a unique vision of wellbeing guided by the principles of Buen Vivir, under which the wellbeing of society and nature are equally integral to one another. Socio-Eco Wellbeing is thus a collective and holistic vision that includes quality of life (health status, work–life balance, education and skills, social connections, civic engagement and governance, environmental quality, personal security, and collective wellbeing) (OECD), the wellbeing of the community, and environmental wellbeing, while also encompassing the personal and subjective.

Despite its endogenous nature, the state does play an important role in Buen Vivir. In the progressive countries in Latin America including Ecuador and Bolivia, policy and regulation are key elements, but so far political action has failed to effect real change. While there is local acknowledgement that Latin America needs to break away from the neoliberal development approach and implement its own approach to developing sustainably, so far this has only resulted in government rhetoric and theoretical academic analyses. This is the case in Ecuador and Bolivia, where Buen Vivir was the key focal point for constitutional reforms; with Ecuador codifying the "Rights of Nature." Both countries have implemented plans for Buen Vivir but continue with their extractivist policies of the past, albeit in a new fashion.

Extractivism has a long history, and although the activity itself is ancient, the modern mode of accumulation by extractivism was borne out of the colonisation of the Americas and Africa which used slaves in the extraction and production of raw materials for export (Acosta 2013). Because of large-scale extractivism's interference with ecosystems, it is incompatible with concepts like Buen Vivir. It is understood as incompatible because of Buen Vivir's biocentrism, being defined as "a conception of the world whereby everything forms part of nature and implies a plural value to nature beyond its economic dimension as natural capital, reaching other dimensions such as ecological, aesthetic, cultural, religious, etc." (Cubillo-Guevara, Hidalgo-Capitán & García-Álvarez 2016).

Historically, in the pursuit of Sustainable Development, we have learnt that policy and academic discourse is not enough to achieve wellbeing and ecological sustainability, as long as the status quo dominates the dialogue. We cannot simply reframe the issues at stake in the old language of development, we need a fundamental shift in direction from the bottom-up. As Peter Block (2007) asserts, "We cannot problem solve our way into fundamental change, or transformation. This is not an argument against problem solving; it is an intention to shift the context and language within which problem solving takes place… It is about changing our idea of what constitutes action."

For such a non-linear concept, there has been a linear course leading up to the need to search for alternatives to Sustainable Development, but the time is ripe to change the way of thinking and doing development, in particular Sustainable Development. In that respect, Buen Vivir shows considerable promise.

Ecuador and Buen Vivir

While several versions of Buen Vivir exist throughout Latin America, there are two countries that have led the way in making it an alternative to traditional development: Bolivia and Ecuador. The context surrounding the Ecuadorian government's interpretation is often considered the most robust in meeting the challenge of becoming a viable alternative to the neoliberal development model (Escobar 2012; Gudynas & Acosta 2011; Radcliffe 2012) because of the presence of a legal framework over Bolivia's moral framework. The former Correa government was also instrumental in making Buen Vivir visible as a policy option in the global arena. It created a Ministry of Buen Vivir, with its appointed Minister Fredy Elhers working diplomatically for the recognition of Buen Vivir as an alternative by various governments around the world.

For such a small country, Ecuador has a huge diversity of landscapes, people, and Indigenous groups. For this study I have chosen Cotacachi County, with a focus on the Intag Valley, for several reasons: Demographics, environment, politics, and current practices and beliefs which provide perspective on various contexts – allowing for its wider resonance. Here my own epistemological background also comes into play.

While Buen Vivir originates from Indigenous cosmology, the way it has come to be conceptualised broadens its meaning and practice beyond Indigenous communities and territories. It is therefore important to examine Buen Vivir in this wider cultural context. Demographically, Cotacachi is home to a variety of communities from urban to rural, and from Indigenous to mestizo.

Environmentally, Intag is one of the world's most biodiverse and ecologically rich regions. The region contains an internationally protected area, the Cotacachi-Cayapas Reserve. It is also home to two of the world's 35 internationally recognised biodiversity hotspots, the Tropical Andes and Tumbes-Choco-Magdalena. Topographically, the Tumbes-Choco-Magdalena hotspot is remarkably diverse, ranging from mangroves, beaches, rocky shorelines, and coastal wilderness, and some of the world's wettest rainforests (Kocian, Batker & Harrison-Cox 2011). The Tropical Andes is known for being one of the most biologically rich and diverse regions on earth, but one whose habitats are under extreme threat from extractivist projects (Kocian, Batker & Harrison-Cox 2011).

Large-scale extractivism threatens the fragile balance of that biodiversity and poses various challenges to communities and the environment. Moreover, it is wholly incompatible with a biocentric Buen Vivir. Extractive activities in Intag have posed a threat to the Cotacachi-Cayapas Reserve and spurred ongoing grass-roots mining resistance to the possible impacts on livelihoods, communities, and the environment. Mining resistance in Intag is led by local communities and is argued in support of Pachamama, the environment, and social justice for wellbe-ing, and based on solidarity and community (Avci 2012). Extractive activities are a threat to their ability to continue their livelihoods and meet the needs of their future generations. As community president of Rio Verde Carmen Proaño stated, "We can't sell our children's future by letting a mining company come in and contaminate our beautiful river" (D'Amico 2011).

The Intag region is also home to one of the country's most active environ-mental organisations, DECOIN (Ecological Defence and Conservation of Intag). Outlining Intag's support for an alternative to neoliberal development, DECOIN's current President, Carlos Zorrilla stated,

> It's wrong to say we're getting in the way of the country's development. What I and others represent is a different vision, a proposal for another way of living, a way of life that has more to do with Sumak Kawsay (Buen Vivir) than a development depending on the extraction of minerals. We're not naive or destabilisers, we've seen the results of mining in Peru, and believe me, they're not pretty. Here in Intag we've got another vision of the future.
>
> (Coffrey 2014)

Inteños (inhabitants of Intag) continually demonstrate their fervour for Buen Vivir – the foundation of which is biocentricity and collectivism. "Inteños depend upon the natural world for their livelihoods and have developed a unique culture that stresses values of mutual interdependence that complement collective and individual rights" (D'Amico 2011).

Politically, national policies for Buen Vivir are implemented provincially. Under the country's national plan for Buen Vivir at the time of research, Ecuador has been divided into nine "deconcentrated zones" to territorialise public policies for Buen Vivir to satisfy the needs specific to distinct territories (SENPLADES 2010). Imbabura, the province within which Cotacachi is located, along with Esmeraldas, Carchi, and Sucumbíos, was established as Zone 1. The focus on the county level of governance over provincial is because the county is sufficiently close to the people to support the definition, discussed shortly, of "community," but not too close for the vision and understanding of Buen Vivir to become nar-row; it is at the county level that communities share a similar identity and similar issues related to Buen Vivir. In addition, the county government has instituted its own version of Buen Vivir in its policies, pertinent to the culture and geography of Cotacachi.

The principles underlying Buen Vivir that I identify in this research therefore represent the similarities between grassroots, policy, and academia that can be implemented in different community contexts. For Buen Vivir to become a viable, practical alternative to Sustainable Development that ensures ecological sustain-ability and increased environmental and social wellbeing, it must be analysed and applied on the ground at the community level, with community-identified needs as a core element because the exogenous approach has not worked thus far.

What exactly the term "community" entails, however, is problematic to define. As Tesiero and Ife mention, citing Bella and Newby, in 1971 there were 98 different definitions of community. By now, there are surely more. Based on the current knowledge of Buen Vivir I ascribe to Tesoriero and Ife's (2010) understanding of a geographical community, which is appropriate for Buen Vivir's emphasis on localness, communal mindset, participation, plurality, and the role of institutions. It includes the five following characteristics:

- Human-scale: Closest to the people, it involves "sufficiently small structures" to enable communities to own and manage their own processes.
- Identity and belonging: Invokes a sense of value and acceptance within a group.
- Obligations: Involves an active level of participation that entails rights and responsibilities as a member of the community.
- *Gemeinschaft*: Entails a structure that allows and even encourages people to interact with each other, as a "whole people."
- Culture: Unique characteristics of a community that define it while encouraging diversity and broad-based participation.

Community in this sense removes vague borders. Simultaneously, it is important to understand how the key actors in the context of community define Buen Vivir and investigate the role institutions and the state play in realising Buen Vivir.

Reading this book

There are several core concepts used throughout this book that I wish to explain upfront. The first is neoliberalism, that is, the ideology, belief, and policies associated with laissez-faire economics. Neoliberal ideas are at the core of development thinking, which emphasise the importance of the individual and economic growth for human prosperity, supported by free-market capitalism.

The failure of neoliberal Sustainable Development has been a core tenet of post-development theory, which critiqued it and subsequently called for alternatives to neoliberal development. The concept of extractivism comes into the equation as a development tool used to increase economic growth. It can be defined as the extraction and removal of natural resources for export to satisfy a capitalist market. This is not limited to mining and oil, but also includes forestry, farming, and fishing, and even large-scale renewables if they seek to support a capitalist model. An extractive economy cannot by its nature lead to sustainable outcomes – neither environmentally nor socially.

Buen Vivir has been labelled one such alternative to development in the hopes of a more socially and ecologically just world. Buen Vivir, however, has been embroiled in vague meanings and contradictory government policies. This has been its greatest weakness as an alternative thus far. With a lack of coherent understanding of what Buen Vivir is has come a lack of understanding of its challenges at the coalface. These are all part of what has led to the research behind this book.

In Chapter One, I start this book with a look at how we have arrived at the current situation, how development and subsequently Sustainable Development have failed to achieve their aims. The first chapter therefore discusses a brief history of development towards the emergence of Sustainable Development. This chapter is a critique of how these ideas have failed to come to fruition and where the problems lie.

In Chapter Two, I then look at the growing legitimacy of "alternatives to development," as introduced by post-developmentalists. This discussion begins with a brief history of post-development in Latin America, which has led to the search for alternatives to the neoliberal Western conceptions of development led by extractivist policies – a Latin American paradox. This post-developmental move by progressive countries like Ecuador has led to neoextractivist policies, whereby the state has more involvement in extractive activities. At the same time there has been a political push for Buen Vivir. I conclude Chapter Two with an introduction of Buen Vivir as one such alternative to development, derived from the ground up.

In Chapter Three, I continue the discussion on Buen Vivir, first taking a brief look at how Buen Vivir has evolved, from its Indigenous origins to policy. The way in which Buen Vivir has been co-constructed by various actors, along with the Indigenous vision for Buen Vivir, has led to a "plural" approach, meaning all knowledges matter and play a role. I discuss this plurality, subsequently leading to a merger of the common core principles arising from its multiple contested definitions. The missing link at this point, however, is that Buen Vivir is identified as an endogenous approach, yet there is a lack of concrete understanding of how that plays out at the coalface, which takes me to the second part of this book.

My ethnographic study in Cotacachi County bridges that gap, looking at ways in which Buen Vivir is both articulated and practised. Chapter Four begins Part II based on the empirical evidence for Buen Vivir. In this chapter, I discuss the ways in which Buen Vivir is understood by the key actors. These interpretations complete the missing pieces of the puzzle for how Buen Vivir can be a practical and viable alternative to Sustainable Development. Without the grassroots understandings, it risks being relegated as a mere discourse critique. While discourse is important in leading change, to achieve the type of transformative change needed for Socio-Eco Wellbeing, we need concrete frameworks for action.

In this chapter I close the gaps between theory, policy, and practice and merge the understandings into a set of 17 principles for Buen Vivir. The key actors in the study discuss the importance of needs satisfaction in achieving Buen Vivir. Given the place the question of needs holds in the definition of Sustainable Development, it is vital to discuss what that looks like under Buen Vivir. I therefore analyse the grassroots perspective of needs, which plays into the way the economy is conceptualised under a Buen Vivir approach.

Chapter Five considers Buen Vivir's plurality. There is a clear difference between Buen Vivir in policy and the notion of Buen Vivir that is practised on the ground. This chapter discusses that difference as a key finding, enabling the practical implementation of Buen Vivir at the community level. I look at examples of what Buen Vivir looks like in practice in Cotacachi County, and conclude with a discussion on the role of the different key actors (community, governments, and organisations).

Attaining Buen Vivir does not come without its challenges, so Chapter Six begins with a look at the key challenges to implementation. The most significant of these is large-scale extractive policy and activities. Cotacachi County has had its own experience with extractivism – both perceived and lived – and so to bring context to the impacts extractivism can have on a community's Socio-Eco Wellbeing, I continue by examining the situation there, and discuss the neoextractive approach taken in policy to delve into the tensions between community, government, and extractive activities.

The role that nature plays in human wellbeing for these communities is critical in understanding their point of view. Far from being anchored only in the context of Cotacachi, this understanding of nature's role underlines the entire premise of Buen Vivir. It is what differentiates it from other alternatives to development. To that end, I investigate some of the socio-eco impacts from extractivism on wellbeing to better illustrate its incompatibility with Buen Vivir. I conclude this chapter with some examples of the various economic alternatives to extractivism put forth in Cotacachi County towards a post-extractive future.

In Chapters Four, Five, and Six, I present you with the particular, taking Cotacachi County as a case study. Chapter Seven moves towards the big picture by starting to look at the global connectedness of even small communities. It would indeed be naïve to assume that Buen Vivir stands as an alternative within and of itself. In today's globally connected society issues such as climate change and social disparity are not geographically isolated. There is an interplay between the local and the global that must be considered if Buen Vivir is to be a viable alternative to Sustainable Development.

In Chapter Seven, I therefore present the political implications of Buen Vivir. I explain how pursuing an endogenous approach through Buen Vivir may simultaneously allow governments to position themselves to meet their global sustainability commitments and responsibilities. I start this chapter by recalling the need for an alternative to Sustainable Development. I then discuss the Sustainable Development Goals (SDGs), and the failure of past efforts for Sustainable Development. I continue by examining the differences and synergies between Buen Vivir and Sustainable Development.

One cannot argue for an alternative to Sustainable Development without considering how or if that alternative can be measured. Chapter Eight is dedicated to that task. I begin by discussing the feasibility of measuring a non-linear alternative, before finally presenting a framework for its implementation with the dual aims of: 1) providing communities with a practical tool to move forward; and 2) providing governments with ways to plurally align national and global policy objectives for sustainability with local processes while changing their approach to allow communities direct their own path.

Chapter Nine concludes this book by examining how Buen Vivir can be implemented, distilling the features of Buen Vivir that demonstrate its viability as a practical alternative to Sustainable Development. In respecting its plurality and biocentricity, I revisit the roles of the key actors, and the implications for policy and for community in an approach that values the needs of both nature and humans equally. I conclude by discussing how the features of Buen Vivir that make it a practical alternative can be implemented in any context.

This book is aimed both at communities and policy-makers to provide a better understanding of what Buen Vivir is all about, to help make implementation possible. It may also be useful to students, development professionals, and organisations involved with communities to set in motion the wheels for making change sustainable for the long-term. For Buen Vivir to be achieved, there is a need for all actors to understand their respective roles. It is my hope that this book helps fulfil that need and help set a viable path for practical action.

References

Acosta, A 2013, 'Extractivism and neoextractivism: Two sides of the same coin', in M Lang & D Mokrani eds., *Beyond development: Alternative visions from latin america*, Fundacion Rosa Lumxemburg, Quito, Ecuador, pp. 61.

Avci, D 2012, 'Politics of resistence against mining: A comparative study of conflicts in Intag, Ecuador and Ida, Turkey', *International Institute of Social Sciences* ISS PhD Theses. Erasmus University Rotterdam.

Block, P 2007, *Civic engagement and the restoration of community: Changing the nature of the conversation*, A Small Group. <http://www.asmallgroup.net/pages/images/pages/CES_jan2007.pdf>.

Coffrey, G 2014, *Enemy of the state: The battle over sustainable development in intag, ecuador*, Upside Down World, viewed 10 January 2015, <http://upsidedownworld.org/main/news-briefs-archives-68/4644-enemy-of-the-state-the-battle-over-sustainable-development-in-intag-ecuador>.

Cubillo-Guevara, AP, Hidalgo-Capitán, AL & García-Álvarez, S 2016, 'El buen vivir como alternativa al desarrollo para américa latina', *Iberoamerican Journal of Development Studies*, vol. 5, no. 2, pp. 30–57.

D'Amico, L 2011, 'El Agua es Vida/Water Is Life': Community Watershed Reserves in Intag, Ecuador, and Emerging Ecological Identities', in *Water, cultural diversity, and global environmental change*, eds., BR Johnston, L Hiwasaki and IJ Klaver, pp. 433–452. Springer.

Escobar, A 2010, 'Latin America at a crossroads', *Cultural Studies*, vol. 24, no. 1, pp. 1–65.

Escobar, A 2012, 'Más allá del desarrollo: Postdesarrollo y transiciones hacia el pluriverso', *Revista de Antropología Social*, vol. 21, pp. 23–62.

Gudynas, E & Acosta, A 2011, 'La renovación de la crítica al desarrollo y el buen vivir como alternativa', *Utopia y Praxis Latinoamericana: Revista Internacional de Filosofia Iberoamericana y teoria Social*, vol. 16, no. 53, pp. 71–83.

IPCC 2015, *Climate change 2014 synthesis report*, Intergovernmental Panel on Climate Change, Geneva.

Kocian, M, Batker, D & Harrison-Cox, J 2011, *An ecological study of ecuador's intag region: The environmental impacts and potential rewards of mining*, Earth Economics, Tacoma, WA.

Mische, P 1993, 'Ecological security in an interdependent world', *Update L. Relat. Educ.*, vol. 17, p. 52.

World Commission on Environment and Development (WCED) 1987, *Our Common Future*, Oxford University Press, Oxford and New York.

Radcliffe, SA 2012, 'Development for a postneoliberal era? Sumak kawsay, living well and the limits to decolonisation in ecuador', *Geoforum*, vol. 43, no. 2, pp. 240–9.

SENPLADES 2010 *1 agenda zonal para el buen vivir: Propuestas de desarrollo y lineamientos para el ordenamiento territorial*, Secretaría Nacional de Planificación y Desarrollo Quito, Ecuador.

Tesoriero, F & Ife, JW 2010, *Community development: Community-based alternatives in an age of globalisation*, 4th edn., Pearson Australia, Frenchs Forest, NSW.

Part I

1 A brief history of development and Sustainable Development

Development is not a new concept. It has its roots in early thinking on progress in the 18th century with philosophers like Nicolas de Condorcet, Georg Wilhelm Friedrich Hegel, and Auguste Comte. Gardner and Lewis (1996) argued that it started with Larrain, who reasoned for the idea of social and economic progress in his "age of competitive capitalism," 1700–1860. Adam Smith also played a key role in establishing the modern capitalist market thought in 1776 with his book *Wealth of Nations*, in which he argued that the "invisible hand" of the market (individual consumers making buying decisions based on self-interest) would result in economic growth, wealth, and therefore prosperity for all (Opello & Rosow 1999). Some scholars, however, believe that development started in the pre-Enlightenment period with Plato and Aristotle.

Modern development started at the end of World War II when former US President Harry Truman took office (Esteva 2010). On the day he took office, 20 January 1949, Truman changed the way the world understood development by introducing the term "underdevelopment" to distinguish the poorer economic regions from those more prosperous economically (Cerdán 2013). This distinction has had profound consequences on the way development has been conceptualised and carried out since (Esteva 2010). Today, we politically refer to underdeveloped regions as the periphery, Global South, or Third World. The idea of underdevelopment thus refers to countries in the periphery, which have historically been considered "lesser" because of their lack of industrialisation and economic growth.

Since that day in 1949, development as a theory has grown into the Western neoliberal ideal of economic growth as a means of "developing" the "underdeveloped" to achieve quality of life and wellbeing for all, albeit narrowly defined. Traditional neoliberal development is anthropocentric, meaning that human wellbeing is the core focus. It links economic growth to human progress, and wellbeing is commonly measured by a country's Gross Domestic Product (GDP). Economically, it is underlined by capitalism. However, it has failed at its primary objectives: Poverty reduction and improving quality of life for everyone on the planet.

Post-developmentalists like Arturo Escobar see neoliberal development as a driver for the core's colonial and neo-colonial desire for domination over the South (Escobar 1995; Gardner & Lewis 1996). Whichever viewpoint one takes, development has become synonymous with progress, an idea which has both negative and positive connotations depending on one's ideological stance; but one thing is certain: It has created greater inequalities.

The international community introduced Sustainable Development as a reaction to the failure of traditional neoliberal development, with a recognition that we must start to consider the impact of development on the natural environment and aim for intergenerational ecological sustainability. We can understand it as a development alternative because it takes the aims of development and reframes them for greater environmental sustainability – that is, economic growth, within the limits of the environment.

Yet, Sustainable Development as a development alternative has not sought to address the root of the problem; instead it has upheld the status quo of neoliberal development. As a result, it has not achieved its own core aims. In fact, climate change has destabilised ecological sustainability and social disparities have amplified. The only objective that has been achieved (albeit unequally) is increasing economic growth, which is argued to be the cause of the aforementioned failures in the first place (Acosta 2012; Harcourt 2013; Ruttenberg 2013).

Underdevelopment and the myth of progress

It is now widely acknowledged that the Western construct of "progress," underlining development and its alternative derivatives, is seriously flawed (Gardner & Lewis 1996). The idea of progress, of "having more and more," started around 500 years ago in Europe; it has since been perpetuated by capitalism, a system which places nature external to humanity (Villalba 2013), and has been believed to be a sure way to overcome the "curse" of underdevelopment. Former President Truman influenced well-meaning populations in the West and turned the desire for progress and consumption into a need to find a solution to a problem that could hamper that progress:

> More than half the people of the world are living in conditions approaching misery. Their food is inadequate. They are victims of disease. Their economic life is primitive and stagnant. Their poverty is a handicap and a threat both to them and to more prosperous areas.
>
> (Morse 2008)

Let us examine that last phrase. The intention here was to not let the lack of economic progress in the periphery hamper prosperity in the core. It was again this anthropocentric, individualist way of thinking that drove the desires for what we now call "development." Esteva (2010) argues that diversity was lost, and the world homogenised, on 20 January 1949, when suddenly "two billion people… were transmogrified into an inverted mirror of others' reality."

This unique era that we are living in has contextually shaped modern ideas of poverty, promoted by the neoliberal economy (Haslam, Schafer & Beaudet 2012). Post-developmentalists are now calling for a deconstruction of that idea, and a reconceptualisation of what is actually going on. Haslam et al. (2012) note that there are two important and distinct understandings of the idea: Relative poverty, which is quantifiably measured against societal standards, and absolute poverty, which is measured against benchmarks like living costs, literacy, and the like. There is a further distinction between extreme and moderate poverty, the former of which prevents people from meeting their basic needs for survival (Haslam, Schafer & Beaudet 2012).

Whether or not one ascribes to the idea that poverty is real or perceived, absolute, or relative is irrelevant here. This does not imply ignoring the problem, far from it. We need to address the roots of the issue, and to do so it is unhelpful in the desire to overcome the ills of development to frame the argument in terms of poverty and underdevelopment, as it brings the debate right back into the framework of neoliberal development. This would necessarily hamper any efforts to look beyond, to the root of the problem. Post-development therefore calls for "new paradigm thinking" (Tesoriero & Ife 2010), a different way of perceiving the world than the way society sees itself now. Real needs rather than "progress" must be at the forefront.

The Western neoliberal development expectation that countries on the periphery must focus on economic growth has resulted in an exploitative and unbalanced unilateral resource flow that has supported the proliferation of neoliberal thinking that continues today (Cobey 2012). We have created the situation as it is now, in the name of development: A deteriorating environment and growing social injustice. The failure of development is that it has been reduced to economic growth (Gardner & Lewis 1996) at all costs, but there are limits to this pursuit of growth.

The failure of development and the path to alternatives

Let us not beat around the proverbial bush: Development has failed in colossal terms at what it was trying to achieve. One must only look at the series of measures that development has introduced and the failure to meet their own objectives.

> Like a towering lighthouse guiding sailors towards the coast, "development" stood as THE idea which oriented emerging nations in their journey through post-war history… Today, the lighthouse shows cracks and is starting to crumble. The idea of development stands like a ruin on the intellectual landscape. Delusion and disappointment, failures and crimes have been steady companions of development and they tell a common story: it did not work.
>
> (Rahnema & Sachs 1992)

Yet pro-growth supporters have actively sought alternative development models that still uphold their ideals of growth and progress, including Another Development (*What Now – The 1975 Dag Hammarskjöld Report on Development and International Cooperation* 1975); Human Development (UNDP); Community Development; and Sustainable Development. García-Álvarez (2013a) calls this the "development concept crisis."

A critique of the economic growth approach led to the introduction of the Human Development paradigm. Human Development is the basis of the UN's Human Development Report which assesses countries on a people-based policy approach – emphasising capabilities over economic growth (*Human development index*). Human Development was born primarily out of the work on human capabilities and functionings of Nobel laureate and economist Amartya Sen. Martha Nussbaum later built upon this capabilities framework, linking capabilities to her work on human rights (Nussbaum 2009).

Where Human Development is problematic is that it prioritises individual capabilities over collective capabilities (Tortosa 2011; Unceta 2013). Indeed Stewart (2013) argues that an approach to capabilities must go beyond the individual, and states, "individuals are so bound up with others that it can be difficult to disentangle them and treat them as separate" (Stewart 2013).

Human wellbeing is emphasised under the HD paradigm but as with all alternative development approaches, it has a "strong anthropocentric bias" (Gale 2018) and as such the wellbeing of the environment is not considered with enough weight (Monni & Pallottino 2015). While Nussbaum's core capabilities do consider the need to live with other species in harmony, it prioritises human needs above all else (Pepper 2017).

Development alternatives have also failed to effect the kind of transformative change needed for Socio-Eco Wellbeing. The problem is that the principles underlying the development alternatives were never questioned; they were just reframed (Acosta 2012). Sustainable Development exemplifies that logic – where economic growth and a decoupling of the environment from society are the foundations, and a clear legacy from the development era. Instead, what we should be doing is decoupling the environment and society from economic growth.

The Millennium Development Goals (MDGs) were the attempt in development to address its own failures, but those too were futile in meeting targets by 2015 (UNDP 2014). Now, the "countries of the world," heavily pushed by those in the core, have reformulated those goals into the Sustainable Development Goals, which build on the MDGs post-2015 but apply to all countries, albeit with the same capitalist and neoliberal mechanisms being used to achieve them.

That goes to show just how persuasive and persistent "development" is as a concept (Gardner & Lewis 1996). Despite numerous failures through the various development alternatives including Sustainable Development, the world is still using development as a tool (however reformulated and revolutionised) to tackle "underdevelopment" and global poverty, rather than analysing the root cause. Let us now take a closer look at Sustainable Development.

Sustaining growth: The emergence of Sustainable Development, critiques, and limits

Sustainability and Sustainable Development seem to be used interchangeably these days, despite not being one and the same. Sustainability refers to the maintenance of all ecosystems and humanity in the long term (Tesoriero & Ife 2010).

Sustainability is not a new idea, and indeed some version of sustainability can be traced back to as early as the 1960s. Some argue that Rachel Carson's book *The Silent Spring* (1962), warning of the environmental problems we were to face, was the beginning of the global environmental movement. Since then, however, the term "sustainability" has evolved into new and complex meanings.

Tesoriero and Ife (2010) rightly argue that the term is in danger of losing its substantive meaning. In fact, true sustainability requires a radical transformation of the global system, moving away from unbridled growth and consumption (Tesoriero & Ife 2010), but the term's downfall is that it has fallen victim to a power game whereby particular knowledge becomes reality.

The Brundtland Report (*Our Common Future*) in 1987 (WCED 1990) brought new emphasis to the meaning of sustainability, and it was then that sustainability was framed within the neoliberal concept of Sustainable Development (Tesoriero & Ife 2010). With a global acknowledgement that the world's resources were in danger, it was originally intended as a way to repair the discrepancies between development and environmental degradation (Rogers, Jalal & Boyd 2008). Some scholars like Svampa (2013) argue that Sustainable Development has only resulted in a "diluted" version of sustainability that looks to shift the limits imposed by environmentalists.

The meta-narrative of Sustainable Development is thus an ever-controversial, ever-contested concept. It has gone through a dynamic process of change since it was conceptualised almost three decades ago at the United Nations Conference of the Environment and Development in 1992. Since then, there has been much public, academic, governmental, civil society, and private sector debate about what Sustainable Development means, how we can measure it, and what the end goal should look like. The lack of agreement on its meaning and implementation is part of its downfall. One constant in the definition of Sustainable Development is the three-pronged approach, first developed by former World Bank economist Mohan Munasinghe in 1993: Economic, ecological, and socio-cultural (Rogers, Jalal & Boyd 2008).

The Brundtland Commission Report introduced perhaps the most-cited definition of Sustainable Development today. This definition has been reused and reaffirmed on many occasions, including in the Rio Declaration of 1992 (UN 1992). Unfortunately, contradictions and inconsistencies in this idea of sustainability hamper any efforts in its achievement. In fact, the Global Sustainable Development Report (2019) has affirmed that not only are recent trends in several dimensions "not moving in the right direction," but those including climate change, biodiversity loss, waste from human activity, and rising inequalities are actually moving us towards a tipping point. Yet, the SDGs still employ language like "ensuring no-one is left behind," which indicates expectations for a universal (Western neoliberal) level of development.

However well-meaning the original notion of Sustainable Development, it has become a victim of terminology, paradoxically equated with the idea of growth because of the way it has been interpreted in neoliberal policy debates. Despite the contested nature of Sustainable Development as a theoretical concept, in practice it has been widely articulated as neoliberal development and distilling the otherwise contested term to a singular notion of sustainability. Hence, with the lack of consensus in theory, and a mainstream association with the status quo in practice, has come a lack of widespread political will to bring about the transformative change needed to address the underlying issues at stake, not seeking to change anything about development but its rhetoric. The "needs" aspect of Sustainable Development consequently is not being met.

Now, "needs" is as skewed as the term "sustainability." The Brundtland Report did not give concrete context to the principle of needs, and indeed it is widely disputed. Despite its deficiencies, this definition is the most practical point of departure for social and environmental action, but further conceptualisation is required, such as refining what is meant by needs, contextualisation, participation, self-sufficiency, harmony, and wellbeing. Similar points have been made in the first Global Sustainable Development Report (2019) which pinpointed several deficiencies of the SDGs, including a consideration of spiritual and cultural values attached to natural resources; cultural context; and the political processes that allow dominant voices to be heard over others such as Indigenous and other marginalised communities. Considering these aspects would allow for an endogenous definition of needs, real needs, rather than placing needs within the expectations of a neoliberal form of sustainability which relies on economic growth.

Rogers et al. (2008) debate the Kuznetsian vision that argues that "sustainability will take care of itself as economic growth proceeds," a view that believes that the more income you earn, the better able you are to look after the environment. This falsity is debated on a number of premises, in particular when you consider alternative worldviews like Buen Vivir, whose proponents (namely Indigenous, not economically wealthy societies) have been practising a version of the concept well before (and apart from) capitalism, yet whose entire philosophy is grounded on respect for the environment.

This comes back to the poverty argument, and those well-meaning, but ultimately neo-colonial, neoliberal ideas that to tackle environmental issues we must eradicate poverty, and that this can only be done by using the system that created the dilemma in the first place. To add fuel to the proverbial fire, the belief that most environmental degradation is caused by poverty is a myth (Rogers, Jalal & Boyd 2008). In fact, ten percent of the world's most affluent countries produce half of all global carbon emissions through lifestyle consumption, in large part due to the global economic inequality that persists which sees the emissions of poorer countries in the periphery linked to the production of goods for richer countries in the core (Gore 2015).

The International Panel on Climate Change (IPCC 2015) found a direct link between anthropogenic emissions and population size, economic wealth, lifestyle, energy use, and land use patterns. The global economy doubled in the last quarter of the 20th century, while CO_2 emissions have risen 40 percent from 1990 levels (Laville 2014; UNFCCC 1997) and 60 percent of the world's ecosystems have been destroyed (Laville 2014). Moreover, by 2005 approximately 60 percent of global ecosystems including water, air, climatic stability, nitrogen, and species were already degraded to non-renewable levels (Jackson 2011; Laville 2014). Between 2010 and 2015 32 million hectares of primary or recovering forest in highly diverse tropics were lost; and by 2016 over 9 percent of domesticated breeds of mammals used for food and agriculture had become extinct with at least 1,000 more threatened (Díaz et al. 2019).

Neoliberalists promote the importance of economic growth, and maintain that sustainability and growth are completely compatible, but the facts cited by climate change science demonstrate the contrary. Back in 2009, Rockström et al. argued that we had already crossed three of nine planetary boundaries they identified as responsible for generating "unacceptable environmental change," due to human development (Rockström et al. 2009), linked to an accumulation of wealth. It is evidently a vicious cycle: More development via the generation of more material wealth requires even more extractivism, which degrades the environment even further. Yet the growth imperative persists. In neoliberal circles there is no justification for the scope, speed, and limits to that growth. It is the "world problematic," as the Club of Rome (1972) called it, that even with all the knowledge we have, we still do not fully comprehend the significance and interrelationships of the problem, thereby rendering us incapable of formulating effective solutions. The Club of Rome "Limits to Growth" (1972) thesis was concerned with the elements that were consequential to economic growth: Population, food production, industrialisation, pollution, and consumption. It argued that with exponential growth we are surpassing the earth's carrying capacity and this will have serious and catastrophic consequences (Meadows & Club of Rome 1972). "The whole is more than a sum of its parts" (Meadows & Club of Rome 1972).

A recent manifestation of this is evident in the creation of the "Green Economy," otherwise known as the green growth argument. When it was clear that the Sustainable Development debate was becoming worn, the international community, dominated by neoliberal development thinking, conceived the Green Economy as a renewal of the concept (Vanhulst & Beling 2013). The Green Economy was conceptualised by the UN Rio+20 with the aim of finding a pragmatic solution to the environment–growth nexus (Vanhulst & Beling 2014). The aim therefore is to continue to exploit natural resources for economic growth, but in a manner that is considered more "sustainable." Technology is integral in the Green Economy, which utilises technological advances to create solutions. Such solutions include, for example, carbon capture and storage or emissions offset projects which seek to ensure that we can continue with the Western material values of consumption and growth, exploiting renewal resources to our advantage.

Neoliberal intellects hail the Green Economy or green capitalism as a "green revolution." In 2008, Achim Steiner stated, "The new green economy would provide a new engine of growth, putting the world on the road to prosperity again. This is about growing the world economy in a more intelligent, sustainable way" (Jackson 2011).

Yet, the term is an oxymoron. It sees nature as capital for public benefit, and especially for the aims of poverty reduction (UNEP), but it is impossible to continue growing exponentially while maintaining ecological integrity. The Green

Economy has essentially legitimised the idea that the role of nature is for the exploitation of human society in the pursuit of quality of life – or "living better" – albeit at the cost of others and of the environment (Álvarez 2013b; Thomson 2011; Villalba 2013). Nature therefore becomes a commodity to exploit, not a relationship to nurture. This exploitation is to purely satisfy the whims of modern society and the habits of consumption. Wellbeing is then subjectively equated with consumption and material means, rather than in its holistic sense. This is amplified in a Green Economy.

It is this commodification of natural resources upon which extractivism depends, which in turn supports neoliberal development; and it is that commodification that is going against the original objectives of sustainability. Our environment, as Huanacuni (2010) affirms, cannot handle any more so-called "green revolutions," or regurgitations of development couched in environmentally friendly language: "It is not just our species that is in danger, but it has also compromised the equilibrium of all ecosystems" (Huanacuni 2010).

The Green Economy thus remains blindsided by the traditional model of development, a "single model... which does not account for cultural diversity and refuses to recognise Mother Earth as a subject of rights" (Samaniego 2012; Vanhulst & Beling 2014). It is nonsensical that the commodification of our natural resources is controlled and managed by the same people that created the environmental crisis in the first place (Acosta 2012). The environmental limits of capitalism and the ways to overcome them are of vital importance in the development debate. Economist Tim Jackson (2011) calls this the "growth dilemma." Rather than economic growth leading to wellbeing, it is actually having the opposite effect, and resource consumption and its corresponding environmental costs are having profound impacts on social wellbeing (Jackson 2011).

Now, I would like to emphasise that I do not propose that we consume nothing. In modern society we continue to shop at supermarkets, live in modern houses, and entertain ourselves. Even alternatives to development advocate a certain level of consumption for health and wellbeing, but one that is completely disconnected from the levels of consumption that we practice today. However, the levels of consumption in the core – the idea of more, bigger, and best (and cheapest) – are unsustainable. The competitive notion of "keeping up with the Joneses" is destroying us and our planet. There is no counter-argument; it is just a fact. In fact, sustainability expert Elizabeth Laville states that in 2014 humanity consumed the total capacity of its ecological budget by August of that year (2014). That means it surpassed the planetary capacity to renew its resources in just eight months, living instead on ecological "credit" (Laville 2014).

It is both unsustainable and paradoxical to advocate that those in the periphery seek the same path to development. As Galeano (1997) notes, what would happen if everyone lived on the same levels of consumption as those in the core? There would be nothing left. If we continue at today's levels of consumption, we will need two planets by 2050 (Laville 2014). It would surpass catastrophe. But the "precarious equilibrium of the world, which is poised on the brink of an abyss, depends on the perpetuation of injustice. The deprivation of the majority is necessary so that the waste of a few is possible" (Galeano 1997).

Comparing green capitalism with Buen Vivir, Vanhulst and Beling (2014) state that its anthropocentricity situates the green economy contrary to Buen Vivir which is founded on biocentric principles and on needs. Post-developmentalists argue that the Green Economy places needs satisfaction in the realm of the market and increased consumption, so that only those needs that can be addressed by material means are satisfied. Needs that are defined by neoliberal economic growth, instead of wellbeing, is a major point of contention. In the words of Mahatma Gandhi, "this world has enough [resources] to meet the 'needs' of everybody, but not the 'greeds' of everybody" (Rogers, Jalal & Boyd 2008). The question therefore must be asked: What are needs, who defines them, and how can we satisfy them? The starting point would therefore be to move away from the top-down analysis of needs popular in traditional development that focuses on economic growth and a Western culture of desires as needs. But this is proving to be a challenge.

The predicament is thus two-fold: Sustainable Development is still anthropocentric; and it is still based on the neoliberal idea of progress through economic growth to meet needs. Not only is an anthropocentric approach detrimental, it is also contradictory to its aims. Principle 1 of the Rio Declaration (1992), for example, affirms that, "Human beings are at the centre of concerns for sustainable development. They are entitled to a healthy and productive life in harmony with nature." The problem is, though, as has been demonstrated throughout modern history, if society focuses purely on human wellbeing, with nature being subordinate, the exploitation of the latter is destructive to the former. And so it leads us to this vicious cycle: The exploitation of nature has led to the demise of human wellbeing, and it has started a cycle of ecological destruction.

So, what is called for now is radical, transformative action. This sentiment has also been echoed by the World Commission on Environment and Development, that "the time has come to break out of past patterns… attempts to maintain social and ecological stability through old approaches to development and environmental protection will increase instability" (Carvalho 2001). As Naomi Klein (2015) argues, the current political approach to addressing climate change and sustainability has only resulted in "uninterrupted backsliding" over the past 20 years. As long as business-as-usual persists, the climate will continue deteriorating at an alarming rate, and social tensions will increase from direct and non-direct impacts of climate change. What is important now is to work towards retrieving, identifying, and articulating the underlying original objectives of Sustainable Development, rather than just criticising it or reframing it. This will require a serious consideration of alternatives.

The unsustainability of Sustainable Development: Why we need an "alternative to development"

Tesoriero and Ife (2010) state that the move away from a resource-heavy perspective to alternative models has led to a rise in the "ecological perspective" in development thinking. The ecological perspective is non-linear, interdependent, and rests on four principles: Holism, sustainability, diversity and equilibrium. Tesoriero and Ife (2010) refer to this challenge to the dominant paradigm as "new paradigm thinking" – essentially a new way of seeing and approaching the world, humanity, and its problems. In post-development logic, this means going beyond the dominant paradigm of neoliberal "development" and envisioning alternatives to development as possible solutions (Escobar 2012).

To paraphrase Laville (2014) many critics and opponents to the alternatives argument believe that it is only crazy radicalists and revolutionaries that would call into question the need for economic growth. In concluding this section, however, I echo Laville's three main (and simple) reasons to support the alternatives debate: 1) Rising inequality; 2) declining stocks of natural resources; and 3) happiness at half-mast. In that light, I recall the original objectives of Sustainable Development which sought to eradicate inequality, ensure the continuance of ecosystems and ecological sustainability, and increase wellbeing.

First, let me discuss rising inequality in global terms. Now the idea of poverty as a Western construct does not deny the existence of catastrophic conditions in countries in the periphery. It does not negate the fact that every 3.6 seconds someone dies because of hunger, or that around 4,000 children perish every day because of a lack of clean, safe water (UNICEF). It does, however, link the existence of these conditions to a post-colonial era, and the dominance of the core over the natural resources in the periphery. Post-colonially (notwithstanding precolonial forms of power), suddenly millions of people in many communities that often had access to natural resources to satisfy their own basic needs have had those resources taken out from the ground beneath them, and their water sources polluted by large-scale extractive activities and industrialisation in the West. It cannot be denied that the problems that exist as what we call "poverty" today have been created by Western-style development, all in the name of "progress." Certainly, this has been argued extensively in development literature. As Ed Begley Jnr. ("Over-population, over-consumption in pictures" 2015) said, "when we destroy something made by man we call it vandalism, but when we destroy something created by nature we call it progress."

Instead of looking at it as a singular issue, we need to understand the interconnections between nature and society. Then the least that can be done is to return the control and management of resources to the communities that possess them in the first place, in a kind of "ecological community development" (Tesoriero & Ife 2010). This brings me to the next point: Declining stocks of natural resources.

Humanity's ecological footprint surpassed the earth's carrying capacity back in the 1970s, meaning that humans are consuming natural resources faster than the earth can renew them (WWF 2010). We are continually overshooting our planet's ecological capacity. Alternatives to development decouple themselves from economic growth, and as such generally promote themselves as having minimal impacts on the environment. Degrowth, for example, aims to reduce ecological pressures while increasing wellbeing by limiting Western-style consumption. Buen Vivir goes even further to harmonise nature with society so that neither has the monopoly over the other. It is about respecting the environment and having a realistic understanding of how growth and consumption are counterproductive to environmental protection because of their dependence on the earth's natural resources, both renewable and non-renewable.

The final point is one of happiness, or subjective wellbeing. It is not dissimilar to the idea of Socio-Eco Wellbeing; rather it is one part of it. There is increasing evidence (Cummins 2000; Levy-Carciente, Phélan & Perdomo 2014) that economic growth, and hence rising consumption, do not lead to greater levels of subjective wellbeing; rather they can have the opposite effect in that there has been a stagnation and even decline of wellbeing in industrialised countries since 1970, despite rising wealth (Laville 2014).

While the concept of subjective wellbeing is a commonly used measure, I argue that it is too constrained, as collective human and environmental wellbeing have strong connections and thus a subjective approach cannot account for the complexity of the nature–society continuum. This has spill-over effects on individual wellbeing and vice-versa. Happiness is subjective and contextual. It varies across cultures and community contexts. In fact, the concept of subjective wellbeing refers to how people judge the quality of their own lives (Diener et al. 1999). But subjective wellbeing is too narrow a concept. So, it is important to distinguish between subjective wellbeing as an individualist, human-centred concept based on happiness, and the broader construct of Socio-Eco Wellbeing which includes both subjective and objective aspects, and transcendent factors like environmental concerns.

Buen Vivir leads to Socio-Eco Wellbeing. So, considering the above definition, it is non-sensical to argue for wellbeing from a top-down approach. As a key outcome of Buen Vivir, Socio-Eco Wellbeing needs to be contextual and approached from the bottom-up. Moreover, in a biocentric concept like Buen Vivir, it is not only human wellbeing that is considered but environmental wellbeing as well.

Laville's three-pronged conundrum invokes the question: Why is the world still continuing with the status quo at the expense of social equality, environmental health, and wellbeing? The justification in support of the status quo is rather weak, as demonstrated earlier. In an argument not too far-flung from the idea of Buen Vivir, economist Tim Jackson (2011) maintains that we have it all wrong, that prosperity has become equated with economic growth, when in fact it originally alluded to having a good life. A different vision is now needed, "one in which it is possible for human beings to flourish, to achieve greater social cohesion, to find higher levels of well-being and yet still to reduce their material impact on the environment" (Jackson 2011).

There is now growing support from both sides of politics that what is needed now is an "alternative to development," rather than more "alternative development" models that act as a band-aid to the neoliberal ideal (Morse 2008). Because, as Escobar (2011) has succinctly summed up, "flawed from the start, the Sustainable Development movement can be said to have arrived to its natural end." Sustainable Development had the right intentions originally (Cobey 2012), but the problem was in its interpretation and implementation, which was further amplified in the neoliberal conception of Sustainable Development by throwing sustainability into the realms of the anthropocentric logic that dominates traditional development thinking.

References

Acosta, A 2012, *The buen vivir: An opportunity to imagine another world, inside a champion: An analysis of the Brazilian development model, democracy*, Heinrich Böll Foundation, Berlin, Germany.

Álvarez, S 2013a, *Sumak kawsay o buen vivir como alternativa al desarrollo en ecuador. Aplicación y resultados en el gobierno de rafael correa (2007–2011)*, thesis, Departamento de Economía Aplicada I Universidad Complutense de Madrid.

Álvarez, S 2013b, 'Sumak kawsay or wellbeing: Perspective and results in ecuador 2007–12', *Annual EAEPE conference*, Paris.

Carson, R 1962, *Silent spring*, Fawcett Publications, Greenwich, CT.

Carvalho, GO 2001, 'Sustainable development: Is it achievable within the existing international political economy context?', *Sustainable Development*, vol. 9, no. 2, pp. 61–73. doi: 10.1002/sd.159.

Cerdán, P 2013, 'Post-development and buen vivir: An approach to development from latin-america', *International Letters of Social and Humanistic Sciences*, vol. 10, pp. 15–24. doi: 10.18052/www.scipress.com/ILSHS.10.15.

Cobey, R 2012, *Living the good life? An analysis of ecuador's "plan nacional para el buen vivir" development model as an alternative to a neoliberal global framework*, MA thesis, East Carolina University.

Cummins, RA 2000, 'Personal income and subjective well-being: A review', *Journal of Happiness Studies*, vol. 1, no. 2, pp. 133–58. doi: 10.1023/A:1010079728426.

Díaz, S, Settele, J, Brondízio, E, Ngo, H, Guèze, M, Agard, J, Arneth, A, Balvanera, P, Brauman, K & Butchart, S 2019, *Summary for policymakers of the global assessment report on biodiversity and ecosystem services of the intergovernmental science-policy platform on biodiversity and ecosystem services*, IPBES Secretariat, Bonn, Germany.

Diener, E, Suh, EM, Lucas, RE & Smith, HL 1999, 'Subjective well-being: Three decades of progress', *Psychological Bulletin*, vol. 125, no. 2, p. 276. doi: 10.1037/0033-2909.125.2.276.

Escobar, A 1995, *Encountering development: The making and unmaking of the third world (new in paper)*, Princeton University Press, Princeton, NJ.

Escobar, A 2011, 'Sustainability: Design for the pluriverse', *Development*, vol. 54, no. 2, pp. 137–40. doi: 10.1057/dev.2011.28.

Escobar, A 2012, 'Más allá del desarrollo: Postdesarrollo y transiciones hacia el pluriverso', *Revista de Antropología Social*, vol. 21, pp. 23–62. doi: 10.5209/rev_RASO.2012.v21.40049.

Esteva, G 2010, 'Development', in W Sachs, ed., *The development dictionary*, Zed Books, London.

Gale, F 2018, *The political economy of sustainability*, Edward Elgar Publishing, Cheltenham.

Galeano, E 1997, 'To be like them', in M Rahnema and V Bawtree, eds, *The post-development reader*, Zed Books, London.

Gardner, K & Lewis, D 1996, *Anthropology, development and the post-modern challenge*, Pluto Press, London.

Gore, T 2015, *Extreme carbon inequality*, Oxfam International, Nairobi, Kenya.

Harcourt, W 2013, 'The future of capitalism: A consideration of alternatives', *Cambridge Journal of Economics*, vol. 38, no. 6, pp. 1307–28. doi: 10.1093/cje/bet048.

Haslam, PA, Schafer, J & Beaudet, P, eds 2012, *Introduction to international development: Approaches, actors, and issues*, Oxford University Press, London.

Huanacuni, F 2010, *Buen vivir/vivir bien*, Coordinadora Andina de Organizaciones Indígenas, Lima, Peru.

Human development index 2015?, United Nations Development Programme, viewed 21 March 2018, <http://hdr.undp.org/en/content/human-development-index-hdi>.

Independent Group of Scientists appointed by the Secretary-General 2019, *Global sustainable development report 2019: The future is now – science for achieving sustainable development*, United Nations, New York.

IPCC 2015, *Climate change 2014 synthesis report*, Intergovernmental Panel on Climate Change, Geneva.

Jackson, T 2011, *Prosperity without growth : Economics for a finite planet*, Pbk. ed., Earthscan, London.

Klein, N 2015, *This changes everything: Capitalism vs. The climate*, Simon and Schuster, New York.

Laville, E 2014, *Vers une consommation heureuse*, Allary Éditions, Paris.

Levy-Carciente, S, Phélan, LM & Perdomo, J 2014, 'From progress to happiness: Measurements for latin America', *Social Change Review*, vol. 12, pp. 73–112. doi: 10.2478/scr-2014-0004.

Meadows, DH & Club of Rome 1972, *The limits to growth: A report for the club of Rome's project on the predicament of mankind*, Universe Books, New York.

Monni, S & Pallottino, M 2015, 'Beyond growth and development: Buen vivir as an alternative to current paradigms', *International Journal of Environmental Policy and Decision Making*, vol. 1, no. 3, pp. 184–204. doi: 10.1504/IJEPDM.2015.074300.

Morse, S 2008, 'Post-sustainable development', *Sustainable Development*, vol. 16, no. 5, pp. 341–52.

Nussbaum, MC 2009, 'Creating capabilities: The human development approach and its implementation', *Hypatia*, vol. 24, no. 3, pp. 211–5. doi: 10.1111/j.1527-2001.2009.01053.x.

Opello, WC & Rosow, SJ 1999, *The nation-state and global order: A historical introduction to contemporary politics*, Lynne Rienner, Boulder, CO.

Over-population, over-consumption in pictures, 2015, The Guardian, viewed <http://www.theguardian.com/global-development-professionals-network/gallery/2015/apr/01/over-population-over-consumption-in-pictures?CMP=soc_567>.

Pepper, A 2017, 'Beyond anthropocentrism: Cosmopolitanism and nonhuman animals', *Global Justice: Theory, Practice, Rhetoric*, vol. 9, pp. 114–133. doi: 10.21248/gjn.9.2.114.

Sachs, W 1992, *The Development Dictionary: A Guide to Knowledge as Power*, Zed Books, London.

Rockström, J, Steffen, W, Noone, K, Persson, Å, Chapin Iii, FS, Lambin, EF, et al. 2009, 'A safe operating space for humanity', *Nature*, vol. 461, p. 472. doi: 10.1038/461472a.

Rogers, PP, Jalal, KF & Boyd, JA 2008, *An introduction to sustainable development*, Earthscan, London.

Ruttenberg, T 2013, 'Wellbeing economics and buen vivir: Development alternatives for inclusive human security', *Fletcher Journal of Human Security*, vol. XXVIII, pp. 68–93. <https://fletcher.tufts.edu/Praxis/~/media/Fletcher/Microsites/praxis/xxviii/article4_Ruttenberg_BuenVivir.pdf>.

Samaniego, J 2012, '*La sostenibilidad del desarrollo a 20 años de la cumbre para la tierra: Avances, brechas y lineamientos estratégicos para américa latina y el caribe*, CEPAL, Santiago.

Stewart, F 2013, *Capabilities and human development: Beyond the individual-the critical role of social institutions and social competencies*, UNDP-HDRO Occassional Papers, 2013/3, UNDP, New York.

Svampa, M 2013, 'Resource extractivism and alternatives: Latin american perspectives on development', in Lang M and Mokrani D, eds, *Beyond development*, Rosa Luxemburg Foundation, Berlin.

Tesoriero, F & Ife, JW 2010, *Community development: Community-based alternatives in an age of globalisation*, 4th ed., Pearson Australia, Frenchs Forest, NSW.

Thomson, B 2011, 'Pachakuti: Indigenous perspectives, buen vivir, sumaq kawsay and degrowth', *Development*, vol. 54, no. 4, pp. 448–54. doi: 10.1057/dev.2011.85.

Tortosa, JM 2011, 'Vivir bien, buen vivir: Caminar con los dos pies', *OBETS. Revista de Ciencias Sociales*, vol. 6, no. 1, pp. 13–7. doi: 10.14198/OBETS2011.6.1.01.

U.N. 1992, *Agenda 21*, United Nations Dept. of Public Information, New York.

Unceta, K 2013, 'Decrecimiento y buen vivir ¿paradigmas convergentes ? Debates sobre el postdesarrollo en europa y américa latina', *Revista de Economía Mundial*, vol. 35, pp. 197–216.

UNDP 2014, *Post-2015 development agenda*, United Nations Development Programme, viewed 1 April <http://www.undp.org/content/undp/en/home/mdgoverview/mdg_goals/post-2015-development-agenda/>.

UNFCCC 1997, *Kyoto protocol*, United Nations Framework Convention on Climate Change, Kyoto.

Vanhulst, J & Beling, AE 2013, 'Buen vivir: La irrupción de américa latina en el campo gravitacional del desarrollo sostenible', *Revista Iberoamericana de Economía Ecológica*, vol. 21, pp. 1–14. http://desarrollo.sociologia.uahurtado.cl/wp-content/uploads/2013/03/2013-Buen-Vivir-y-Desarrollo-sustentable.pdf.

Vanhulst, J & Beling, AE 2014, 'Buen vivir: Emergent discourse within or beyond sustainable development?', *Ecological Economics*, vol. 101, pp. 54–63. doi: 10.1016/j.ecolecon.2014.02.017.

Villalba, U 2013, 'Buen vivir vs development: A paradigm shift in the andes?', *Third World Quarterly*, vol. 34, no. 8, pp. 1427–42. doi: 10.1080/01436597.2013.831594.

WCED 1990, *Our common future*, Australian ed., Oxford University Press, Melbourne, VIC.

What now – the 1975 dag hammarskjöld report on development and international cooperation, 1975, Development Dialogue, Hammarskjöld Foundation, Uppsala.

WWF 2010, *The living planet: Biodiversity, biocapacity and development*, World Wildlife Fund, Gland, Switzerland.

2 Towards an alternative to development

The growing legitimacy of post-development

Post-development emerged in the search for alternatives to neoliberal development that would ensure sustainability, improve quality of life, and increase wellbeing. Post-development, however, mainly focuses on the critique of traditional development, economic growth, and the current neoliberal economic system, which means that it only questions a discourse, and does not offer concrete practical solutions (Gudynas 2013a).

In terms of discourse, there have been three major pieces of work on post-development thought: *The Development Dictionary*, published in 1992, edited by Sachs (2009); Escobar's *Encountering Development* (1995); and *The Post-Development Reader* (Rahnema & Bawtree 1997). The body of literature that has emerged since the 1980s in post-development has consistently stated that there is no interest in *development alternatives* like Sustainable Development; instead post-developmentalists call for an outright rejection of the paradigm, seeking "alternatives *to* development" (Escobar 1995).

According to Ziai (2007) post-development theory focuses on the following four aspects: 1) An opportunity to create an alternative discourse to development; 2) that the "objects" of development become the "subjects" of knowledge production; 3) a need to change the practices of knowing and doing; and 4) achieving the above by mobilising the resistance of local peoples and highlighting the alternative strategies that they produce. These aspects imply a concrete strategy, but what alternatives look like in practice have remained vague.

While development thinkers tout neoliberal theory as a solution to the problems and inequalities in the global system, post-development scholars posit that development has done extraordinarily little in this respect. Acosta (2012) raises the point that since the conception of modern development, how many projects have succeeded in achieving their objectives? Realistically very few.

Regardless, neoliberalists still critique the pursuit of post-development aims. Escobar (2000) identified three main (albeit flawed) critiques of post-development: 1) Development is generalisable and essentialist; 2) post-developmentalists romanticise the "local," ignoring global power relations that sway local development; and 3) they fail to acknowledge the social reality on the ground.

What post-developmentalists strongly emphasise is the need to focus on wellbeing and sustainability instead of economic growth. Such alternatives are contextual, closer to the people, and as such have a greater ability to take into consideration realities on the ground.

This leads us to Buen Vivir, which post-developmentalists argue is an alternative to development because, unlike neoliberal development, it denounces economic growth as an indicator of wellbeing, and it is biocentric instead of anthropocentric. The ultimate outcome is collective Socio-Eco Wellbeing through a plural, yet endogenous, approach, implemented in practice and policy. This renders it incompatible with the policies of extractivism that have historically supported neoliberal development aims as a tool in the pursuit of economic growth.

Henceforth, I will examine Buen Vivir in the context of extractivism to better understand what challenges an extractive economy poses on the achievement of Buen Vivir. The impacts of extractivism on social *and* environmental wellbeing have been well documented; however, progressive countries in Latin America, such as Ecuador, have abandoned their traditional extractivist policies of the past in favour of neoextractivism, which is essentially a continuum of the process of accumulation based on primary exports, but with increased involvement of the state in its management as well as profit and wealth distribution (Acosta 2012).

Post-development in Latin America

In Latin America, discussions of post-extractivism and post-development have featured at the state level, as well as amongst civil society and academics; however, progressive developmental policies couched in neoliberal language have caused a tense impasse as radical demands for change have continually been toned down in practice.

Latin American scholars like Escobar and Esteva have been instrumental in influencing the global post-development debate. The revolt against neoliberal development in Latin America, has been first and foremost a "discourse critique" (Gudynas 2013a), and can be understood to be post-developmentalist in origin, but its progress in policy and practice has failed to follow through.

Galeano (1997), who may be seen as overtly critical of the development debate in Latin America, has a few solids points that have led to the renewed push for post-development alternatives in the continent. He discusses how many of those looking at development in Latin America from an exogenous perspective may recall its "successes." In Bolivia, for example, the "Bolivian miracle" saw the country going from being one of the poorest in the region to an illustrative model of developmental "success" (1997). But, as Galeano states, "Technocracy only sees statistics, not people... Now the village of Llallagua has no water, but there is an antenna with a television dish on the summit of Mount Calvario" (Galeano 1997). These oversights may be mere collateral damage to neoliberal developmentalists, but they have not gone unnoticed by the people of Latin America. In the past three decades there has been somewhat of a revolution to return to traditional values and way of life based on the fundament of Buen Vivir.

The insurrection of neoliberalism in Latin America today can be linked back to two scenarios (Gudynas 2011). First, in the 1900s a political process was put in motion akin to post-development thought, as a reaction to neoliberal market reforms. At the same time, the emergence of several progressive countries in Latin America saw the rise of an Indigenous movement roused by the emancipation of the Indigenous rights, knowledge, and cultures that were previously oppressed. In light of this, Indigenous communities started to mobilise at the national level across Latin America, but were more concentrated in Ecuador and Bolivia whose respective Indigenous organisations like *Confederación de Nacionalidades Indígenas de Ecuador* (CONAIE) and *Confederación de Pueblos Indígenas de Bolivia* (CIDOB) started to lend Indigenous voices to the political processes through state reform.

The consolidation of this movement with its propositions for social inclusion and plurality was a decisive factor in the rise of alternatives coming from the popular classes. The Indigenous movement spurred on a popular movement, which was undoubtedly the start of the post-developmental shift that can be noted in Latin American politics and mindsets today, manifested in Buen Vivir and touted as an alternative to neoliberal development.

Buen Vivir, based on the Indigenous worldviews of Sumak Kawsay or Suma Qamaña, thus became the driver for shifting the political spaces towards a post-development framework. Policy-makers have advocated Buen Vivir as a change of paradigm from the "monocultural" neoliberal agenda to a post-development, post-neoliberal socio-economic transformation (Radcliffe 2012). And in line with post-development thinking, as a concept it critiques the "Otherising" of poverty (Radcliffe 2012) that is prevalent in development discussions, bringing control back to the people at the lowest level and away from the government elite. The legitimacy that Latin American post-development has given to the possibility of finding a viable solution to the development legacy is unprecedented. Buen Vivir has played an important role in that shift.

In the search for "alternatives to development"

The idea of an "alternative to development" has become an important trend in the search for a practical solution rather than a pure discourse critique. Buen Vivir has been most critical in Ecuador and Bolivia. Other alternatives that could be argued to be more mainstream in post-development literature have also made an important contribution, most notably degrowth (conceptualised in France and diffused around Europe), which has parallels with Buen Vivir. For that reason, it is important to briefly examine what the commonly misunderstood concept of 'degrowth' means.

Degrowth

Like post-development, the concept of degrowth also calls for a complete paradigm shift. It radically questions the "spirit" of capitalism: Consumption and development as economic progress (Latouche 2012) in the name of human well-being and the environment. Latouche (2012), a prominent French intellectual in the degrowth space, says, "The aim of the movement for 'degrowth' is precisely to let other voices be heard again and to open up alternative paths." As a concept predicated on wellbeing and the environment, it rests on two key principles: 1) That economic growth must not surpass the biophysical limits of the planet; and 2) that human wellbeing takes precedence over the pursuit of wealth (Whitehead 2013).

Degrowth has grown in popularity since the Global Financial Crisis (GFC) of 2008, in a social uprising against the capitalist failings that caused the crisis in the first place. But it is not a new idea. As an intellectual and political theory, it first was introduced in the 1970s by André Gorz and Nicholas Georgescu-Roegen, but it wasn't until the 2000s (particularly following the GFC) that it started to gain ground as a popular social movement (Gudynas 2013b).

Supporting the assumption by Martinez-Alier et al., Unceta (2013) points out that there are two main themes running through degrowth. On the one hand, there is degrowth *á la française* represented in conjunction with two perspectives: One derived from political ecology and the other from a general critique of development. On the other hand, there is the idea of sustainable degrowth, which some would link to ecological economics (Unceta 2013).

Degrowth's main problem, however, is in its terminology (Unceta 2013). It does not refer to a backwards slide or decline in growth as the prefix suggests; rather it rejects economic growth as a basis for attaining quality of life. Latouche (2012) states that it has wrongly been interpreted, as the French *decroissance* has more positive connotations that the English "degrowth." Using an environmental analogy, he asks (Latouche 2012), "What could be more fortunate than the fact that after a disastrous flood, a river returns to its normal flow?"

Latouche's premise, therefore, is that *decroissance* does not equal negative growth, as that would only plunge societies into darkness, and compromise wellbeing and quality of life (Chassagne & Everingham 2019). While that is important to bear in mind, sustainable degrowth goes one step further in that it does not promote a literal decline in growth in all areas of society. The need for this approach has been echoed by several proponents of post-development: "The over-consumption of some groups, for example, the very rich, has to decrease. In that sense, there will indeed be less growth. But, on the other hand, some sectors do need to continue to show growth, for example, education and sanitation" (Cordaid 2012).

There will eventually come a point where degrowth is no longer an option, for example peak oil which will result in "self-limiting growth" (Garcia 2012). The 2019 novel coronavirus (COVID-19) demonstrated the need to shift growth from consumption sectors to areas like health and sanitation to prevent grave public health issues from future global pandemics. At the time of writing there have also been preliminary discussions about this "self-limited" economic growth in times of global crisis such as COVID-19.[1] Sooner or later, we will be forced to change as the system collapses on itself.

The proposition of Buen Vivir as an alternative has juxtaposed it with degrowth. Gudynas (2011), however, sees degrowth neither as a comparison concept to Buen

Vivir, nor as an objective of Buen Vivir, but rather as a consequence. The problem is that degrowth remains a political and theoretical idea, whereas Buen Vivir has more practical promise, as Part II of this book will demonstrate. Therefore, degrowth might not necessarily be a practical alternative to development that will result in real transformative change, but it may have some ideas to support Buen Vivir in practice[2] and move us towards a post-extractive era.

Ending the age of extractivism

Taken out of the neoliberal context, the ancient act of extraction itself is not a negative activity since the use of natural resources has sustained life on this planet for millennia. It is the method, scale, and purpose of extraction that are the culprits. Extractive activities on a massive scale have large detrimental social and environmental impacts. Water pollution from mining water run-off, air and noise pollution from open-pit mining operations, the clearing of land and habitats, soil contamination and expropriation of land from entire communities are very tangible problems that regularly cause conflict between communities, extractivist companies, and governments, as well as within the communities themselves.

Extractivists will argue that there are many positive aspects of extractivism – one of them being the opportunities provided by the market for income creation and wealth. This, however, is a very anthropocentric viewpoint, which turns nature into a commodity for the objective of increasing human wellbeing. If the economic aspects of extractivism had such a positive economic impact, the grave inequalities that we see between the periphery and the core would cease to exist. More often, extractivism leads to disproportionate wealth distribution and does not deliver on the creation of employment on a scale as large as is promised (Acosta 2013). Moreover, it leads to the degradation of the natural environment and its ecosystems. This expropriation of nature places human beings at dire odds with the environment.

This nature–society dualism will only lead to the former's destruction, and it is only by living in harmony with nature that we can recover the true dimensions of sustainability (Acosta 2012; Arsel & Angel 2012). In that respect, extractivism is incompatible with Buen Vivir. Even the former Correa government acknowledged that it challenges the ability to attain "Good Living," "because it reproduces a pattern of unequal accumulation and irrational exploitation that degrades the ecosystem" (SENPLADES 2009). Given the persistence of neoextractivism in Latin American politics, any realistic analysis of Buen Vivir as an alternative to development therefore must be examined within the context of this new extractivism. This brings with it its own set of challenges, as I will discuss in Chapter Six.

"A Latin America paradox": A very brief history of extractivism in Latin America

Modern extraction and accumulation in Latin America can be traced back to the conquest of the Americas. While pre-Columbus extractive operations in the region relied on human labour and technological advances on a large scale, it was largely for the benefit of the region. Colonial and post-colonial extraction, on the other hand, exploits the region's resources for the benefit of the West. In an analysis of these "new geographies of extractive industries," Bebbington and Bury (2013) argue that Columbus's diaries from his expeditionary force in 1492 demonstrate the mindset of colonial control that still dominates Western development today: An obsession with the abundance of gold and how it can be extracted on a large scale for the advantage of Western civilization.

Despite what we already know about its causal effect on climate change, extractivism is increasing (Bebbington & Bury 2013). The latest commodity boom in Latin America has seen the development of new mining pits, exploration, drilling installations, and large-scale plantations (Schorr 2019).

It is evident, as Escobar (2010) states, that Latin America is at a crossroads in terms of development and its dependence on extractivism. According to Acosta (2013), this has been a mechanism of colonial appropriation. Like most countries in the periphery the region has been subject to what is called the "paradox of plenty" or the "resource curse," whereby the abundance of natural resources has led to a social and ecological "perverse state of affairs" (Acosta 2013). The exploitation of Latin America's resources for the advantage of countries in the core has not gone unnoticed by governments in the region, who are now turning to what has been termed "neoextractivism" to regain greater control of the region's natural resources (Gudynas 2010; Svampa 2013).

The Birth of neoextractivism: The progressive politics paradox

The term "neoextractivism" was coined by Eduardo Gudynas in 2009, and refers to a continuum of the process of accumulation based on primary exports, but one that contains both new and old features: An increased involvement of the state in its management, as well as profit and wealth distribution (Acosta 2012). It is this involvement of the state that is the most important aspect of the neoextractivist approach, particularly in the context of Buen Vivir. In Ecuador, for example, the former Correa government used neoextractive policies as a premise to attain the economic means to implement social policies under Buen Vivir. This is contradictory and, as Acosta argues, it reduces Buen Vivir to a product or a slogan, without genuine intent for change.

This turn towards the nationalisation of resources is seen as the cornerstone of post-development in Latin America, yet the very nature of large-scale extractive activities, be they nationalised or not, seems to contradict post-development objectives. Ecuadorian neoextractivism is promoted in the 2008 Constitution, whereby "the State reserves the right to administer, regulate, oversee and manage strategic sectors, following the principles of environmental sustainability, precaution, and efficiency" (Constitución de la república del ecuador 2008 art. 313). Yet, neoextractivist policies have been part of the main cause of tension between the state and civil society in Ecuador. This "new extractivism" can even be considered anti-constitutional, highlighting the contradictions present in the

Ecuadorian government's approach. For example, article 14 recognises the "right of the citizens to live in a clean environmental that is ecologically balanced, that guarantees sustainability, Buen Vivir and *Sumak Kawsay*" (Constitución de la república del ecuador 2008).

Within neoextractivism, the continual commodification of nature poses the greatest problem. It conflicts with the biocentric principles underlying Buen Vivir that demand respect for the environment and harmony between human beings and nature. Placing an economic figure on nature is inherently problematic and unsustainable.

Whichever policy approach governments take to extractive activities, large-scale modern extractivism points to a process that is destructive by nature. It is an economic growth activity based on an idea of infinite resources, ignoring the ecological limits of that growth. As Alvarez mentions, "its impulse provides little space to care for the environment, to promote social economy and to sustain food sovereignty" (Álvarez 2013). These are all critical elements of Buen Vivir. Moreover, extractivism in Latin America has a sour reputation for the appropriation of Indigenous land, environmental destruction, ecological crises, and adverse social impacts affecting communities, individuals, and entire ways of life.

In the search for practical alternatives, we need to transition towards a post-extractive economy. Buen Vivir does so with values of plurality, complementarity, and a reciprocity with nature. As Brightman and Lewis (2017) assert:

> The challenge of sustainability demands much more than the protection or preservation of communities or nature reserves, and more than technical fixes for CO_2 production or resource limitations: it requires re-imagining and reworking communities, societies and landscapes, especially those dominated by industrial capitalism, to help us build a productive symbiosis with each other and the many nonhumans on whom we depend.

Buen Vivir: A path towards Socio-Eco Wellbeing

Buen Vivir thus provides us with an opportunity to reimagine the way we understand development. So far, I have discussed the history of development, argued why we need an alternative, and laid the foundations for arguing Buen Vivir as one such alternative; yet the conceptual puzzle is still incomplete. Buen Vivir has been hailed by post-developmentalists and ingrained in progressive policy, but many gaps remain in our knowledge of just how it can be a viable and practical alternative – one that promises transformative change, not just discourse and rhetoric.

Buen Vivir seeks Socio-Eco Wellbeing which brings us back to the original objective of sustainable and intergenerational needs satisfaction specified by the Brundtland Commission. The satisfaction of needs for both present and future generations has been jeopardised by the inconsistencies and contradictions in the vague definition of "needs" specified by the Brundtland Commission, and its use in neoliberal Sustainable Development (Vanhulst & Beling 2013). Despite these issues, however, the satisfaction of needs is still the core objective of Sustainable Development programs. Policy-makers rely on indicators to measure how actions impact those needs. On the issue of measurement, Munasinghe, an economist from the World Bank, argues for the importance of maintaining social and cultural systems when considering needs for sustainability (Rogers, Jalal & Boyd 2008). While this is not the general focus of most economists, it is a vital aspect of Buen Vivir. But how can one calculate such stability?

The idea that sustainability needs to be quantifiably measured is deeply ingrained in development thinking and therefore the issue of measurement needs to be examined, if Buen Vivir is to be a viable alternative to Sustainable Development. And as a plural approach, it is open to incorporating aspects of other alternative approaches to enable viable operationalisation, but the only way it can do so is by marrying the conceptual with the empirical, examining the way in which it is understood, defined, and practiced by the key actors.

In the words of Arturo Escobar, in the "pursuit of alternatives" we must indeed make contact with "those whose 'alternatives' research is supposed to illuminate" (Escobar 1995). Alternatives must be sought in their local settings. Buen Vivir is no exception. After all, Buen Vivir is not only a theoretical paradigm but also a social practice that should serve as inspiration to transform the current reality (Unceta 2013).

Buen Vivir invites us therefore to delve deeper. It aims for transformative and holistic change. It can provide the opportunity to understand the whole, not just the sum of its parts – the interrelationships, the origins, and all of its dimensions – so that we may find an effective, practical, and viable solution to our environmental and social woes. That being said, before moving onto its practical analysis, it is time to explore a more profound conceptual foundation of Buen Vivir.

Notes

1　The "time of writing" was in the middle of the COVID-19 global pandemic; therefore it is too soon to thoroughly analyse the consequences, but it is certain that more events of this nature will force structural changes to the global economy. See Chassagne (2020).
2　See, for example, Chassagne and Everingham (2019).

References

Acosta, A 2012, *The buen vivir: An opportunity to imagine another world, Inside a champion: An analysis of the Brazilian Development Model, Democracy*, Heinrich Böll Foundation, Berlin, Germany.

Acosta, A 2013, 'Extractivism and neoextractivism: Two sides of the same coin', in M. Lang & D. Mokrani (eds.), *Beyond development: Alternative visions from latin america*, Fundacion Rosa Lumxemburg, Quito, Ecuador.

Álvarez, S 2013, 'Qué es el sumak kawsay o buen vivir', *Economia y buen vivir*, viewed 5 February 2014, <http://buenvivir.eumed.net/wp-content/uploads/2013/04/sumak-kawsay-concepto.pdf>.

Arsel, M & Angel, NA 2012, '"Stating" nature's role in Ecuadorian development: Civil society and the yasuni-itt initiative', *Journal of Developing Societies*, vol. 28, no. 2 pp. 203–27. doi: 10.1177/0169796x12448758.

Bebbington, A & Bury, J 2013, 'New geographies of extractive industries in latin America', in A Bebbington & J Bury, eds., *Subterranean struggles: New dynamics of mining, oil, and gas in latin america*, University of Texas Press, Austin, TX. doi: 10.7560/748620.

Brightman, M   2017, 'Introduction: The anthropology of sustainability: Beyond development and progress', in M. Brightman & J. Lewis (eds.), *The anthropology of sustainability*, Palgrave Macmillon, New York.

Chassagne, N 2020, 'Here's what the coronavirus can teach us about tackling climate change', *The Conversation*, <https://theconversation.com/heres-what-the-coronavirus-pandemic-can-teach-us-about-tackling-climate-change-134399>.

Chassagne, N & Everingham, P 2019, 'Buen vivir: Degrowing extractivism and growing wellbeing through tourism', *Journal of Sustainable Tourism*, vol. 27, no. 12, pp. 1909–25. doi: 10.1080/09669582.2019.1660668.

Constitución de la república del ecuador 2008, Registro oficial 449, 20 October 2008, Quito.

Cordaid 2012, *Buen vivir, the good life (imagining sustainability −6)*, CIDSE, viewed 11 December 2013, <http://www.cidse.org/articles/rethinking-development/growth-and-sustainability/buen-vivir-the-good-life-imagining-sustainability-6.html>.

Escobar, A 1995, *Encountering development: The making and unmaking of the third world (new in paper)*, Princeton University Press, Princeton, NJ.

Escobar, A 2000, 'Beyond the search for a paradigm? Post-development and beyond', *Development*, vol. 43, no. 4, pp. 11–4. doi: 10.1057/palgrave.development.1110188.

Escobar, A 2010, 'Latin America at a crossroads', *Cultural Studies*, vol. 24, no. 1 pp. 1–65. doi: 10.1080/09502380903424208.

Galeano, E 1997, 'To be like them, in M Rahnema and V Bawtree, eds., *The post-development reader*, Zed Books, London.

Garcia, E 2012, 'Degrowth and buen vivir (living well): A critical comparison', *Third international conference on degrowth for ecological sustainability and social equity*, Venice, Italy.

Gudynas, E 2010, *Si eres tan progresista ¿por qué destruyes la naturaleza?: Neoextractivismo, izquierda y alternativas*, CAAP, Quito.

Gudynas, E 2011, 'Buen vivir: Today's tomorrow', *Development*, vol. 54, no. 4 pp. 441–7. doi: 10.1057/dev.2011.86.

Gudynas, E 2013a, 'Debates on development and its alternatives in latin america: A brief heterodox guide', in Lang M and Mokrani D, eds., *Beyond development*, Rosa Luxemburg Foundation, Quito.

Gudynas, E 2013b, 'Development alternatives in bolivia: The impulse, the resistance, and the restoration', *NACLA Report on the Americas*, vol. 46, no. 1 pp. 22–6. doi: 10.1080/10714839.2013.11722007.

Latouche, S 2012, 'Can the left escape economism?', *Capitalism Nature Socialism*, vol. 23, no. 1 pp. 74–8. doi.org/10.1080/10455752.2011.648841.

Radcliffe, SA 2012, 'Development for a postneoliberal era? Sumak kawsay, living well and the limits to decolonisation in ecuador', *Geoforum*, vol. 43, no. 2, pp. 240–9. doi.org/10.1016/j.geoforum.2011.09.003.

Rahnema, M & Bawtree, V (eds), 1997, *The post-development reader*, Zed Books, London.

Rogers, PP, Jalal, KF & Boyd, JA 2008, *An introduction to sustainable development*, Earthscan, London.

Sachs, W 2009, *The development dictionary*, 2nd new ed., Zed Books, Limited Macmillan [Distributor], London, Gordonsville.

Schorr, B 2019, 'Extractivism in latin america: The global-national-local link', *Latin American Research Review*, vol. 54, no. 2, pp. 509–516. doi: 10.25222/larr.392.

SENPLADES 2009, *Plan nacional para el buen vivir 2009–2013 : Construyendo un estado plurinacional e intercultural*, Secretaría Nacional de Planificación y Desarrollo, Quito, Ecuador.

Svampa, M 2013, 'Resource extractivism and alternatives: Latin American perspectives on development', in Lang M and Mokrani D, eds., *Beyond development*, Rosa Luxemburg Foundation, Berlin.

Unceta, K 2013, 'Decrecimiento y buen vivir ¿paradigmas convergentes ? Debates sobre el postdesarrollo en europa y américa latina', *Revista de Economía Mundial*, vol. 35, pp. 197–216.

Vanhulst, J & Beling, AE 2013, 'Buen vivir: La irrupción de américa latina en el campo gravitacional del desarrollo sostenible', *Revista Iberoamericana de Economía Ecológica*, vol. 21, pp. 1–14. <http://desarrollo.sociologia.uahurtado.cl/wp-content/up loads/2013/03/2013-Buen-Vivir-y-Desarrollo-sustentable.pdf>.

Whitehead, M 2013, 'Editorial: Degrowth or regrowth?', *Environmental Values*, vol. 22, no. 2 pp. 141–5. doi: 10.3197/096327113x13581561725077.

Ziai, A 2007, *Exploring post-development: Theory and practice, problems and perspectives*, Routledge, London.

3 Sustaining the "Good Life"

Buen Vivir as an alternative to
Sustainable Development[1]

"We have gold. It flows in our rivers. We don't want it," I was once told by a *campesino* in the highlands of Ecuador speaking of the encroachment of extractive companies on their doorstep. "We don't want the problems you have in the West," I was told by another. "If we look after Mother Earth, she will look after us." And such is the philosophy of Buen Vivir: Where nature and society are inseparable and the utmost respect for Pachamama is required to achieve Socio-Eco Wellbeing.

Buen Vivir, however, still lacks coherency (Giovannini 2014a; Walsh 2010). So far, we know that it is as much ecological as it is social; has a more integrated, holistic approach to meeting needs than that of Sustainable Development; and considers both human and environmental needs. Its principal aims are achieving Socio-Eco Wellbeing through a bottom-up, endogenous approach to identifying and meeting needs, as opposed to a top-down exogenous perception of needs.

As demonstrated in Chapter Two, Sustainable Development's neoliberal status quo discourse has so far not ensured collective wellbeing and long-term sustainability. It is at this juncture that Buen Vivir offers an attractive solution, as a post-development "alternative to development," instead of another reformulation of the old neoliberal model. However, as Gudynas argues, while post-development theory questions a discourse, it does not offer any concrete solutions (2013). Nonetheless, post-development provides us with a useful platform to begin to understand Buen Vivir theoretically, before we can analyse it practically.

The previous chapters discussed the critiques of Sustainable Development in the literature; however, in this chapter I would like to highlight the conceptual strengths of Buen Vivir to tackle the areas where Sustainable Development has failed – acheiveing Socio-Eco Wellbeing. This chapter is a critical review of the discourse on Buen Vivir, including policy as well as Indigenous and academic literature,[2] and analyses how it can seek to achieve the common aims of sustainability and wellbeing, albeit from a different perspective. I focus on putting the pieces of the conceptual puzzle together through a synthesis of the core common principles, to begin to examine how it could become a practical alternative to Sustainable Development, as a plural solution for change. Like Vanhulst and Beling (2014), in the analysis in this chapter, I thus take the perspective of a "discursive field" endorsed by Sachs; and I use Dryzek's (1997) categorisation of environmental discourses as "status quo," "reform," or "transformation" to evaluate Buen Vivir discourse.

Both Buen Vivir and Sustainable Development aim for sustainability and well-being through "transformation" (UNGA 2015) with two fundamental differences: 1) Buen Vivir is an endogenous approach allowing for contextual change to start from the bottom-up, while Sustainable Development is universal and top-down, disallowing for differences in culture, geography, and socio-economic circumstances; and 2) the former places the highest value on the reciprocal relationship between nature and society, whereas the latter puts human needs above all else.

Villalba (2013) cautions against comparing Buen Vivir and trends in Western alternatives, to avoid co-optation by the dominant discourses of development. As Vanhulst and Beling (2014) argue, using Buen Vivir as an attack on Sustainable Development will result in it being a "short-lived discursive enterprise" rather than a practical and viable alternative. So, in the logic of Houtart (2011; Villalba 2013), what we need is "dialectic thinking to guide solutions that are neither the linear model of traditional development, nor a return to a fundamentalist Indigenous past." Rather than creating polarised political arguments by using Buen Vivir as an "offensive" (Caria & Domínguez 2016) we need to examine what it is we are trying to achieve and come to a cooperative and plural solution.

The plurality of Buen Vivir has two contexts. The first notion of plurality comes from the Indigenous interpretation, and is later adopted in policy. It revolves around its biocentricity (SENPLADES 2009) – that is plurality of being for all living things. The second is a plurality of knowledge and vision – present in Indigenous and post-development literature – that Buen Vivir should be implemented in cooperation, with all epistemologies involved, including the Western scientific and the technical knowledge that Sustainable Development espouses (Delgado, Rist & Escobar 2010). Arutro Escobar (2017) sums this up, arguing:

> While indigenous traditions have an important role to play in this endeavor, so does a transformed understanding of science, one which would help humans reinterpret their place at the species level within a new universe story. By placing it within a reinterpreted cosmology, science would move beyond the dominant technical and instrumental comprehension of the world to be reintegrated with the phenomenal world and so it would contribute to humans' reencounter with the numinous universe.

In a resolution for a "2030 Agenda for Sustainable Development," the UN partly recognised plurality in the SDGs, albeit from a policy perspective: "We recognise that there are different approaches, visions, models and tools available to each country, in accordance with its national circumstances and priorities, to achieve sustainable development" (UNGA 2015 art. 59). However, the post-2015 global framework for Sustainable Development to ensure a "just, equitable and inclusive" world by 2030 provided no blueprint for how to achieve that with contributions from local communities (Howard & Wheeler 2015). This recognition provides a unique opportunity for an approach like Buen Vivir to find a practical place within the global framework. Therefore, I am proposing that rather than considering Buen Vivir as an opposing, ideological alternative to the dominant paradigm, it should be understood as a positive practical tool or resource for endogenous, community-led change. To do so, let us look at where it started.

Indigenous origins to political discourse

The Ecuadorian interpretation of Buen Vivir originates from Indigenous cosmovision, loosely translated in Spanish from the Kichwa term "Sumak Kawsay." Its Bolivian counterpart *vivir bien* is translated from the Aymaran *suma qamaña*. Both concepts have gained traction in popular discourse since the region's Indigenous movements in the 1990s (Álvarez 2013), which has subsequently had profound impacts on political and intellectual fronts.

Huanacuni (2010) has broken down the translated terms from both Kichwa and Aymara into Spanish: "*Sumak*" or "*suma*" meaning "plenitude" or "sublime," and "*kawsay*" meaning "life" or "to be living," roughly translate into "a life in plenitude." Both concepts lose their tacit meaning when translated into Spanish, and even further so when translated into English (Huanacuni 2010).

Both Sumak Kawsay and Suma Qamaña have impacted on policy with progressive governments in Latin America employing them as a political reaction to the failure of Western-style development (Gudynas 2011); though they have led to differed policy interpretations. The Bolivian government's Vivir Bien resulted in a set of ethical guidelines for government; whereas the Ecuadorian government's Buen Vivir is considered the most robust interpretation in terms of meeting the challenge of becoming a viable alternative, because of the inclusion of the "Rights of Nature" (articles 71 and 74) in the 2008 Constitution (Constitución de la república del ecuador 2008). It is this plural set of rights that provides the Ecuadorian Buen Vivir with a stronger policy framework for ecological sustainability, though their inclusion, argue Villalba and Etxano (2017), is "more rhetorical than operative" because of the contradictions between government policy and practice.

The former Correa government operationalised the constitutional changes in the *Plan Nacional para el Buen Vivir (PNBV: 2009–13, and 2013–17)*, based on neoextractive strategies. It is arguably in this process, however, that Buen Vivir has become ambiguous (Merino 2016), which renders it at risk of being co-opted for various political interests. Nonetheless, each contribution to the concept of Buen Vivir has been important in shaping the way we understand it. In that respect the Ecuadorian PNBV, which also includes specific targets, is more compelling than the Bolivian moral interpretation, and provides a sound practical base from which to examine the role of government institutions in implementing it. This is the reason why I focus my attention on Buen Vivir over the Bolivian Vivir Bien.

Buen Vivir is a "work-in-progress" because of the assimilation of Indigenous worldviews with the ensuing political and academic definitions, making it a plural "platform" for alternative visions (Gudynas 2011), because of this ongoing fusion between its Indigenous underpinnings and the way it is shaping and is shaped by politics and academia. Guardiola identified two approaches for Buen Vivir (Guardiola & García-Quero 2014): The extractivist approach supported by the government through neoextractive endeavours, which views extractivism as a means for achieving Buen Vivir; and the ecological approach, supported by Indigenous and post-development literature.

The former Correa government's intention to achieve Buen Vivir through social redistribution policies, acknowledging the Rights of Nature, and through economic diversification (Villalba & Etxano 2017), by building economic capacity in other areas such as knowledge and technology to transition away from the exportation of raw materials, (SENPLADES 2009) seemed like a positive step. Yet, there was (and continues to be with the new government) a clear contradiction between policy and practice (Deneulin 2012), demonstrating its extractivist approach. The Correa administration argued that a neo-extractive model aims to bridge the gap between current neoliberal development practices and future Buen Vivir. On the one hand, the PNBV identified a need for "endogenous development with strategic relation to the world system to satisfy basic needs" (SENPLADES 2009); but on the other hand, it failed to acknowledge that a top-down analysis of needs situated within an extractive-dependant economic system geared for growth is antagonistic to the objectives of Buen Vivir. Extractive activities pose a serious challenge to the attainment of Buen Vivir due to their impacts on the environment. They are fundamentally inconsistent with the principle of reciprocity with nature, upon which Buen Vivir is founded.

This new approach to extractivism was labelled as "21st Century Socialism" and pitched against the dominant ideology of neoliberalism. Some scholars will argue that we cannot have political discourse without the inference to political ideology (Monni & Pallottino 2015). However, once something has been labelled under a particular ideology, it has the potential to become co-opted for certain interests. Ideology, in this way, becomes a "mobilising utopia" sought as an "offensive weapon against hegemonic ideals" (Caria & Domínguez 2016), though this will only create a polarising defence instead of working in cooperative and plural ways for effective solutions. The outcome is that the concept either becomes radicalised, or weak and rhetorical. In global Sustainable Development discourse the latter has been realised, as the dominant ideology has become an "interest syndicate" (Caria & Domínguez 2016) for pursuing the status quo, acting contrary to its own principles.

In Ecuador the PNBV absorbed the new direction of the government and states that "Good Living cannot be improvised, it must be planned" (SENPLADES 2013), which means from the top-down. But this fails to acknowledge that so much of the very idea of Buen Vivir depends on context. As Kauffman and Martin state, it is not a "preformulated route to sustainable development... it involves dialogue within and among communities to determine the best pathways" (Kauffman & Martin 2014). Beyond that, it comes from the bottom-up, which necessarily incorporates local realities.

In the political discourses of Buen Vivir, participation is viewed as a way to understand communities' experiences on the ground, and an attempt to meet their real needs. In theory, this brings development decisions closer to the people, but it is still driven by top-down objectives. To truly be consistent with the principles of Buen Vivir, it is essential for needs to be determined from the bottom-up based on a non-linear realisation of Socio-Eco Wellbeing and not economic growth: Living well, *not* living better.

The ecological approach, on the other hand, calls on the need to emphasise Indigenous origins of Buen Vivir; however, the Indigenous notion of Buen Vivir is something very different to what is found in political discourse and academia (Merino 2016). It is anchored in culture and a belief system, with more profound meaning than can be articulated in language. From this perspective Buen Vivir is an endogenous alternative to neoliberal development (Delgado, Rist & Escobar 2010) and this endogenous emphasis provides the opportunity to understand, define, and satisfy the real needs of communities, instigating bottom-up change (Escobar 1992; Giovannini 2014a). Inevitably such an endogenous approach has deep implications for both global and national policy (Merino 2016).

What I propose is an approach that honours Buen Vivir's Indigenous origins for its ethos, values, and aims, while not seeking to retrofit specific cultural values articulated only within Indigenous communities. That is, learning from its Indigenous origins but emphasising the importance of plurality and community context. This approach does not maintain that communities must apply it in isolation, but rather that the process should derive from the ground up, and not be imposed from the top-down. As Delgado et al. (2010) state, "if communities could create Buen Vivir for themselves entirely, it would have already been done." Agostino and Dübgen (2012) add that it cannot be achieved by individuals, it must be a collective action, in cooperation with all actors involved without diluting it. Buen Vivir is indeed a conceptual puzzle and it is important to note the key part each interpretation plays in bringing the puzzle together. The challenge is how to translate Buen Vivir into a practical community resource without it becoming another rhetorical tool for self-interested policy. The key lies in this core principle of plurality.

A plural alternative to Sustainable Development

One point that many now agree on is that to achieve sustainability, we require a radical transformation of the global system, moving away from unbridled growth and consumption (Redclift 2002; Tesoriero & Ife 2010). This will require a plural approach to move away from the status quo.

A recognition of the situation has evoked renewed global action with the SDGs. The SDGs associate Sustainable Development action with climate change, but nonetheless are grounded in the same neoliberal, anthropocentric system of economic growth that has failed the current model of development. The stated desire to break away from the traditional concept of "development" (SENPLADES 2009) seems to follow what Dryzek calls an "imaginative reformist departure" in environmental discourses, where "the environment is brought to the heart of society and its cultural, moral and economic systems" (Dryzek 1997). This discourse seeks to reform old approaches to environmental problems as economic opportunities. It is far from the radical transformative departure proposed by Buen Vivir. It is no longer a compelling case that countries need "developing," because wellbeing and quality of life cannot be supported by unbridled economic growth. "Growth is not making us happier. It is creating dysfunctional and unequal societies, and if it continues as is it will make large parts of the planet unfit for human habitation" (Harcourt 2013).

Growth, though, is very much central in the conception of human wellbeing in Sustainable Development (Guillen-Royo 2015). Wellbeing in this respect still relies on a top-down approach to break "the poverty trap" (Ruttenberg 2013) which ignores the diverse realities and needs of local communities. It also emphasises wellbeing in the individual, rather than the community. While wellbeing in Sustainable Development is often equated to levels of happiness, happiness relies on the subjective individual. Though individual happiness does affect community wellbeing and vice-versa, the notion of wellbeing prescribed by Buen Vivir focuses on communal wellbeing over individual wellbeing. This notion is subjective in that it rests on a community's identification of needs rather than an exogenous perception of needs. Wiseman and Brasher (2008) define community wellbeing as a "combination of social, economic, environmental, cultural, and political conditions identified by individuals and their communities as essential for them to flourish and fulfill their potential." Buen Vivir is innovative for sustainability in terms of wellbeing, in that it also requires environmental wellbeing, practiced by behaviour and beliefs and guaranteed by the Rights of Nature; its communal, holistic wellbeing considers context.

In reference to the first point of difference with Buen Vivir mentioned earlier, post-developmentalists say that the broad approach ascribed by Sustainable Development dominated by global institutions with a Western bias fails to consider local context, aiming for conformity to exogenous Western ideals (Smyth 2011). As Esteva and Prakash (1997) state, "local proposals[,] if they are conceived by communities rooted in specific places, reflect the radical pluralism of cultures and the unique cosmovision that defines every culture."

On the second point of difference, if we continue on the path towards Buen Vivir as an endogenous alternative that decouples itself from the growth imperative and the nature–society dualism of Sustainable Development, we will by default attain more sustainable outcomes than we will on the current trajectory. An alternative perspective is therefore essential – one that post-developmentalists ascribe plurally embraces sustainability and holistic wellbeing.

Plurality is relatively easy to incorporate in Buen Vivir as it is under a process of co-construction. As Cerdán (2013) asserts, even within Latin America "there is a wide recognition that Buen Vivir is not a homogenous philosophy; rather, it incorporates a diversity of knowledges [sic] and philosophies." In the same vein, Vanessa Bolaños (2012) asserts that "processes of change are not constructed from one lone actor, but always from the articulation of a correlation of forces: Both within the country and the construction of new socio-political economic schemas." The viability of Buen Vivir as an alternative will thus be revealed in how it is understood in practice.

In acknowledging the vital importance of plurality, one of the key challenges for Buen Vivir is its multiple interpretations. If Buen Vivir is a construction of multiple epistemologies, the theoretical argument needs to be less about which vision is right, and more about uniting the similarities to enable us to move forward cooperatively and plurally in practice, not just in discourse; because as Cubillo et al. (2014) argue, the polemic surrounding the contested interpretations "threatens to prevent, in practice, Buen Vivir from being consolidated as a way of life and living in harmony with nature and others." Overcoming this starts with challenging the dominant norms and opening new spaces for thinking about Socio-Eco Wellbeing.

Buen Vivir: Equal aims, contested definitions

Both Buen Vivir and Sustainable Development are big ideas with conceptually loose boundaries. On Sustainable Development, Connelly once stated it has different conceptions due to its "widely accepted but vague core meaning" (2007) and that this lack of consensus prevents contributions to its practice. Just as Sustainable Development has been identified as an essentially contested concept so is Buen Vivir in that it is underlined by "legitimate, yet incompatible and contested interpretations of how the concept should be put into practice" (Connelly 2007). Contrary to Sustainable Development which has a universal definition but is contested by its loose economic, environmental, and social principles, Buen Vivir lacks a single definition but contains a set of common core principles.

In the words of Lukes and Runciman (1974), "essentially contested concepts must have a common core; otherwise, how could we justifiably claim that the contests were about the same concept?" This does not mean homogenising the different interpretations into a single definition but synthesising the main common principles to develop a practical tool for change, rather than another rhetorical policy goal. Villalba and Etxano (2017) argue that there is no "doctrine on the foundations and central elements of Buen Vivir." Cubillo-Guevara et al. (2016), however, identified three different "streams" of Buen Vivir – Indigenous, socialist (political), and post-developmentalist (academic) – within which they argue three common elements of Buen Vivir: Identity, equity, and sustainability. While the current scholarly research does provide an analysis of different interpretations and origins of Buen Vivir, it does not offer this synthesis of the core principles, common across its different interpretations.

To that end, I now move to coalesce the principles that are constant in Buen Vivir, and that could contribute to a contextual and practical resource by taking a step towards understanding what the concept entails. Although loose principles have been recognised in both the Bolivian Constitution and the Ecuadorian PNBV, these have been decided by the state, and therefore contradict the idea of Buen Vivir being an endogenous yet plural construction from actors at all levels. In a plural concept, all interpretations must be considered. This "common core" acts to anchor the notion of Buen Vivir, to create a platform from which to understand its applicability as a plural and contextual concept.

The overarching ethos of Buen Vivir is a life in harmony with nature, Pachamama, or Mother Earth (Huanacuni 2010). Several authors describe nature–society pluralism as "reciprocity"; and so human beings must acknowledge and pursue this to ensure life in all forms continues (Acosta 2010). Cubillo-Guevara et al. (2016) define Buen Vivir as a "form of life in harmony with oneself, society and nature," though if the term "definition" means to assign exact meaning to a concept, Buen Vivir is more complex than that, given its contested interpretations. While an overarching description can serve as a guide for policy, for flexibility in implementation it is important to synthesise the common principles across the multiple contested definitions rather than referencing a single universal definition to be able to use Buen Vivir as a viable and practical tool for communities. So then, we may rightly ask: What does Buen Vivir entail?

Just as Sustainable Development is defined by the triple pillars of economic, social, and environmental as categories for focus, Delgado et al. (2010) define three main pillars for Buen Vivir that serve to categorise the principles rather than define the approach: Social, spiritual, and material. Unlike Sustainable Development's growth-centred economic pillar, this "material" pillar includes a more holistic vision for economic activity. The "spiritual" pillar refers to transcendence rather than religion.[3] Ecuadorian scholar Santiago García-Álvarez (2013) built upon these, identifying six common dimensions of Buen Vivir: Livelihood, equity, sustainability, empowerment, capabilities, and social cohesion.[4] These dimensions can be understood as "sub-categories" of each of the three pillars. Table 3.1, below, provides a definition of these dimensions specific to Buen Vivir.

The principles in Table 3.2 identified through a critical scoping review of academic, Indigenous, and political discourse bring together existing knowledge on Buen Vivir, to better understand what it involves at the conceptual level and where the gaps may lie. Table 3.2 demarcates the core principles found in the literature into these dimensions and their corresponding pillars mentioned by Álvarez and Delgado et al. by an analysis of the definitions provided below by Álvarez.

I allocated the principles to a corresponding dimension by analysing how each principle was discussed in the literature in the context of Buen Vivir, and how that relates to Álvarez's description of the dimensions. For example, while complementarity as a principle in support of social balance and justice has been

Table 3.1 Definition of dimensions adapted from Alvarez (2013)

Dimensions	Definition
Equity	Diversity, social balance, and social justice
Social cohesion	Living in harmony with others
Sustainability	Mutual respect for the environment and living in harmony with nature
Empowerment	Participation and respect for cultural systems
Livelihood	A plural and alternative economy supporting a dignified life
Capabilities	Expanded human capabilities where collective wellbeing is fundamental

Table 3.2 Principles of Buen Vivir (literature)

	Principles of Buen Vivir					
	Social		Spiritual		Material	
	Equity	*Social cohesion*	*Sustainability*	*Empowerment*	*Livelihood*	*Capabilities*
Core principles	• Plurality[5] • Non-linear progress • Complementarity	• Community • Harmony	• Reciprocity • Nature	• Decolonisation[6] • Culture	• Food sovereignty[7] • Sustainable use of resources[8]	• Wellbeing • Quality of life • Contextuality[9]

described in the literature as "relationality between human beings," reciprocity in Buen Vivir has been described by Deneulin (2012) as "relationships of service and reciprocity towards each other and towards nature," destabilising the hierarchy of society as above nature in Sustainable Development. On that reciprocal relationship Acosta (2010) notes that "ensuring sustainability is [thus] indispensable to ensuring human life on the planet." On wellbeing, Ruttenberg (2013) describes it as enhancing community capability, "supporting the development of human potentialities through meaningful livelihoods, strengthening social relations and promoting ways of life in harmony with nature." The idea of living in harmony with nature is constant but does not negate societies' need to use natural resources; it just requires that it is approached differently. The sustainable use of resources was often discussed as a way to ensure livelihood through an alternative economy with a consequence of greater environmental and social sustainability, "in contrast to neoliberal production" (Agostino & Dübgen 2012).

The discourse highlights the possibility for much-needed transformation away from the status quo by demanding, for example, reciprocity and communal wellbeing over individual wellbeing and human needs attained by economic growth. Additionally, while sustainability in Sustainable Development is manifested through the commodification of nature, Buen Vivir requires mutual respect for the environment and includes the Rights of Nature in its ambit. Likewise, capabilities that rely on collective wellbeing and particular to context, rather than individual needs based on Western-derived development metrics, can help address social inequalities. Social inequalities arise in the pursuit for linear-style progress linked to growth. The principle of non-linear progress espoused by Buen Vivir under the dimension of equity can therefore help lead to more social balance and justice.

Supporting these principles is the endogenous approach, which favours practice over discourse; and by thinking of these principles as being practically applied, we can start to envisage how Buen Vivir promises to ensure sustainability where Sustainable Development has failed by embracing plurality, and a biocentric, communal approach to wellbeing. However, to move from discourse to practice, certain challenges need to be overcome, including transitioning to a post-extractive economy (Villalba & Etxano 2017).

A grassroots solution to wellbeing and sustainability?

The literature raised two challenges for Buen Vivir in translating a concrete model that can be put into practice endogenously. The first is by Tortosa (2011) who discusses the issue of possible indicators to strengthen the conceptual debate and support its implementation and measurement. This issue of measurement has been raised by several authors as a major challenge in taking Buen Vivir forward as a concrete proposal for community action (Phélan 2011; Unceta 2013) – one that can meet the global aspirations of quantitatively driven governments. Taking the linear perspective from a concept like Sustainable Development where the path towards sustainability requires us to track progress, it is only logical that a non-linear alternative would have to demonstrate its efficacy to achieve what Sustainable Development has failed. This argument calls for on-the-ground research to understand the implications of possible indicators for Buen Vivir; therefore this is further canvassed in Chapter Eight.

The other point is raised by Phélan (2011) who argues that for Buen Vivir to be put into practice, it would require work from multiple perspectives: Institutions and communities, macro, and micro. This point supports Buen Vivir's plural approach.

Furthermore, I identify three additional implementation challenges: 1) Its contested nature; 2) the political attribution of ideology; and 3) its existence within an extractive economy. On the first implementation challenge, if we acknowledge its Indigenous origins and the importance that plurality plays, then we understand that for it to become a viable alternative to Sustainable Development we need to consider all interpretations. Couple this with the reality that exogenous solutions to endogenous issues are problematic in that they provide a "narrow conception of need" (Giovannini 2014b) and jeopardise sustainable outcomes (Gudynas 2009); Buen Vivir is thus an alternative with endogenous motives using plural approaches.

As for the second implementation challenge, the political definition is concerned with a reformist discourse that frolics with ideology – it can be viewed as more utopian than practical. Policy-makers could better reflect on the primary endogenous norm of Buen Vivir, as Villacís et al. (2015) conclude: "the State must continually think about the epistemes of Good Living beyond a political speech, and as a representative example that exposes the bases of the new post-2015 agenda." The implications would allow governments to position themselves for sustainability, paving the way forward for a convergence of meanings, and offering a platform for its plural achievement. Lastly, however, as long as extractivism remains at the core of development policies, there will be tensions regarding what Buen Vivir means and how best to implement it (Merino 2016) because an extractive or neoextractive approach is antagonistic to Buen Vivir on a structural level and inherently obstructive to the nature–society continuum. A post-extractive transition could be the only way to achieve Buen Vivir (Villalba & Etxano 2017). This involves all actors.

"To effect change means to effect a 'change in the order of discourse,' to open up the 'possibility to think reality differently'" (Pieterse 2000). Analysing the discourse has been vital as a foundation to better understand Buen Vivir and how it differentiates from Sustainable Development; but using discourse alone turns it into an "ideological platform [which] invites political impasse and quietism" (Pieterse 2000). As Pieterse (2000) affirms, it is possible to share post-development's observations, without a total offensive on development. So, in his words, "Let's not quibble about details... What do you have to offer?" It involves having the resolve to transform behaviours and thinking away from neoliberal development to one of endogenous capacity, needs, and environmental practices. But transformation takes time, education, and societal and political will.

In conclusion, the most fundamental differences between Sustainable Development and Buen Vivir are that the former is modelled on a system that values exponential economic growth as an indicator of wellbeing and within that is the notion that natural resources are commodities to be exploited and traded for profit; whereas the latter rejects both of these notions. Its contextuality and plurality are key strengths in translating Buen Vivir into a community tool that promises to bridge the divide between Indigenous worldview and modernity, filling the gaps where Sustainable Development has failed. For environmental and social wellbeing there is no one-size-fits-all model; it depends on the context (Marti et al. 2013). Regardless, there is a real gap in knowledge of how such a tool might be prescriptive enough to provide us with the concrete steps to achieve sustainability and wellbeing, yet flexible enough to consider context.

Faced with these challenges and gaps, one must then find out: What does Buen Vivir look like in practice on the ground, at grassroots level, within an extractive economy? How can it be successfully implemented as a tool for communities to achieve change? And as an alternative, what is the point of convergence with Sustainable Development discourse, to allow it to meet the common aims of sustainability and wellbeing and achieve real future outcomes rather than just rhetoric?

Change cannot be achieved through discourse critique alone; it requires a practical approach. While the literature on Buen Vivir discusses the Indigenous, political, and academic interpretations, one piece of the puzzle is missing on the path to implementation: Community practice and understanding of the core common principles. What it means in practice, and to whom, remains (at the time of research) largely unanalysed. Given that there is such academic consensus regarding the ambiguity of Buen Vivir, there is a surprising lack of empirical research into understanding its core principles in practice.

For the realisation of Buen Vivir, there is a critical need for a bottom-up practical alternative with global applicability beyond niche circles (Monni & Pallottino 2015). To achieve this, instead of pigeonholing Buen Vivir into a political ideology or theory, it could be considered as a plural tool for communities that has wider policy implications, and one where all key actors have a role to play. In the following chapter, therefore, I will take this understanding of which principles are constant across the various contested interpretations and compare them to how they align with an understanding of Buen Vivir on the ground, and what they mean in practice. If it is examined from grassroots practices and understandings, not just limited to discourse, then Buen Vivir has a viable way forward, towards new horizons for Socio-Eco Wellbeing.

Notes

1 This chapter first appeared as a peer-reviewed academic article, published in the *Community Development Journal*, republished by permission of Oxford University Press: Chassagne, N (2018), "Sustaining the 'Good Life': Buen Vivir as an Alternative to Sustainable Development," *Community Development Journal*, Volume 54, Issue 3, July 2019, Pages 482–500, https://doi.org/10.1093/cdj/bsx062.
2 In a similar vein to Cubillo et al. (2014) who argue that while there is no single homogenous definition of Buen Vivir in the literature, there are three contested "streams": indigenous, socialist (political), and post-developmentalist (academic); all three are discussed in this chapter.
3 Transcendence in this context should be understood as a "psychological state of selflessness" (Gorelik & Shackelford 2017). Transcendent "values are more likely to have pro-environmental beliefs and norms and to act pro-environmentally while the opposite is true for those who strongly endorse self-enhancement values" (Clayton 2012).

4 These dimensions are based on García-Álvarez's analysis of Sumak Kawsay as Buen Vivir, which acknowledges the indigenous origins of Buen Vivir, as well as its endogenous nature. For a political proposal for Buen Vivir, Cubillo-Guevara, Hidalgo-Capitán, and García-Álvarez (2016) provide an analysis of the main "elements": identity; spirituality; statism; equality; sustainability; and localism.
5 As the peaceful existence of diversity.
6 The process of which supports a respect for cultural systems.
7 Assumes access to food as a human right, providing dignity to all in the food system, from producers to consumers.
8 Relates to the satisfaction of needs through livelihood, rather than the perusal or wants pertaining to economic growth.
9 Supports the notion of Buen Vivir as being tailorable to each community based on its capabilities.

References

Acosta, A 2010, 'El buen vivir en el camino del post-desarrollo. Una lectura desde la constitución de montecristi', *Policy Paper*, vol. 9, pp. 63–72.

Agostino, A & Dübgen, F 2012, 'Buen vivir and beyond', *Degrowth conference, real Utopias. From solidarity economy to the 'Buen Vivir'*, Venice, Italy.

Álvarez, S 2013, 'Qué es el sumak kawsay o buen vivir', *Economia y buen vivir*, viewed 5 February 2014, <http://buenvivir.eumed.net/wp-content/uploads/2013/04/sumak-kaws ay-concepto.pdf>.

Bolaños, V 2012, *Organizaciones sociales: Actores del cambio más allá del gobierno*, Corriente Alterna, 1 Fundación Tierranueva, Quito.

Caria, S & Domínguez, R 2016, 'Ecuador's buen vivir a new ideology for development', *Latin American Perspectives*, vol. 43, no. 1 pp. 18–33.

Cerdán, P 2013, 'Post-development and buen vivir: An approach to development from latin-America', *International Letters of Social and Humanistic Sciences*, vol. 10, pp. 15–24. doi: 10.18052/www.scipress.com/ILSHS.10.15.

Clayton, SD 2012, *The Oxford handbook of environmental and conservation psychology*, Oxford University Press, Oxford.

Connelly, S 2007, 'Mapping sustainable development as a contested concept', *Local Environment*, vol. 12, no. 3 pp. 259–78. doi: 10.1080/13549830601183289.

Constitución de la república del ecuador 2008, Registro oficial 449, 20 October 2008, Quito.

Cubillo, AP, Hidalgo, AL & Domínguez, JA 2014, 'El pensamiento sobre el buen vivir. Entre el indigenismo, el socialismo y el postdesarrollismo', *Revista Del CLAD Reforma Y Democracia*, vol. 60, pp. 27–58.

Cubillo-Guevara, AP, Hidalgo-Capitán, AL & García-Álvarez, S 2016, 'El buen vivir como alternativa al desarrollo para américa latina', *Iberoamerican Journal of Development Studies*, vol. 5, no. 2 pp. 30–57.

Delgado, F, Rist, S & Escobar, C 2010, *El desarrollo endógeno sustentable como interfaz para implementar el vivir bien en la gestión pública boliviana*, Plural, La Paz.

Deneulin, S 2012, 'Justice and deliberation about the good life: The contribution of Latin American buen vivir social movements to the idea of justice' in *International development and well-being*, Vol. 17, CDS-University of Bath,

Dryzek, JS 1997, *The politics of the earth: Environmental discourses*, Oxford University Press, Oxford.

Escobar, A 1992, 'Reflections on 'development': Grassroots approaches and alternative politics in the third world', *Futures*, vol. 24, no. 5, pp. 411–36. doi: 10.1016/0016-3287(92)90014-7.

Escobar, A 2017, 'Sustaining the pluriverse: The political ontology of territorial struggles in latin America', in M. Brightman & J. Lewis (eds.), *The anthropology of sustainability*, Springer, New York.

Esteva, G & Prakash Suri, M 1997, 'From global thinking to local thinking', in M Rahnema & V Bawtree, eds., *The post-development reader*, Zed Books, London.

Giovannini, M 2014a, 'Indigenous community enterprises in Chiapas: A vehicle for buen vivir?', *Community Development Journal*, vol. Advanced access, pp. 1–17. doi: 10.1093/cdj/bsu019.

Giovannini, M 2014b, *Indigenous peoples and self-determined development: The case of community enterprises in Chiapas*, thesis, University of Trento.

Gorelik, G & Shackelford, TK 2017, 'What is transcendence, how did it evolve, and is it beneficial?', *Religion, Brain & Behavior*, vol. 7, no. 4, pp. 361–5. doi: 10.1080/2153599X.2016.1249928.

Guardiola, J & García-Quero, F 2014, 'Buen vivir (living well) in ecuador: Community and environmental satisfaction without household material prosperity?', *Ecological Economics*, vol. 107, pp. 177–84. doi: 10.1016/j.ecolecon.2014.07.032.

Gudynas, E 2009, 'Diez tesis urgentes sobre el nuevo extractivismo', *Extractivismo, política y sociedad*, pp. 187–225, CLAES, Montevideo.

Gudynas, E 2011, 'Buen vivir: Today's tomorrow', *Development*, vol. 54, no. 4 pp. 441–7. doi: 10.1057/dev.2011.86.

Gudynas, E 2013, 'Debates on development and its alternatives in latin America: A brief heterodox guide', in Lang M & Mokrani D, eds., *Beyond development*, Rosa Luxemburg Foundation, Berlin.

Guillen-Royo, M 2015, *Sustainability and wellbeing: Human-scale development in practice*, Routledge, London.

Harcourt, W 2013, 'The future of capitalism: A consideration of alternatives', *Cambridge Journal of Economics*, vol. 38, no. 6, pp. 1307–28. doi: 10.1093/cje/bet048.

Houtart, F 2011, 'El concepto de sumak kawsay (buen vivir) y su correspondencia con el bien común de la humanidad', *Revista de filosofía*, vol. 69, no. 3, pp. 57–76.

Howard, J & Wheeler, J 2015, 'What community development and citizen participation should contribute to the new global framework for sustainable development', *Community Development Journal*, vol. 50, no. 4, pp. 552–70.

Huanacuni, F 2010, *Buen vivir/vivir bien*, Coordinadora Andina de Organizaciones Indígenas, Lima, Peru.

Kauffman, CM & Martin, PL 2014, 'Scaling up buen vivir: Globalizing local environmental governance from ecuador', *Global Environmental Politics*, vol. 14, no. 1, pp. 40–58.

Lukes, S & Runciman, WG 1974, 'Relativism: Cognitive and moral', *Proceedings of the Aristotelian Society, Supplementary Volumes*, vol. 48, pp. 165–208. doi: 10.2307/4106865.

Marti, IP, Wright, C, Aylwin, J & Yanez, N 2013, 'Introducción: El debate del desarrollo', in S Marti I Puig, C Wright, J Aylwin, & N Yanez, eds., *Entre el desarrollo y el buen vivir: Recursos naturales y conflictos en los territorios indígenas*, Catarata, Madrid.

Merino, R 2016, 'An alternative to 'alternative development'?: Buen vivir and human development in andean countries', *Oxford Development Studies*, vol. 44, no. 3, pp. 1–16. doi: 10.1080/13600818.2016.1144733.

Monni, S & Pallottino, M 2015, 'Beyond growth and development: Buen vivir as an alternative to current paradigms', *International Journal of Environmental Policy and Decision Making*, vol. 1, no. 3, pp. 184–204. doi: 10.1504/IJEPDM.2015.074300.

Phélan, C 2011, 'Revisión de índices e indicadores de desarrollo: Aportes para la medición del buen vivir (sumak kawsay)', *Obets: Revista de Ciencias Sociales*, vol. 6, no. 1. pp. 69–95.

Pieterse, JN 2000, 'After post-development', *Third World Quarterly*, vol. 21, no. 2, pp. 175–91. doi: 10.2307/3993415.

Redclift, M 2002, *Sustainable development: Exploring the contradictions*, Routledge, London.

Ruttenberg, T 2013, 'Wellbeing economics and buen vivir: Development alternatives for inclusive human security', *Fletcher Journal of Human Security*, vol. XXVIII, pp. 68–93. <https://fletcher.tufts.edu/Praxis/~/media/Fletcher/Microsites/praxis/xxviii/arti cle4_Ruttenberg_BuenVivir.pdf>.

SENPLADES 2009, *Plan nacional para el buen vivir 2009–2013: Construyendo un estado plurinacional e intercultural*, Secretaría Nacional de Planificación y Desarrollo, Quito, Ecuador.

SENPLADES 2013, *Plan nacional para el buen vivir 2013–2017*, Secretaría Nacional de Planificación y Desarrollo, Quito, Ecuador.

Smyth, L 2011, 'Anthropological critiques of sustainable development', *Cross Sections*, vol. 7, pp. 78–85.

Tesoriero, F & Ife, JW 2010, *Community development: Community-based alternatives in an age of globalisation*, 4th edn., Pearson Australia, Frenchs Forest, NSW.

Tortosa, JM 2011, 'Vivir bien, buen vivir: Caminar con los dos pies', *OBETS. Revista de Ciencias Sociales*, vol. 6, no. 1, pp. 13–7.

Unceta, K 2013, 'Decrecimiento y buen vivir ¿paradigmas convergentes ? Debates sobre el postdesarrollo en europa y américa latina', *Revista de Economía Mundial*, vol. 35, pp. 197–216.

United Nations General Assembly 2015, *Transforming our world*, Resolution. *A/Res/70/1*, United Nations/New York. https://www.un.org/ga/search/view_doc.asp?symbol=A/ RES/70/1&Lang=E.

Vanhulst, J & Beling, AE 2014, 'Buen vivir: Emergent discourse within or beyond sustainable development?', *Ecological Economics*, vol. 101, pp. 54–63.

Villacís, MA, Mora, MF & López, R 2015, *Alternatives for development or alternatives to development?*, Southern Voice on post-MDG international development goals, Occasional paper series 23, Centre for Policy Dialogue, Dakah Bangladesh.

Villalba, U 2013, 'Buen vivir vs development: A paradigm shift in the andes?', *Third World Quarterly*, vol. 34, no. 8, pp. 1427–42. doi: 10.1080/01436597.2013.831594.

Villalba, U & Etxano, I 2017, 'Buen vivir vs development (ii): The limits of (neo-) extractivism', *Ecological Economics*, vol. 138, pp. 1–11. doi: 10.1016/j. ecolecon.2017.03.010.

Walsh, C 2010, 'Development as buen vivir: Institutional arrangements and (de)colonial entanglements', *Development*, vol. 53, no. 1, pp. 15–21. doi: 10.1057/dev.2009.93.

Wiseman, J & Brasher, K 2008, 'Community wellbeing in an unwell world: Trends, challenges, and possibilities', *Journal of Public Health Policy*, vol. 29, no. 3, pp. 353– 66. doi: 10.1057/jphp.2008.16.

Part II

4 Understandings of Buen Vivir in Ecuador's Cotacachi County

Imagine a place rich in biodiversity, where communities have a profound respect for nature manifested in a reciprocal relationship with the land. This place is Cotacachi County, located 100 kilometres north of the capital Quito in the mountainous region of the Ecuadorian Highlands, and the subject of the fieldwork underlying this book.

The connection to the land of Cotacacheños – both Indigenous and non-Indigenous – manifests in a worldview based on Buen Vivir and in the ensuing local politics, which strives to enable a life in harmony with nature. In Cotacachi, says Joaquín, an Indigenous local government employee, "there is a practice of wanting to conserve, to take care of, to respect the earth – and with a relationship that is not only purely material but also spiritual." Within that philosophy is the connection to community, and the values that come with living a communal rather than an individually oriented lifestyle. Although most people here have a tacit understanding of Buen Vivir, it is more of a lived than a communicated philosophy. It is often referred to interchangeably as "Sumak Kawsay." Even in policy Buen Vivir is not effectively or concretely defined.

Local government employee Leandro, for example, argues that this debate around what Buen Vivir is, does not extend to the people; it needs to be asked, "'But what is Sumak Kawsay?' and to follow that in the debate. The debate does not go to them [the people] and ask, 'Let's see, what do you think about Sumak Kawsay and how do you analyse it to be able to say we can achieve Sumak Kawsay?'"

This is precisely the aim of this second part of the book. In this chapter I garner grassroots understanding of Buen Vivir and its core principles, as well as evidence of what this looks like in practice, and how it fits into the discussion of "needs." This analysis is triangulated with the conceptualisation I discussed in Part I, to build upon this set of core principles towards a practical community tool for change.

Cotacachi County has a population of approximately 40,036 habitants, 78 percent of whom live in a rural area (*Actualizacion pdyot cotacachi 2015–2035* 2016); 55 percent are Indigenous (Saltos 2008), mainly Kichwa, which is one of the largest concentrations of Indigenous people in Ecuador. Possibly for this reason, the county has a strong affiliation with the ethos of Buen Vivir or Sumak

Kawsay and over the past two decades the affection for Buen Vivir has grown stronger through communal practices as well as community and local government campaigns.

The county has a unique model of democratic participation instituted through a participatory budget, introduced by Indigenous Former Mayor Auki Tituaña. Through these processes, the people of Cotacachi voted for the county to be declared an "Ecological County" – the first in Latin America – in order to protect the area's biodiversity. For these reasons it is the ideal case study for an examination of Buen Vivir as an alternative for achieving Socio-Eco Wellbeing.

As noted by Arturo Escobar (1995), "The nature of alternatives as a research question and a social practice can be most fruitfully gleaned from the specific manifestations of such alternatives in concrete local settings." Inherent in Buen Vivir is the emphasis on community and endogenous-led change. To properly understand the epistemology and ontology of Buen Vivir at the local level – that is, the social, cultural, and historical drivers behind the phenomenon – it is necessary to seek the "insider's view" (Mason 2002). In the case of Buen Vivir, that extends to the three main categories of key actors: Community, government, and local civil society organisations.

For this reason, I chose my key informants using purposive sampling which means "selecting groups or categories on the basis of their relevance to your research question, your theoretical position and analytical framework, your analytical practice and... the argument or explanation that you are developing" (Mason 2002). The idea is to target individuals with specific knowledge or perspectives. Key informants therefore were chosen for the potential richness of information they could provide, their knowledges and lived experiences. All key informants are referred to by pseudonyms throughout, to protect their privacy.

The most pressing questions arising from the conceptual analysis in Part I are: What is Buen Vivir and how can it be implemented? One cannot prescriptively define what Buen Vivir means, simply because as discussed in Chapter Three it is a "concept under construction" which can be defined differently depending on who interprets it, and that is part of its allure as an alternative. An endogenous-focused Buen Vivir is the antithesis to the current development model, albeit a plural one that is implemented cooperatively in different realities and within various contexts.

As I demonstrated in the previous chapter, Buen Vivir can become a viable and practical alternative to Sustainable Development provided that certain conditions are met. Its flexibility to be tailored to cultural, linguistic, historic, and geographic contexts is possibly its greatest strength, against the universal, top-down imposition of traditional development of which Sustainable Development is part. It provides descriptive meaning founded on a set of core principles which delivers a direction for change, but leaves the prescriptive elements up to the communities themselves.

One of those conditions is creating a solid understanding of what it means in practice, on the ground at the community level. This chapter is thus dedicated to addressing that by examining understandings of Buen Vivir in Ecuador's

Cotacachi County. What follows in the next four chapters is the "what" of Buen Vivir, with Chapter Eight explaining the "how."

What does Buen Vivir entail?

The vague notion of what Buen Vivir entails both in policy and the literature partly arises because of its complexity, and partly because of its contested nature. Cubillo-Guevara et al. (2016) describe it as "a form of life in harmony with one-self, with society and with nature" and by now we also understand that Buen Vivir entails "building multiple realities that exist plurally under Buen Vivir itself, that would take meaning only within the boundaries of each society." Until now, what that looks like is practice has been ambiguous, so with that in mind, I propose the following set of principles, triangulating the conceptual analysis with the field data including semi-structured interviews with key informants, observations, and document analysis to form a more coherent and practical picture.

The principles of Buen Vivir

Interviews with key informants, together with the conceptualisation in the literature, have confirmed that Buen Vivir means different things to different people. The advantage of this contextuality is cemented in the principle of plurality, referring to both a plurality of knowledge and a plurality of being. However, key informants felt that while the former Correa government introduced a policy of Buen Vivir, it failed to concretely set out its core principles in a manner that can help guide practice and be used as a practical tool by communities in the pursuit of Buen Vivir.[1] Interchanging the language of Buen Vivir and Sumak Kawsay, local government employee Leandro states, "The slogan is there [in policy], but the basic idea is not... the problem is that they never knew what Sumak Kawsay is."

The key premise of Buen Vivir is that it needs to come from the bottom-up, rather than top-down. Furthermore, as a plural concept, its co-construction should incorporate all epistemologies necessary in order to move forward. In that light, it is my aim for the following set of principles to help determine a concrete path for its application at the community level, in any community context. While one individual definition may differ from the next, there are principles which are common in Buen Vivir, and which can help guide a more just and sustainable society.

Luis, an employee of a local cooperative which works with local producers internationally, explains that while everyone has their own definition, there are variables which connect Buen Vivir together as one concept: "There are things that for all humanity are necessary. Yes, there are some fundamental principles that I think people can agree on what Buen Vivir is... For example, it can be health, access to food, a community. I personally believe that there is no one who can say 'I don't want this in my life'."

In Table 4.1, I identified a total of 17 principles based on the understandings of Buen Vivir at the local level, in dialogue with the principles discussed in Chapter Three. These principles are both interdependent and interconnected. In this table,

Table 4.1 Core principles of Buen Vivir

Principles of Buen Vivir					
Social		*Spiritual*		*Material*	
Equity	*Social cohesion*	*Sustainability*	*Empowerment*	*Livelihood*	*Capabilities*
• Equality • Holistic rights	• Community • Harmony • Solidarity	• Reciprocity • Healthy environment • Food security	• Self-determination • Respect • Participation	• SSE economy • Decent work • Leisure time	• Good health • Culture • Education

I have taken the same base framework of pillars and dimensions used in Chapter Three, to include a set of core principles that build upon that original framework with an on-the-ground understanding of the principles to address the aforementioned gaps. There is no hierarchy between the principles; therefore, the discussion below is not ordered by principle, but, because of their interconnectedness, I discuss the principles by their relevant dimension.

Social cohesion

The idea of community in Buen Vivir is the turning point from an individualistic notion of neoliberal development to the idea of seeking holistic communal wellbeing and sustainability. This principle of community refers to aligning one's values to prioritising the community above the individual. In places like Latin America there is still a strong notion of community, unlike in many Western countries. The community is what ties everyone together and provides support, which positively affects both communal and individual wellbeing. Though two other principles must be present for a community to function: Harmony and solidarity. Without those two, there is no community spirit. Rodriguez, a local farmer in the Intag Valley, explains: "A community is the second home, because a community is everything. You cannot be part of a community if you are isolated from others. My home is where my family is, and my second home is the community, which we must defend and fight for and try to give the best within."

The value of family was frequently discussed, and for many is the foundation of wellbeing and a part of community, though that does not necessarily mean that for one to obtain wellbeing one must be part of a traditional family unit. For some, that is simply not possible. However, for most key informants "community" signifies that the involvement of families (not just individuals) in community life enriches community cohesion and solidarity. Rafael, a senior employee at a National Ministry of the Correa government, explains: "They do not have to be blood. What I believe is that we all need to talk. Talk and agree on the best solutions [to community problems]." This signifies solidarity.

Complementing this vision is the idea that community and harmony between people is necessary for wellbeing, and therefore Buen Vivir. Felipe, founder of a local organisation, explains: "That's what wellbeing is for many people, absolutely – you get along with your neighbours. You can't live and say that you're experiencing Sumak Kawsay if you're fighting with your neighbours."

Sustainability

Reciprocity, the principle built on relationships, is crucial to Buen Vivir. Two-thirds of key informants say that it is the cornerstone of Buen Vivir; this differentiates it from other alternative approaches. Reciprocity here is defined as the integral relationship between human society and the natural environment that heeds a sentiment of greater ecological respect than the current development model. As a biocentric concept, the principle of having a healthy environment is central to wellbeing. A society which pays greater respect to the cyclical nature of our relationship with the environment will have a heathier environment as a result. That supports a sustainable use of resources, over their commodification for economic growth, with the understanding that humans need the environment in order to survive (Acosta 2012). As Diego, a political activist and respected community member, asserts: "There is a relationship between man and nature and when one does not respect the other, it's difficult to live in an environment where there is no mutual respect… The possibility between man and nature gives us rights to give and receive [from nature]; and we also give and receive."

Felipe (2014) speaks of keeping a certain harmony between all living beings, "emphasizing a full life with access to what is sufficient and necessary with absolute correspondence with the wellbeing of Mother Nature and of other human beings." Mother Nature is how the Indigenous key informants prefer to refer to the environment (Pachamama), criticising the Spanish translation of "environment" for its lack of commitment to all living and non-living things. In Spanish, the word "environment" (*medioambiente*) is separated into two parts: "*Medio*" (medium, middle, or half) and "*ambiente*" (atmosphere or surroundings). Leandro explains: "The environment, everything is the environment. That is what environment means. So, I do not comprehend *medioambiente*. Because half is half. It's *ambiente* for us. It is important to have an environment [*ambiente*]. The environment is not only nature." Pachamama thus encompasses more of an biocentric approach as opposed to the human-centred values system under traditional development. Juan, a farmer and writer in the Intag Valley, asserts, "It is very important," then asks jokingly, "where is the other half?" He continues, "Do you believe that we live in a half-environment or a whole-environment?"

A healthy environment which hosts fertile, uncontaminated land also helps ensure food security. The State of Food Insecurity (FAO 2001) defined food security as "a situation that exists when all people, at all times, have physical, social and economic access to sufficient, safe and nutritious food that meets their dietary needs and food preferences for an active and healthy life." This is closely aligned with the idea of "intergenerational needs" highlighted by the Brundtland definition of Sustainable Development. It also aligns with the metanarrative for neoliberal Sustainable Development. The post-modern perspective on food security, however, highlights the complexity, diversity, and flexibility needed in thinking about food security (Maxwell 1996), which is more in line with the notion of Buen Vivir. The post-modern shift takes the above definition and nuances it to focus on the subjective not objective metanarrative of food security; it includes the livelihoods of individuals and communities rather than a "food first" attitude, and includes bottom-up, participatory approaches to food interventions (Maxwell 1996). When the issue of a healthy environment is raised, it is usually followed by a need for food security and the fact that food security cannot be ensured without a healthy environment. In places like Intag, this issue is raised in relation to the impacts of extractive activities on agricultural land. Food is a central part of Ecuadorian social life, but the ability to cultivate and harvest food is especially valued in the rural areas of Ecuador like Intag.

The right to healthy food and the right to property to fulfil social and environmental function and guarantee food security is codified under the 2008 Constitution, and it is also the objective of the recently introduced Law of Rural Land and Ancestral Territories (Ley orgánica de tierras rurales y territorios ancestrales república del ecuador national assembly 2016). To those in urban areas it means having access to safe and healthy quality produce, without the risk of transgenics and chemical use. For Indigenous community member Maria, who lives in a semi-rural Indigenous community, access to land and the capacity to work it is vital to her wellbeing and survival, as an Indigenous person but also as a woman. Food security in rural Ecuador thus denotes access to land, as well as to learn to work the land, yielding one's own produce, and providing a livelihood, despite impacts from climate change. Maria explains: "To achieve Buen Vivir we must encourage women to work our lands. Right now, if I do not work I do not eat… if everyone went to work [in a white collar sense] all over the world and earned money… When you stop working Pachamama in agriculture, what do we eat? The dollar bill? *No.*"

Empowerment

The ability and capacity for a community to manage its own resources endogenously and determine its own path to development is the basis for community self-determination. A respect for others' opinions and situations helps foster a healthy society where participation and self-determination can flourish and endogenous solutions to local problems can arise. "The power is in local communities" ("Una oportunidad insólita de cambiar el mundo" 2010).

Stated in the PNBV is Ecuador's objective to promote endogenous development to improve "the people's capacity for self-determination in their public decisions, and in their political, territorial, food, energy, economic, financial, commercial and cultural matters" (SENPLADES 2009) through food and economic sovereignty "and the achievement of balances between production, work and environment, with self-determination, justice and sovereign international relations" (SENPLADES 2009). Economic sovereignty refers to the strengthening of actors and processes which allow direct participation in public decision-making.

Participation can be understood as a necessary requirement for self-determination, and both of these principles can be understood as a necessary precondition to achieve Buen Vivir endogenously. As Leandro affirms, "not one person decides any one thing; but we all decide, we all have to participate. Participate in all senses of the word." For youth leader Sofia, participation is all-inclusive and equitable. She argues, "Buen Vivir is participation for everyone, that everyone is treated equally: The elderly, the disabled – that there is no discrimination. It should be the opinion of all and the union of all."

Equity

Equity in participation is also a crucial element and helps provide equality of opportunity regardless of ethnicity, gender, religion, or other factors. Diego argues that, for him, community wellbeing "is society, community, sharing values, principles, and rights for all on an equal footing." Equal opportunity is expressed as a fundamental right, but equity is also a principle in its own right, which gives entitlement to rights.

Fundamental rights potentially cover all of the core principles, but rights are equally important as a principle in their own right to expressly ensure that fundamental rights are upheld equitably in order to achieve Buen Vivir. Fundamental rights are a set of legal protections in the context of a particular jurisdiction and include rights to which all human beings are fundamentally entitled (*Universal declaration of human rights* 1948). While the argument for universal and individual rights seems contradictory to the contextual and communal in Buen Vivir, the rights contained in most modern constitutions are similar to those contained in the International Bill of Rights (Gardbaum 2008), which includes the Universal Declaration of Human Rights, International Covenant for Social and Economic Rights, and the International Covenant for Civil and Political Rights. The difference in those rights necessary to obtain Buen Vivir is that they emphasise "rights for all," refocusing the communal wellbeing objective, and also include the Rights of Nature. The Rights of Nature are codified in the 2008 Constitution under articles 71 to 74, which institute those rights, provide the right to restauration, and apply the principle of precaution; article 74 additionally allows the people to benefit from the use of these resources to obtain Buen Vivir (Constitución de la república del ecuador 2008).

This is not to negate that the individual has rights, but these rights should be regarded in the context of communal and sustainable Socio-Eco Wellbeing. Because of this emphasis on communal wellbeing over the individual, and the inclusion of the "Rights of Nature," I refer to the equitability of rights as "holistic rights" to justly encompass the notion of Socio-Eco Wellbeing, as opposed to individualistic and human-centred fundamental rights. Thus, holistic rights under Buen Vivir not only include human-centred rights, but also those delegated to nature.

Luis argues that rights in this sense are fundamental for intergenerational ecological sustainability, and require the sustainable use of resources with reciprocity in mind:

> It is achieving long-term as a human collective power a healthy environment for generations to come. You can maintain that good relationship with the environment without destroying it completely. No need to use all the resources we have now to have a good quality of life.

Capabilities

Despite a general respect for the environment in these communities, many key informants recognise that an awareness of the effects and consequences of certain practices and ways of life on the environment is not purely instinctive; it is cemented with education. There is also a feeling in communities that people's behaviours and attitudes towards this have changed for the better since the recent government laws and campaigns, returning to ancient practices combined with utilising modern technology and knowledge to protect and conserve land. Of his environmental work, regional representative of a national government ministry Mateo says:

> Northern Ecuador including up to Esmeraldas used to be called the "green province" because it conserved 50 to 80 percent of its forests. Then that's when this law came in that 50 percent of your land should be worked. If you were in possession of 100 hectares of forest, the same state forced you to "work" it. You had to prove you're working on that site by clearing 50 percent of the forest. That is, of the 100 hectares, 50 you had to uproot, and then you could settle the title. That law is dead now, and we have started to raise people's awareness. But if we talk about the environment it is not only taking care of the trees or looking after water. It's changing attitudes ranging from the child, to the parent, to society itself. Then changing it [the attitude] requires a lot of work. So, ensuring a healthy and balanced environment is the biggest task of all.

The right to education is a fundamental right (SENPLADES 2009), and likewise is a core principle of Buen Vivir. It is also by education that we learn values as a society. Therefore, education is not only vital to create future opportunities, but also it is helps create values and a *savoir vivre*, and as mentioned, an awareness of Buen Vivir. Mateo argues, "I believe that education is one of the most important, fundamental pillars that there is because it cultivates values and principles. If I'm well educated, I will have values and these values I will also pass on to my children." Moreover, education can improve social wellbeing, providing wide-ranging benefits to a community by promoting active citizenship (OECD 2013). Education considers the context of culture. The practice and respect of culture through education is crucial to Buen Vivir and ensures that communities retain their particular capabilities at no detriment to their culture. As Felipe states, for many people culture is an important part of Buen Vivir, "so cultural identity is important for many people... for Indigenous people it becomes [even] more of a central issue."

Maintaining good health, like culture, is a major resource for communities and is seen as a basic capability for wellbeing (Fukuda-Parr 2003). According to Mateo, "the right to health is the most important thing for human beings." Public health issues can have detrimental impacts on the economy and can affect community capabilities, especially if issues relate to mental health. In the midst of COVID-19, for example, we can clearly see the effects of public health crises on capabilities. A Buen Vivir approach can help manage these impacts in a more socially and ecologically sound manner than neoliberal economic fixes.

In the pursuit of Socio-Eco Wellbeing, Sen's capability approach was apt in that it claimed the moral requirement for the freedom to achieve wellbeing (Sen 2001). This freedom means increasing citizens' participation and access to things like good health, culture, education, and the environment. But where it differs from capabilities understood within the context of Buen Vivir is in how that freedom for wellbeing is understood in terms of individual capabilities. Where Sen was concerned with the ability of development to expand individual capabilities, Buen Vivir is more concerned with collective capabilities of a community to achieve Socio-Eco Wellbeing. It reaffirms that the principles of Buen Vivir are interrelated. Capabilities are thus also intrinsically linked to livelihood.

Livelihood

One economic aspect that can impact on mental and physical health is that of having access to decent work opportunities. The issue of decent work was revealed as a core principle of Buen Vivir, not only for key informants but also for government policy. However, decent work for oneself encapsulates not only having financial security, but also a sense of personal fulfilment in one's work.

For key informants, decent work not only means a fair income, job security, and decent working conditions but also includes having leisure time to enjoy outside of work. For local organisation representative and Indigenous woman Laura, one is implicated in the other; and it is especially an issue for women. She says, "I personally think that [Buen Vivir] means to be tranquil and well within oneself. Then, those two things mean a lot of other things. As a woman, that is how you ensure yourself access to job opportunities, academia, social security, taking advantage of your own time."

Access to decent work and leisure time are economic issues, and while the ethos behind Buen Vivir denounces economic growth above all else, the economy is still an important factor for achieving it. The difference is that there a focus on a social and solidarity economy (SSE) rather than a capitalist market economy, the latter being a priority for traditional development.

An SSE is concerned with collective capabilities in the realisation of an alternative economy. Thus, collective capabilities are intrinsic to the material pillar. Moreover, capabilities reinforce livelihood, and vice-versa. Scarlato (2013) argues that the SSE, in particular social enterprise, emphasised under a Buen Vivir approach can help enhance capabilities. Scarlato (2013) describes "social enterprise as a means of supporting grassroots mobilisation to emphasise the concept of collective capabilities." She further argues that "the concept of collective capabilities helps to reconcile the individualist orientation of the human development approach with the principles of reciprocity and collectivity that underlie the buen vivir vision." For the majority of key informants, capabilities and livelihood are central concerns and are understood as a question of meeting fundamental needs while retaining rights, community, and self-determination. Meeting fundamental needs is thus imperative to attaining Buen Vivir.

A Grassroots perspective of needs

In Chapter One I asked the question: "What are needs, who defines them, and how can they be satisfied?" If needs are not satisfied, then the principles of Buen

Vivir cannot be met, and vice-versa. While there is a set of core principles, the different interpretations of Buen Vivir revert to the issue of needs satisfaction. As community is the basis for Buen Vivir, different conceptions of needs must be discussed on that level, not in an individual sense. In other words, each community's needs are different and therefore that determines what Buen Vivir looks like to any particular community. On meeting those fundamental needs, however, it is important to consider the grassroots perspective, rather than to take a Western developmental (that is to say, exogenous) approach to needs.

According to Indigenous community leader Gabriela, more can be done on that level to achieve Buen Vivir. She states that we need to understand "what would be the best mechanism to work more [cooperatively] with our people; mostly with young people to change their materialistic ideas." That is, the much-needed change away from materialistic wants as a façade of actual fundamental needs. Governments must facilitate that change, rather than drive it. In the case of Indigenous communities, Gabriela believes that "the government should allocate a resource for organisations to start to strengthen ancestral knowledge. But one that is not based on the government's need but our *real* needs. So then, we decide how we want define Sumak Kawsay."

The issue of needs is a complex one, and in order to be able to satisfy needs under Buen Vivir, there must be governmental support for an endogenous approach like Buen Vivir. Needs, in a contested concept, is complex terrain; however, there was a consensus in the data – supported by the literature – that needs should be determined by the people themselves based on actual needs and not identified exogenously in relation to an individualistic, consumerist or Western-based vision of needs.

Felipe calls into question the modern, neoliberal idea of needs, which is tied to the economic market and to consumption. It is also part of the complexity of the rhetorical discourse on needs and of identifying, assessing, and satisfying needs as either wants or requirements (Jackson, Jager & Stagl 2008). Jackson et al. make two points about consumerism and needs: One relates to an actual "need," "requirement," "necessity," or "deficiency" while the other can be attributed to "desire," "pleasure," or "love" with related antonyms of "boredom" or "indifference" (Jackson, Jager & Stagl 2008). They state, "In a world in which economic consumption is threatening to erode the integrity of the global ecosystems, it is particularly vital to be able to identify which bits of consumption contribute to human needs satisfaction, and which simply operate as pseudo-satisfiers and destroyers." The latter is closely tied to consumption and economic growth and can inhibit the satisfaction of actual needs. Local government representative Fernando says, "The difference is in buying to meet our needs, then I do not think we will ever meet them… if everyone has to have the best then we will never satisfy our needs. And that's the grave error that we make and [then] we fall into the grand majority."

If we return briefly to the Brundtland Report's use of needs rhetoric in Sustainable Development, as a society one cannot guarantee that current and future needs are met if those needs are based on material consumption, desires, and wants. They must be thought of as actual needs; those needs which are required to be satisfied for human life to continue in a dignified manner, through community-led identification of them. Reaffirmed by local writer Juan, Buen Vivir must be decided by the people themselves.

In Cotacachi, Buen Vivir has not yet been achieved, and though many say that it is very difficult to achieve, meeting needs is a start. Diego says:

> At least I think you can satisfy priority needs: Access to drinking water, access to sewage, electricity, decent work, living in a healthy environment, to have the possibility of freedom of communication and decision. Not to have limits to decide what you want for your life and what is necessary for your life, and not necessarily your life, not to be prosecuted; and neither the political community nor the governance structure be the cause [of that].

In the case of Cotacachi, many community members are concerned for the top-down identification of needs by governments and exogenous organisations, as is common practice in development policy. They point to several failed development projects initiated by either international non-governmental organisations or national government priorities. They were futile, they argue, not because of a lack of good intention, but because they failed to let the communities decide what their actual needs were, instead relegating to an outsider's, perspective of what was needed in the community. These were environmental, economic development, and women's empowerment projects which could have been successfully implemented by other means if the communities themselves had determined their own needs. One such example is an international organisation which donated a commercial oven to a small community hall to provide an opportunity for community members to generate income by opening a dining hall. It remains unused because as one community member told me, "In such a small community we don't need to eat out."

Many in these communities have an alternative conception of needs than in a Western society driven by consumption. Some externally established projects, says local government employee Emanuel, create imagined needs that did not previously exist. Speaking of the World Bank PRODEPINE (Indigenous and Afro-Ecuadorian Peoples Development Project)[2] he tells how "the idea was to bring the Indigenous to power, make them feel the allure of power... the PRODEPINE project and the World Bank gave 20 million dollars directly to the Indigenous, generating other needs. The golden ponchos as they were called here were groups of Indians with gigantic salaries."

This type of mindset is evident in their fight against mining in the county. In informal conversations with community members, I was often told that they are simply not interested in wealth accumulation, as long as they have their needs met. Things like family, community, personal relationships, a healthy environment, and food security are more important than economic progress in the name of development; especially when economic growth is generated by resource extraction, which they say inhibits and even prohibits the ability to meet needs and achieve Buen Vivir.

Basic needs were often cited by key informants as those needs imperative for survival and a dignified life: Food, shelter, clothing, and essential public services as such as clean water, sanitation, public transport, health, and education. Yet, looking at needs only through the basic needs lens poses a risk of falling back into the neoliberal theory of development whereby GDP is the measurement of wellbeing, because, as the theory suggests, economic growth creates the necessary wealth to cover basic needs for all, thereby attaining "development" (Phélan 2011). If this approach has not worked to achieve wellbeing, social justice, and sustainability, then we must seek change.

When I questioned key informants about what they believed the needs of the community were, they explicitly cited basic needs such as those defined above. In Cotacachi, many communities still have unsatisfied basic needs. For Indigenous business owner Valentina, unsatisfied basic needs, as well as a lack of capacity, is what is missing for her community to attain environmental and social wellbeing. She says, "there are communities without clean water. There are communities that do not have all basic services. It makes these communities still lack basic services, such as mains sewage and drinking water." Basic services play a crucial role, therefore so does local government in providing those services. As Fernando says, "Wellbeing is improved with real services. For example, a community without a water quality service cannot really live, cannot have wellbeing."

Likewise, Felipe says that there are basic tangible needs that governments can help satisfy:

> The governments say we got to build more clinics. And many communities will be happy with that. Or we're going to build a road, and many communities will openly accept a road, because that's part of this indoctrination that, that the inhabitants of a country may have: That roads are good, clinics are good, hospitals are good, ah, a big school with fancy equipment is good. So, the physical aspects of wellbeing will be met to a certain point by government. Those are tangible.

However, throughout the interviews it was clear that these needs are not the only needs to be satisfied. Felipe continues, commenting that to achieve Buen Vivir there are many intangible, psychological needs that cannot be satisfied economically. "There are many intangible things that a government can't really give you: This peace with yourself, peace with communities, peace with your environment." The satisfaction of these intangible needs is also essential to ensure Socio-Eco Wellbeing. Psychological needs mirrored in Maslow's Hierarchy of Needs (Maslow & Lewis 1987) such as culture, leisure time, community, and family, and the more spiritual needs such as respect and a sense reciprocity with the environment, are equally as important for both human wellbeing and ecological sustainability.

Another alternative approach to needs satisfaction was conceived by Manfred Max-Neef in 1991 under Human-Scale Development (HSD). The objective of HSD is development that "is focused and based on the satisfaction of fundamental human needs, on the generation of growing levels of self-reliance, and on the construction of organic articulations of people with nature and technology, of global processes with local activity, of the personal with the social, of planning with autonomy and of civil society with the state" (Max-Neef, Elizalde & Hopenhayn 1991). It includes nine axiological needs: Subsistence, protection, affection, understanding, participation, identity, idleness, creation, and freedom; and four existential categories, or "satisfiers," which help in the satisfaction of these needs: Being, doing, having, and interacting (Cruz et al. 2011; Jackson, Jager & Stagl 2008; Max-Neef, Elizalde & Hopenhayn 1991). With respect to Buen Vivir, the needs are the most pertinent aspect of HSD, and can be described as:

- Subsistence: Health, food, shelter, work, living environment
- Protection: Care, freedom of choice, autonomy, social security, health systems, dwelling
- Affection: Being respected, loved, having fun, friends, family, privacy, a relationship with nature
- Understanding: Critical capacity, education, schools, universities, communities, curiosity, investigating, learning
- Participation: Duties, responsibilities, work, collaboration, opinions, freedom of expression, associations, rights
- Leisure: Imagination, fun, games, landscapes, living environment, sports, intimate spaces
- Creation: Boldness, invention, designing, building, skills, innovation, abilities
- Identity: Belonging, esteem, self-knowledge, religion, values, community, language, customs, norms, values, social settings
- Freedom: Autonomy, passion, rights, equality, choice, exploration, awareness (Max-Neef, Elizalde & Hopenhayn 1991).

In Max-Neef's theory, not all satisfiers are equally successful. There are destroyers, which completely fail to satisfy needs; pseudo-satisfiers, which generate a false sense of need satisfaction; and inhibiting satisfiers, which satisfy one need but inhibit the satisfaction of other needs (Jackson, Jager & Stagl 2008).

The approach outlined by Max-Neef based on fundamental needs, rather than basic needs, is the most appropriate in the context of Buen Vivir. These reasons are threefold and are manifested in what we know about Buen Vivir thus far: 1) They allow for contextualisation and particularities in different contexts; 2) they are based on self-determination, participation, and a reciprocal relationship within the community, and the community with nature; and 3) they include both the tangible basic needs and intangible psychological needs.

The fundamental difference between Max-Neef's conception of needs and that of Maslow is that there is no hierarchy in Max-Neef's needs (Max-Neef, Elizalde & Hopenhayn 1994). This is an important distinction in an approach like Buen Vivir because of the interconnectedness of the principles. What is interesting in Max-Neef's argument given the contested nature of Buen Vivir is the need for "transcendence," that is, how needs are satisfied over time and between cultures.

It is the "satisfiers" or the "having," "doing," "being," and "interacting" which change according to culture, context, and circumstance (Cruz, Stahel & Max-Neef 2009). Looking at needs satisfaction through the lens of Buen Vivir rather than traditional development diminishes the risk of the above-mentioned negative satisfiers because of the focus on communal needs with respect for the environment, rather than on individual needs based on "desires and preferences expressed through the market" (Jackson, Jager & Stagl 2008).

The satisfiers allow communities to identify ways in which their needs can be satisfied, not just identifying their needs and then leaving it to institutions or organisations to determine how these should be satisfied. For example, in the context of Intag where the government is closing local schools, the need for "understanding" comes under the principle for education and can be satisfied by providing local schools to minimise the risk to children travelling by foot or shared transport. Local farmer Rodriguez says that these needs have not been considered: "So far what has been done in the community is trying to prevent schools from being closed, but it was impossible... a school is the soul of the community, it is the light of your community because it is your future."

From the governmental perspective there is a direct correlation between the satisfaction of needs and happiness, which the national government along with local organisations believe is the cornerstone of Buen Vivir. For that reason, the former Correa government created the now defunct Ministry for Buen Vivir, whose mandate was to satisfy the basic needs of Ecuadorians. One of the ways it aimed to do so was by replacing GDP with a measure for happiness ("Freddy ehlers: El buen vivir es sinónimo de felicidad" 2015). Former Minister for Buen Vivir Freddy Elhers described Buen Vivir as a "synonym of happiness" ("Freddy ehlers: El buen vivir es sinónimo de felicidad" 2015), though it is more complex than that. Rafael explains, "Buen Vivir enables us to have a happy life. Not always. It may not always be happy but [it allows us] to live with greater happiness." However, as part of wellbeing, happiness can be said to be an outcome of the achievement of Buen Vivir rather than a principle to achieve it; though if both the tangible and intangible needs are satisfied, one can conclude that this will lead to greater levels of overall happiness.

Indigenous community leader Gabriela also includes the satisfaction of basic needs, along with psychological needs, as a driver of happiness: "Being happy is being in harmony with your family at home, that you have your basic necessities, food, that you eat healthily. I know that there are always things that I feel will ensure that my children are well. In other words, that they have decent work and food to eat."

According to the Australian Unity's Australian Wellbeing Index (Australian Unity 2016) happiness is achieved when three elements are present: Relationships, financial security, and good health. The Index measures subjective happiness and equates it to individual wellbeing. Although happiness is considered subjective, under Buen Vivir it is directly related to the cohesion and harmony of a community, as Felipe explains: "It means being happy with who you are, with your work; for example, if you have a good relationship with your neighbours. You can't have Buen Vivir without [them]. I think those are key components: You get along with your community, you like who you are and what you do." The importance of harmony within a community and one's personal relationships demonstrates that if the more psychological needs are satisfied – a sense of community, harmony, and solidarity – then individual happiness will follow, which will have a cyclical effect on Socio-Eco Wellbeing.

Materialism, economy, and Buen Vivir

One element of Buen Vivir that has been identified by both the key informants and policy is that to achieve it and meet fundamental needs, the productive matrix must change, and a new economic model must be adopted (SENPLADES 2013 Objective 10). Thus, the material pillar of Buen Vivir moves beyond material "progress" or wealth accumulation and economic growth and focuses on the principles which are vital to satisfying fundamental needs and achieving the communal vision of Socio-Eco Wellbeing. While Buen Vivir rejects the notion of economic growth and wealth accumulation, the economy is still imperative to a Good Life, though it is based on a reciprocal relationship with the earth, not one that purely views natural resources as economic commodities; meaning that within a Buen Vivir economy, society must truly live within the limits of the earth's capacity. This is reminiscent of the 1972 Club of Rome hypothesis of "Limits to Growth."

It is time to begin looking towards an economic approach that promotes sustainable living because, as Mander and Goldsmith (2014) argue, "we now face chronic, uncontrolled global crises in deforestation, biodiversity loss, climate change, fisheries depletion, soil loss, land degradation and freshwater depletion. Perilously, economic globalization is pushing the Earth beyond its limits." Two thirds of the key informants mentioned that there are biophysical limits to the earth that must be respected, but that are not because of the attitude and consumeristic ways of life in modern society. They believe that it is just as much an issue of awareness and education, and that once people fully comprehend that the resources are running out, they will stop or slow down their materialistic consumption patterns.

Laura, an Indigenous member of a local organisation, states, for many in society, "Resources are something you have, and you take advantage of. That *cannot* continue like that because we are part of nature. At some point the forest is going to end, water sources will be dried up, if we continue as we are." Buen Vivir takes the idea of intergenerational sustainability set out in Sustainable Development seriously, since it underlines the nature–society continuum. Laura continues: "In saying that the resources will not be around forever, we say finally that the resources are not only ours. But we have to be aware that we have children, and possibly will have grandchildren. They no longer will have what we are talking about or what we are calling resources."

This does not mean reverting to an ultra-conservationist approach to resources whereby we stop using them altogether, but it involves a more sustainable approach to resource use than is currently considered under Sustainable Development. As a society, it is about viewing our relationship with nature in a completely different way. Laura recalls an anecdote from another Indigenous colleague:

> What one lady told me seemed to me to be very, very good; she said, "they tell us that sustainability is to take absolutely everything there is, absolutely every little thing, some things more than others but we have to use every little thing." And she said that she does not like that because what they do is rather to use only what they need, and the rest has to stay [unused]. So, it was a very interesting reflection… I think it's a matter of seeing nature not only as a resource [but] as Pachamama [Mother Earth], not just something you use and that is there to serve you.

Felipe explains that this way of viewing nature is a matter of education and awareness: "If you're living this idea of Sumak Kawsay, to be at harmony with, or at peace with, your environment, and if you're aware that your actions will disturb that, you're much less likely to take what you don't need." He argues that it is a learned worldview:

> It's awareness of… your lifestyle, the goods you need to live well, to be aware of what that causes to the environment. Most people don't realise that they need to mine 60–100 tonnes of mineral dirt, subsoil to get one ounce of gold. If they could see the cyanide, if they could see the destruction, they would *not* buy that gold ring. So, awareness is absolutely important in terms of our relationship with natural resources.

It is also a matter of viewing "other" types of wealth than economic as vital to wellbeing, and to place equal importance upon them. This conception of wealth is not comparable to the neoliberal idea of placing monetary value on non-economic aspects, such as the economic value placed on natural resources; rather, it entails a full appreciation of and respect for non-economic aspects of society, such as the environment (including aesthetic value), culture, community. Felipe explains that it is important to make society aware of that fact: "We can really concentrate on making people aware that economic wealth is just one type of wealth, and it's not the most important wealth for achieving Sumak Kawsay. Social wealth is very, very important; cultural, environmental wealth."

Problematically, neoliberal development places an economic value on everything, and that has been part of the problem for attaining Sustainable Development; it is oxymoronic when society turns nature into a commodity. In addition, society's wellbeing has been measured in quantitative economic terms, with Gross Domestic Product (GDP) being the leading indicator of wellbeing, and economic poverty the baseline for development progress. Not all societies see their level of economic poverty as a measure of their happiness and wellbeing. The Indigenous peoples of Latin America, for example, do not view wellbeing in this type of linear fashion, and such is the ethos of Buen Vivir.

The key informants, both Indigenous and non-Indigenous, place greater value on non-material or non-economic wealth and consider that poverty has many dimensions that must be considered, not only economic. Luis, although now an urban resident, is from Intag Valley and understands the strengths and challenges of rural communities, which often have policy priority when it comes to economic poverty alleviation and development. He clarifies:

> Poverty has many parameters. A person can honestly have a good level of economic [security], but if he does not have time to enjoy with his family, he is poor in time. A person can have free time, can have money, but if he does not have anyone with whom to spend time, he is poor socially. Poverty has many factors but is usually always qualified as economic.

The former Correa government introduced new measures in line with the PNBV to measure various forms of poverty in the Multi-Dimensional Poverty Index, which was developed over two years by a Statistical Poverty Commission. It included two key national bodies, INEC (National Institute for Statistics and Census) and SENPLADES (National Secretary of Planning and Development), with support by the Oxford Poverty and Human Development Initiative. The former head of the SENPLADES, Pabel Muñoz, affirmed that "poverty is reflected in multiple dimensions and is the result of multiple factors; the most important inequalities. To eradicate it we must generate equal opportunities, equal access to resources, and economic and social justice" and do so by implementing "profound changes in economic structures and power relations" ("Ecuador presenta su propuesta para medición del índice de pobreza multidimensional").

Within the Ecuadorian government's MPI there are four dimensions: Education; work and social security; health, water, and food; and housing and a clean environment (access to a sewerage system and rubbish disposal) (*Encuesta nacional de empleo, desempleo y subempleo (enemdu)* 2019). If we consider that poverty is the opposite of wealth, however, there are also dimensions of poverty that are not included, but which are vital for Buen Vivir, such as social cohesion, community involvement, and environmental poverty. Luis also spoke of the poverty of being disconnected from the land, and the nature of modern society where we have the convenience of supermarkets, but the deficiency of not knowing where our food comes from, how it is grown, and the quality of the produce. In a globally connected world where the majority of societies are urbanised, ensuring that connection to the land is not an easy task. Many people are disconnected from where their goods – including natural resources and food – come from. At the same time, there is an increasing scepticism of the globalised fast goods and services consumer industry, and we are seeing more movements going "back to roots" such as organic food, slow food, localisation, and slow living (Mander & Goldsmith 2014). As Mander and Goldsmith (2014) note, "The importance of the natural world, in intrinsic terms and for human life, is fundamental. Without it, we cannot survive. Yet we have sufficiently divorced ourselves from it to become capable of devising an economic system that is destroying it."

Felipe recognises that that the idea of using only what is needed is not a novel one borne from Buen Vivir: "I think Gandhi had it right when he said 'there's enough stuff to go around, if people are fair with it. And not nearly enough if we take too much.' So, the idea is to just take what you need from the environment, and that includes the elements, or natural resources. Just what you need."

This involves greater connection to our environment and to nature, but it by no means infers a return to the past (Gudynas & Acosta 2011) (as critics might suggest); rather, it requires new ways of thinking. As Gudynas and Acosta (Cordaid 2012) affirm, "We don't stop building bridges, and we don't reject Western physics and the mathematics to build them. But the size and materials used to build those bridges will be different."

It comes back to the question of fundamental needs satisfaction, and the approach taken under Buen Vivir emphasises needs outside the realm of wealth creation, profit, economic growth, and linear human progress. Returning to the earlier argument by Jackson et al. regarding needs as wants (Jackson, Jager & Stagl 2008), at the community level, an alternative economic approach is required. This is an important point where both practice and policy concur. Javier, head of a local organisation which works with communities on environmental issues, clarifies: "The social economy can be defined in many ways, but it is the alternative economy compared to the dominant model that we know. In this case the economy is conceived from territories, from communities *for* communities, and also *by* communities." For Javier, it increases capabilities; he says, "So, it includes, as well as wealth, commissioning local talent; the use of local resources, local agricultural resources; the respect for local traditions; participation in political decisions; organisation or policy in general; and a very important element is work that is respectful of the environment, not destructive."

Defined separately, the social economy is also seen as the "third sector," and an important, stabilising backbone to counter problems such as economic poverty and social exclusion (Kawano 2013). The solidarity economy on the other hand seeks to radically transform the whole neoliberal social and economic system (Kawano 2013). Together the SSE offers an alternative economy which can work within the current economic system, albeit towards transformative change. RIPESS define the SSE as "an ethical and values-based approach to economic development that prioritises the welfare of people and planet over profits and blind growth" (*Global vision for a social solidarity economy: Convergences and differences in concepts, definitions and frameworks* 2015). It "combines and balances logics of accumulation, redistribution, and reciprocity, expressed in a democratically regulated market, an equitable reassignment of resources by a participating State, and the affirmation of practices of mutual benefit in the framework of a society and a culture of solidarity" (*Global vision for a social solidarity economy: Convergences and differences in concepts, definitions and frameworks* 2015). This understanding of the SSE supports the principles of Buen Vivir, and it can be part of a strategy to concretise Buen Vivir because it identifies economic organizations created by people who freely join to develop economic activities and create jobs on the basis of solidarity, reciprocity, and cooperative relations... This approach implies direct participation by civic society in the decision-making that affects the common good in order to implement concrete economic alternatives.

(Giovannini 2014)

The SSE tends to include cooperatives; social businesses or businesses with a social purpose; fair trade, ethical agri-economy, small-scale, and rural enterprises; and microcredit institutions and charities that trade with a focus on community and reciprocity (Utting, van Dijk & Matheï 2014). There is some tension, though, about whether fair trade should be included because of an unequal distribution of gains (Samba Sylla 2014). Many small producers in Ecuador feel that the fair trade system is not socially and economically just because of the need to pay for hefty certification fees, which most small producers alone cannot do, and without certification their products become unsellable in the face of certified competition. Juan tells how organic certification, like fair trade, puts small producers at a disadvantage: "We [community farmers] organised ourselves to be organic but organic certification is worth USD $5000; but without it, you cannot sell that product. As a farmer you have to spend USD $15,000 to certify your products. So that is a way to stop your initiative."

The SSE, however, is the ideal model of economic development for Buen Vivir because it shares many of the same tenets: Both call for ethical consumption, communal wellbeing, redistribution of wealth, and a system that is inclusive and participatory. Not least, like Buen Vivir, it is founded in endogenous self-determination, usually small in scale, and local. It is a plural economy and Buen Vivir requires plural cooperation on all levels to produce knowledge that can enact long-term change. A plural approach must work cooperatively within the current model, away from "reform" and "status quo" and towards "transformation."

It is an accepted fact that for ecological sustainability and human wellbeing we now need transformation – acknowledged in the UN's 2030 Agenda for Sustainable Development. Using an approach like Buen Vivir with an economic pillar based on SSE can bring the "people dimension" (UNGA 2015) to the global sustainability agenda whilst acting for long-term, effective change endogenously.

In policy, Ecuador's Constitution of 2008 established a "social economy based on the principles of solidarity" (SENPLADES 2009). It "rejects the false dichotomy between State and market promoted by neoliberal thought, and establishes a complex interrelation between the State, the market, society and nature. The market will no longer be the sole engine that promotes development. Instead it will interact with the State, society and nature" (SENPLADES 2009). The former Correa government called for a strengthening of the social and solidarity economy in the 2009–2013 PNBV as "Mechanisms for Inclusion, Social Protection, and Guarantee of Rights in Light of the New Agreement for Coexistence to Strengthen Social and Economic Capacities" (SENPLADES 2009). The plan states that Buen Vivir stresses solidarity, reciprocity, and cooperation, and the concept of "distributing while producing" and "producing while re-distributing." As a result, a popular, social, and solidarity-based economy is the main tool to make (re)distribution and the process of wealth generation inseparable from one another (SENPLADES 2009).

In that respect, productivity is still important under Buen Vivir; it is just the model of productivity that changes as it aims for Socio-Eco Wellbeing over economic growth. Government plays a major role in ensuring that structures are in place for allowing communities to move to this model. Politically, if the new productive structure is undertaken in a genuine attempt for change it will mean transitioning from an extractive economy towards a more diversified and inclusive economy. However, at the policy level there are several contradictions in Buen Vivir policy: 1) That wealth accumulation remains the key objective, akin to neoliberal strategies; and 2) the postponing of transitions to a post-extractive economy rather than starting change now. The PNBV states, "Although accumulation of wealth will depend initially on commodity extraction, the strategy will be to promote new non-polluting industries and diversify exports based on bioproducts and ecological services, which will significantly relieve pressure on the environment" (SENPLADES 2009).

With the climate crisis being fuelled by extractive industries, this change needs to start now. This, I argue, is the turning point between practice and policy, with each actor having a vital role to play.

Notes

1　This last point is important because although the PNBV outlines several principles with certain government targets to be achieved, this is more akin to traditional development in that it is implemented from the top-down. Yet an analysis of the concept asserts that it is endogenous to implement change from the bottom-up. I also reiterate the need to include all key actors in the identification of principles. Additionally, neither the key informants nor the literature believes that the principles outlined by the government are concrete and inclusive enough to provide transformative change. For these reasons, although the government interpretation has informed my analysis, it is not appropriate to have recourse to this for a practical community-led understanding of Buen Vivir.

2　For more information on this project, see World Bank (2003).

References

Acosta, A 2012, *The buen vivir: An opportunity to imagine another world, Inside a champion: An analysis of the Brazilian Development Model, Democracy*, Heinrich Böll Foundation, Berlin, Germany. <http://www.br.boell.org/downloads/Democracy_Inside _A_Champion.pdf#page=194>.

Municipio de Cotacachi, *Actualizacion pdyot cotacachi 2015–2035*, 2016, Cotacachi, Ecuador.

Australian Unity 2016, *Australian wellbeing index*, Australian Unity, Melbourne, Australia, <https://www.australianunity.com.au/media-centre/news-and-media/australian-unity-wellbeing-index-2016>.

Constitución de la república del ecuador 2008, Registro oficial 449, 20 October 2008, Quito.

Cordaid 2012, *Buen vivir, the good life (imagining sustainability −6)*, CIDSE, viewed 11 December 2013, <http://www.cidse.org/articles/rethinking-development/growth-and-sustainability/buen-vivir-the-good-life-imagining-sustainability-6.html>.

Cruz, I, Rauschmayer, F, Omann, I & Frühmann, J 2011, *Human needs frameworks and their contribution as analytical instruments in sustainable development in policymaking*, Routledge, New York.

Cruz, I, Stahel, A & Max-Neef, M 2009, 'Towards a systemic development approach: Building on the human-scale development paradigm', *Ecological Economics*, vol. 68, no. 7, pp. 2021–30. doi: 10.1016/j.ecolecon.2009.02.004.

Cubillo-Guevara, AP, Hidalgo-Capitán, AL & García-Álvarez, S 2016, 'El buen vivir como alternativa al desarrollo para américa latina', *Iberoamerican Journal of Development Studies*, vol. 5, no. 2, pp. 30–57.

'Ecuador presenta su propuesta para medición del índice de pobreza multidimensional', Secretaría Técnica Planifica Ecuador, <http://www.planificacion.gob.ec/ecuador-presenta-su-propuesta-para-medicion-del-indice-de-pobreza-multidimensional/>.

INEC 2019, *Encuesta nacional de empleo, desempleo y subempleo (enemdu)*, INEC, Quito.

Escobar, A 1995, *Encountering development: The making and unmaking of the third world (new in paper)*, Princeton University Press, Princeton, NJ.

FAO 2001, *The state of food insecurity in the world 2001*, Food and Agriculture Organization of the United Nations, Rome, Italy.

Felipe, GO 2014, ITACA, México, Disponible en: http://filosofiadelbuenvivir.com/wpcontent/uploads/2014/05/Utop% C3% ADas_en_la_era_de_la_supervivencia-1-1.pdf>.

'Freddy ehlers: El buen vivir es sinónimo de felicidad', 2015, *El Universo*, 15 May 2015.

Fukuda-Parr, S 2003, 'The human development paradigm: Operationalizing sen's ideas on capabilities', *Feminist Economics*, vol. 9, no. 2–3, pp. 301–17.

Gardbaum, S 2008, 'Human rights as international constitutional rights', *European Journal of International Law*, vol. 19, no. 4, pp. 749–68.

Giovannini, M 2014, *Indigenous peoples and self-determined development: The case of community enterprises in chiapas*, thesis, University of Trento.

Global vision for a social solidarity economy: Convergences and differences in concepts, definitions and frameworks, 2015, Ripess, viewed <http://www.ripess.org/wp-content/uploads/2017/08/RIPESS_Vision-Global_EN.pdf>.

Gudynas, E & Acosta, A 2011, 'La renovación de la crítica al desarrollo y el buen vivir como alternativa', *Utopia y Praxis Latinoamericana: Revista Internacional de Filosofia Iberoamericana y teoria Social*, vol. 16, no. 53, pp. 71–83.

Jackson, T, Jager, W & Stagl, S 2008, *Beyond insatiability: Needs theory, consumption and sustainability*, Elgar Reference Collection, Cheltenham.

Kawano, E 2013, *Social solidarity economy: Toward convergence across continental divides*, United Nations Research Institute for Social Development, viewed 26 July 2016, <http://www.unrisd.org/unrisd/website/newsview.nsf/(httpNews)/F1E9214CF8EA21A8C1257B1E003B4F65?OpenDocument>.

'Ley orgánica de tierras rurales y territorios ancestrales república del ecuador national assembly 2016, SAN-2016- 0398, Registro Ofi cial N° 711', 7 March 2016, El Telegrafo, Ecuador.

Mander, J & Goldsmith, E, eds., 2014, *The case against the global economy. [electronic resource] : And for a turn towards localization*, Routledge, London. doi: 10.4324/9781315071787.

Maslow, A & Lewis, KJ 1987, 'Maslow's hierarchy of needs', *Salenger Incorporated*, vol. 14, p. 987.

Mason, J 2002, *Qualitative researching*, 2nd ed., SAGE, London.

Max-Neef, MA, Elizalde, A & Hopenhayn, M 1991, *Human scale development: Conception, application and further reflections*, Apex Press, New York.

Max-Neef, MA, Elizalde, A & Hopenhayn, M 1994, *Desarrollo a escala humana: Conceptos, aplicaciones y algunas reflexiones*, Icaria Editorial, Barcelona.

Maxwell, S 1996, 'Food security: A post-modern perspective', *Food Policy*, vol. 21, no. 2, pp. 155–70. doi: 10.1016/0306-9192(95)00074-7.

OECD 2013, *Education indicators in focus*, OECD, Paris, France, <https://www.oecd.org /education/skills-beyond-school/EDIF%202013--N%C2%B010%20(eng)--v9%20F INAL%20bis.pdf>.

Phélan, C 2011, 'Revisión de índices e indicadores de desarrollo: Aportes para la medición del buen vivir (sumak kawsay)', *Obets: Revista de Ciencias Sociales*, vol. 6, no. 1, pp. 69–95.

Saltos, T 2008, *The participatory budgeting experience cotacachi - Ecuador*, 2008/02, World Bank, Washington, DC, <http://siteresources.worldbank.org/EXTSOCIALD EVELOPMENT/Resources/244362-1170428243464/3408356-1194298468208/4 357878-1206561986056/TatyanaSaltosPaperSession3Day2.pdf>.

Samba Sylla, N 2014, *Fairtrade is an unjust movement that serves the rich*, viewed <https:/ /www.theguardian.com/global-development/2014/sep/05/fairtrade-unjust-movement-serves-rich?CMP=share_btn_fb>.

Scarlato, M 2013, 'Social enterprise, capabilities and development paradigms: Lessons from ecuador', *Journal of Development Studies*, vol. 49, no. 9, pp. 1270–83. doi: 10.1080/00220388.2013.790962.

Sen, A 2001, *Development as freedom*, Oxford Paperbacks, London.

SENPLADES 2009, *Plan nacional para el buen vivir 2009–2013 : Construyendo un estado plurinacional e intercultural*, Secretaría Nacional de Planificación y Desarrollo, Quito, Ecuador.

SENPLADES 2013, *Plan nacional para el buen vivir 2013–2017*, Secretaría Nacional de Planificación y Desarrollo, Quito, Ecuador.

'Una oportunidad insólita de cambiar el mundo', 2010, *Periodico Intag*, Marzo - Abril, p. 35.

United Nations General Assembly 2015, *Transforming our world*, Resolution A/Res/70/1, United Nations/New York. https://www.un.org/ga/search/view_doc.asp?symbol=A/ RES/70/1&Lang=E.

United Nations General Assembly, *Universal declaration of human rights*, 1948, Resolution 217A, New York.

Utting, P, van Dijk, N & Matheï, M-A 2014, *Social and solidarity economy: Is there a new economy in the making?*, Social Dimensions of Sustainable Development, OPSSE--10, United Nations Research Institute for Social Development, Geneva.

World Bank 2003, *Indigenous and afro-ecuadorian peoples development project*, World Bank, viewed 10 August, <http://www.worldbank.org/projects/P040086/indigenous-af ro-ecuadorian-peoples-development-project?lang=en&tab=overview>.

5 Living Well and Buen Vivir

Practice vs. policy?

The vagueness surrounding what Buen Vivir means has blurred the differences between practice and policy. We know that the way Buen Vivir has evolved, originating from Indigenous worldviews and influenced by academia and policy, is an important aspect of its conceptuality. We also know that it is an endogenous, community-led tool for change, change which stems from the bottom-up, but where all actors have a role to play in plural cooperation.

Until now I have discussed the particulars of Buen Vivir: Its principles, approach to needs, and economic aspect. However, there is one significant research finding which enables communities to work towards attaining Buen Vivir and meeting their fundamental needs practically. It honours Buen Vivir's ascension from grassroots, while emphasising its plurality. That finding is identified as *Vivir Bien* (literally translated as Living Well).

So, what is Vivir Bien and what are its implications for the implementation of Buen Vivir? Vivir Bien involves changing in attitudes and behaviours towards Buen Vivir, through grassroots practice. It is the idea of a community tool epitomised.

The literature on Buen Vivir often discusses Vivir Bien and Buen Vivir interchangeably, with the former referring to the Bolivian conception (based on Suma Qamaña), and the latter to the Ecuadorian conception of the same idea (based on Sumak Kawsay). My research refers to Vivir Bien in a different fashion. Buen Vivir and Vivir Bien are two notably different ideas, albeit with the same Indigenous roots. They do not relate to cultural differences, but rather to conceptual differences. Vivir Bien (or Living Well), as referred to here, originates from the Kichwa term "Ally Kawsay," rather than Aymara "Suma Qamaña." The difference is beyond pure semantics; it is one of attitudes, actions, beliefs, and behaviours. It transcends the argument in the literature for the need for practical guidelines for Buen Vivir, because Vivir Bien is just that. Buen Vivir is a political act based on the idea of Sumak Kawsay, or even a concept that has been co-opted by the government and has no relation to communities' day-to-day reality and the change they are trying to achieve. In other words, Buen Vivir relates to policy, or a utopian goal, whereas Vivir Bien relates to the practice of the principles of Buen Vivir, or the day-to-day actions taken in communities and for communities. Both are integral to one another and can be understood as two strands of the same concept.

When it comes to implementation, the same principles apply to Vivir Bien as to Buen Vivir, albeit from a practical perspective, and, most importantly, from the bottom-up. Javier, like many other key informants, calls Buen Vivir a utopia, but affirms: "Well, you can also have a utopian goal." Javier argues, "Buen Vivir is a goal. I'm not saying that it exists, because it does not. It's a goal, which can also be a utopian goal. It's a goal. It's a path – a path where you have to coalesce principles, ideas [and] bold proposals… and that's the difference because then we have Vivir Bien." Joaquín explains further: "I would say that it [Buen Vivir] is the ultimate [goal] of society, but it's like climbing stairs. I believe that it can be utopian… It is a goal to be obtained."

The need for concrete examples of practice has been discussed by various scholars and intellectuals. These practices cannot be identified in a utopian Buen Vivir or its aspirational political interpretation of "Good Living," but rather in Vivir Bien – the daily practice of "Living Well." For Socio-Eco Wellbeing to be achieved at the grassroots level – by communities, for communities – the focus is not on pursuing an aspirational political ideology, but rather it is about the changes, acts, and decisions that communities make for the future on a day-to-day basis.

In Cotacachi County, Vivir Bien is also a local government campaign for wellbeing and sustainability to reinforce the importance of daily practice for community-led change (*Actualizacion pdyot cotacachi 2015–2035* 2016). Mayor Cevallos states that the construction of Vivir Bien at the local policy level "Involves acting in accordance to the principles and knowledge of our people, who as the highest expression of life, manifest the harmony of their daily actions with nature, the friendly use of the benefits of land and permanent care of water" (*Hidronangulvi* 2016).

Vivir Bien is the epitome of endogenous, people-led change and Buen Vivir is about scaling that up to ensure that the political structures and policies are in place to achieve the end goal: Socio-Eco Wellbeing. The particular, contextual, and practical emphasis of Vivir Bien is the basis for change and transformation emanating from the ground up. Buen Vivir is thus the capacitating tool that communities can use to help realise Vivir Bien at the local level, because it provides the space, the political structures, and the resources to implement the principles in practice, with the co-operation of all actors and in the aim of attaining Socio-Eco Wellbeing. Leandro explains:

> Sumak Kawsay is a climax, to reach a place where everything is beautiful, where we become happy. But it is not the everyday. The quotidian, we call it "Ally Kawsay," which is more common, we are always talking about Ally Kawsay. Of course, the epitome of the two is wellbeing. That is, to live well. We say Ally Kawsay is living well and Sumak Kawsay is good living. But Sumak Kawsay is the space in which we arrive somewhere. You don't take into account the process, but you take into account the act of climax. Ally Kawsay is more day-to-day.

Joaquín clarifies: "Sumak [Kawsay] is high level and Ally Kawsay is very, very detailed… earthlier." It is therefore concentrated in the practices, beliefs, and attitudes of the community, rather than high-level policy. This makes it more amenable to practical implementation in communities, and through an understanding of the principles and challenges to implementation, it can be transformed into a useful tool for communities to achieve Socio-Eco Wellbeing for themselves, on a daily basis with consideration for the long-term.

It must be emphasised that for Vivir Bien to be achieved at the grassroots level, there must be a significant amount of political will. The political structures must be in place to allow this transformation to occur. In Buen Vivir, governments act as facilitating institutions, rather than the main actors. That includes creating the systems and structures necessary for endogenous-led change. The most vital path for creating Buen Vivir therefore is by practice.

Following on the path of Sustainable Development, aspirational goals such as those enacted in international and national policies by the United Nations and various governments have only strengthened the status quo and have not led to the concrete change that society needs. An alternative that can work cooperatively with global and national goals but enact real change at the community level is what is now required; and a hybrid Buen Vivir–Vivir Bien policy–practice approach offers that. People-led change is essential. Emmanuel states: "I think the role of people in living well is fundamental; that is, without people, without the active movements we could not have Vivir Bien or Buen Vivir or anything else."

Miguel explains that both Buen Vivir and Vivir Bien are necessary: "Logically we must have Ally Kawsay to achieve Sumak Kawsay. Logically Sumak Kawsay is always ahead, we are always looking for it, waiting for it. It is the ideal state." In other words, both Vivir Bien and Buen Vivir feed off each other and are necessarily dependant on one another.

In that light, for Vivir Bien to occur, there are four preconditions: Equality; solidarity; participation; self-determination. These are also core principles of Buen Vivir. None of the four preconditions can exist in a political environment hostile to endogenous change. Leandro tells me that both at the level of community understanding of Vivir Bien, as well in local politics, these four points are very important:

> The first [point] is the horizontality of society, that is him and you, to both be equal. We can turn around, we can agree, we can discuss. We can make things very interesting, if you respect my judgment, and I respect your judgment. Minga[1] [collective] work, democratic living teaches us that we live by doing things for others. For us participation is not only being representative of a space, and that the people who suddenly represent me must accept what I say. It is a place where people have the process which also decides those spaces… and self-determination as we understand it, that I get to decide, the space, or model of the space [for participation], so to speak. So those four aspects are fundamental to us achieving Ally Kawsay.

The principles of Buen Vivir underpin practice. At this juncture, if it is determined that Vivir Bien is the practice of Buen Vivir at the grassroots, then it is necessary to look at some examples of what this practice looks like on the ground to complete our understanding of Buen Vivir. The next part of this chapter does so, categorised by the relevant principles, and again demonstrating the interconnectedness of the principles.

Vivir Bien: A look at Buen Vivir in practice

Buen Vivir is applicable outside of the Andean context; however, it is important to bear in mind that these examples are specific to the community or communities in which they are manifested. They illustrate how some of the principles are played out in practice. These examples have been determined not only through responses by the key informants, but also through documents and observations of both rural and urban daily life in the county.

Healthy environment, reciprocity, and education

Environmental practices are by far the most visible, affirming the biocentricity of Buen Vivir in practice. In the communities themselves citizens are partaking in a number of environmental conservation activities. Indigenous leader David says, for example, that in his community in the foothills of Cotacachi city, efforts concentrate on the reforestation of land which was previously obligated to be cleared by governmental regulations.

During a visit to one of the Indigenous communities, I was made aware of how integral their practices are. On one farm facing the Imbabura volcano, perched high up on the hills bordering the Pichincha province, I was given a tour by the owner's daughter. Many of these Indigenous communities capture rainwater for use and reuse on agricultural land, as well as in households. The family is self-sufficient, only needing to go to the supermarket once in a while for items like rice, while on the property fruit, vegetables, and herbs are grown for both food and medicinal purposes. The daughter explained that by default all produce is organic: "For the environment and for good health, it's better without chemicals." Families within the community share produce, because, she explains, "without a strong community, there is no Buen Vivir." Sharing information on practices is also common practice resulting in capacity-building and awareness between families and communities.

All families in rural Cotacachi grow their own produce, and many in urban areas. Where families do not have access to land or skills to do so, there are still many small produce markets which sell organic produce. Communities also create micro-enterprises between families to either swap or buy local produce, creating pockets of local solidarity economies.

Following a round of interviews with key informants one community member gave us a lift back to where we were staying. He was passionate about environmental education, stating that he has noticed a significant change in biodiversity over the past years. One issue is with the extinction of several native species in the region, including the Andean bear. However, he explained, "For the last few years there have been many strong campaigns to teach people about the value of the biodiversity and animals and that we have to look after them. In fact, since, we have seen a significant rise in numbers of lots of the species, so it has worked."

This awareness and education for environmental conservation practices has resulted in a greater connection to the land and a better relationship: Reciprocity with the environment. Laura says, "Daily, I prefer to refer to nature more in terms of Mother Nature. Mother Nature is everything, not only the land that is cultivated... it is the whole environment... and also from my experience, everything I do is going to come back to nature." What goes around, comes around.

In the daily life of Cotacacheños, the presence and/or threat of mining exploration and operations is a major preoccupation; nonetheless most people recognise that paradoxical role that energy plays in the wellbeing of their family and community lives. Community members have thus identified a need for more renewable energy projects as an alternative to non-renewable destructive mining activities. One of the ways in which this has been manifested is in small-scale hydroelectricity plants, such as those developed in cooperation with HidroIntag and the municipal government, including the HidroNangulvi project. Cotacachi Mayor Jomar Cevallos[2] claims that the local hydroelectric energy project HidroNangulvi, for example, is a "clear example of how to build Vivir Bien," albeit with governmental and external cooperation (*Hidronangulvi* 2016). The Nangulvi site is located in the Intag region, where communities have continually voiced their opposition to large-scale extractive projects and searched for alternatives to replace the need for them. Through micro-projects with local watersheds, HidroIntag aims to put the management of local water sources back into the hands of the communities, effectively increasing their self-determination. HidroNangulvi looks to integrate community actors, civil society, and local government in the self-management of watersheds, albeit in accordance with the PNBV, and provides an example of a plurality of actors and knowledges in the pursuance of Buen Vivir.

The HidroIntag project was created as a result of Cotacachi's participatory democracy processes. The micro-projects seek to create "integrated environmental management of watershed[s] and promote a non-extractivist local economy" (HidroIntag 2009) by integrating community actors and civil society to manage their own water resources by "generating investment in rural development, promoting energy efficiency, access to local employment [and] self-management of watersheds" (*Hidronangulvi* 2016). The Nangulvi project in particular helps to conserve over 440 square kilometres of native forest, situated in the buffer zone of the Cotacachi-Cayapas Ecological Reserve, one of the most biodiverse areas on earth (*Hidronangulvi* 2016). Through local government and organisations, the communities define the criteria for the selection of works and the objective is to reinvest the resources generated by the ten mini hydroelectric plants back into the community in economic, social, and ecological projects identified by the communities themselves (HidroIntag 2009).

With a similar concern for maintaining the region's rich biodiversity, local environmental organisation DECOIN has purchased primary and secondary cloud forest in the Intag Valley from the government to create 41 community-owned and -managed reserves, bordering the Cotacachi-Cayapas Reserve. In addition, it has helped create 37 community watershed reserves, creating "genetic banks" for native plants and animals, in cooperation with UK NGO Rainforest Concern (Zorrilla 2010). As part of this project, the communities have planted over 50,000 trees and have received training on how to take, analyse, and interpret water samples, to self-manage the reserve (Zorrilla 2010).

Communities in Cotacachi have taken not only action on environmental issues seriously, but also education. This is demonstrated in many environmental education campaigns by the communities themselves, including one project selected for the local government Program of Support for Decentralised Management of Natural Resources in Northern Ecuador (PRODERENA). The "Citizens *Minga* for Environmental Education" seeks to capacitate 30 participants with local environmental knowledge including community leaders, members of water boards, council members, and general community members in the environmental management of two parish areas in Cotacachi: Imantag and Quiroga. During the project training booklets, maps, and models were developed to inform communities about what is happening with their environment. They included information such as what is happening with the water, how many water boards there are, and how much water is available to communities. The training included topics proposed by communities such as burning, biodiversity, ecological reserve, and waste management (Rivera 2007).

SSE and decent work

Several alternatives to development have been proposed and pursued in the county "in the context of economic and political crisis," also with a view to conserving and protecting its biodiversity, and promoting local talent and participation (*Hidronangulvi* 2016). There are currently 1,200 people directly involved in 34 groups or organisations for economic alternatives in the Intag region alone (*Actualizacion pdyot cotacachi 2015–2035* 2016). One of the most successful alternatives is the Agri-artisanal Association for Coffee Farmers of Rio Intag (ACCRI). ACCRI has been in operation for almost 20 years and helps small coffee producers and families diversify their normal crops to include organic coffee crops for sale both locally and nationally, both of which would be difficult to achieve in small-batch production – there are no large-scale monocultures involved. Representatives at ACCRI say that this project has helped keep communities and families interested in the continuance of agriculture, as well as provide community members with a consistent alternative income, as coffee plantations have a long lifespan.

Small local producers and artisans also have the opportunity to sell to the local and tourist markets through regular "fairs" supported by the national and provincial governments as a part of the social and solidarity economy, and include various sectors, for example food/agricultural produce, artisan handicrafts, community tourism, and textiles. These economic initiatives are held with the strategic aim of operationalising the model for a social and solidarity economy proposed in the PNBV, but also provide small producers with an opportunity to sell their produce outside of their specific community context.

Community-based eco and cultural tourism is another initiative being promoted by the local government, realised through the will of the communities. Tourism has been one of the ways in which the national government has sought to diversify the economy (SENPLADES 2013) alternatively. Many community members have identified small-scale community-based tourism as a possible sustainable alternative to extractive activities (*Actualizacion pdyot cotacachi 2015–2035* 2016). There are more than 30 families who now work together to offer tourism activities such as guided hiking and horseback tours in Intag and the surrounding areas (Olivera 2010). There are also programs of cultural exchange between families in Cotacachi and tourists, organised by several different groups. Local tourism agency Runa Tupari, for example, works with Indigenous communities from the Peasant Organisations Union of Cotacachi to organise volunteer tourism stays with local families to exchange culture and to participate in domestic and agricultural work.

Besides providing economic alternatives to traditional market activities, several artisan groups like *Mujer y Medioambiente* (Woman and the Environment) in Intag work to continue traditions such as handicrafts and other handmade produce with natural materials, giving full consideration to the environmental impact of their craft (Chassagne & Everingham 2019). Working as a cooperative, they sell their produce for a fair price within local communities, as well as to tourist markets, providing an income for the artisans. Luis says alternatives to development projects like the above-mentioned are important for building community solidarity: "What it represents in the initial stage is learning to work together. They [community members] realise that it is easier to work together to achieve quality to later have products which can be sold, and which also represent where they come from" (Chassagne & Everingham 2019).

Culture, community, and solidarity

Cultural conservation is an important aspect of Buen Vivir, and is not limited to the Andean context; it can be applied across various communities, as culture is a vital part of community identity and therefore plays a role in the harmony and solidarity of a community. Although there is a strong element of globalisation in daily life – for example, manifested in popular culture, technology, global brands, the adoption of anglicised expressions into Spanish – the importance of culture is especially evident in cultural traditions and celebrations in Cotacachi, as well as in public spaces such as the *Casa de las Culturas*, which serves to inform not only tourists but local communities. Indigenous community leader David argues that "to recover Sumak Kawsay, Ally Kawsay, one needs to know, to value our customs, our traditions… that is our tradition."

The idea of community is often manifested in the ways in which community members work together, not just for the wellbeing of individuals, but to enhance the social and environmental wellbeing of the entire community. This can be demonstrated in the various *mingas* held in any one community, since a *minga* is defined by community work for mutual gain. For example, many small communities throughout Cotacachi do not have reliable water treatment systems that service the entire community, and often *mingas* are held to ensure that the community has access to clean and quality water. Several community members will gather together at a set time and place and decide on the work that needs to be done, and tasks will be delegated to complete it. There is often an elected community leader to take charge of the work.

This is not just limited to physical environmental work. Rodriguez speaks of the importance of the treatment of "disadvantaged" community members for community wellbeing. Sofia provides the example of building literacy in her community as a way in which Buen Vivir has been pursued. She says, "the elderly who do not know how to read and write, we work in groups [in the community] forming mingas [to teach them]." Communal work, as well as all of the above examples, helps build community, harmony, and solidarity, in the spirit of Buen Vivir.

The element of community is thus a fundament of Buen Vivir which supports one of the main underlying elements of Buen Vivir: Its plurality. To affirm this, I would like to restate that communities themselves cannot achieve Buen Vivir by acting alone. It is thus crucial to also examine the role of government and local organisations as other key actors in Buen Vivir.

The importance of plurality

Plurality is referred to in many senses: A plurality of vision, a plurality of knowledge, a plurality of being, and a plurality of change. In that respect, Buen Vivir as a people-led approach combines with the knowledge and vision of other actors to achieve change. Buen Vivir as a concept is not ignorant in discounting others' input in achieving Socio-Eco Wellbeing, which is crucial in a globally connected world, and in the context within which modern societies live. While all key informants believe that Buen Vivir can be achieved by communities themselves, it must be noted that they do not believe that it can be achieved in isolation.

The previous section outlined some examples of how these communities implement the principles of Buen Vivir through practice, or Vivir Bien. Although it is community-led, governments and organisations have a vital role to play. The question is now: What is their role and to which extent?

On Buen Vivir as an alternative, Ruttenberg (2013) stated that "[c]ommunity-based findings must then be compiled and articulated politically to elicit adequate policy response, thereby ensuring that development policy is designed to address social wellbeing needs as determined at the local level. This process… is of utmost importance to achieve a hybrid two-way symbiosis between bottom-up and top-down approaches to development policy alternatives" (Ruttenberg 2013). So, in the operationalisation of Buen Vivir we require not only endogenous-led change with policy support, but also external cooperation in the form of local, national, or global organisations acting as "moderators" or mediators of a bottom-up approach to ensure that processes do not become co-opted by government or external interests. We then have a hybrid approach whereby communities drive change, with policy support; according to Howard and Wheeler (2015) (paraphrasing Banks et al. 2015), organisations play "their role in the development ecosystem as a vital part of 'multiple bottom-up strategies that link engagement and advocacy in formal spaces with broader social mobilization and coalition building efforts,' rather than merely serving to reinforce the status quo." This approach would transform Buen Vivir into a viable practical alternative, rather than a political slogan or a radical offensive, though this is a fine line.

Buen Vivir: Political slogan or viable alternative?

Buen Vivir risks entering a crisis of legitimacy akin to that of Sustainable Development because of the contradictions between government policy and practice, and that policy endangering grassroots practice. Its legitimacy as a viable alternative to mainstream development has been questioned by intellectuals, and the confusion surrounding its core philosophy has led to it being called an ideology – both in the literature and on the ground – rather than a concrete practice, which is what is required if it is to be a viable alternative. This is partly due to the homogenisation of interpretations: Indigenous, political, and academic.

Felipe (2014) affirms that Buen Vivir is "a utopia which, for its realisation demands acute cultural transformations and a revision of the same bases of modern Western civilization." However, by the term "utopia," Felipe refers neither to the idea of a utopia based on Sumak Kawsay, as discussed by key informants above, nor to the "execution of government projects" (Acosta 2012), but to the political construction that has been interwoven by government, social movements, and academics.

Felipe (2014) argues that utopias exist as opposing dialectics to ideologies, which in the case of neoliberalism only helps to ensure the continuation of the status quo. Those in defence of ideologies, he says, will question a utopia as an "impossible dream" (Felipe 2014). However, he maintains that a utopia is "not simply a dream, but a dream that indispensably aspires to be realised." So, from that perspective, Buen Vivir as a utopian alternative political project has to be separated from ideology to serve a high-level, guiding purpose in which it is possible unite community needs with national and global goals.

Nonetheless, many in Ecuador associate the term "Buen Vivir" with a political campaign on behalf of the government which only delivered contradictions, rather than a path for action. Many key informants therefore see the politicised Buen Vivir as a "political slogan." Head of a local environmental organisation Javier argues, "I believe that the word will be transformed in the very short-term into a tainted word, a slogan. But the propaganda is very good, very beautiful, but that it is full of contradictions." Likewise, local government employee Miguel says, "The way I see this word used… as a slogan. Something that has been gathered from the Andean world and used as an alternative proposal. [But] I think it is the most viable alternative." Indigenous head of a local organisation Laura explains the contradiction: "The President said that to achieve Buen Vivir we need hous-ing, we need *everything*. Where do we get this? 'From our natural resources,' he said. And then that is the justification to continue mining and selling oil blocks. So that is a pretext for extractivism."

In the same light, local government employee Emmanuel states, "Regrettably, Buen Vivir as it is conceptualised today in Ecuador is just a slogan." For him, this also includes the way Buen Vivir has been conceptualised in literature, continu-ing to explain that "those who took this word, [for example] Alberto Acosta and others, have not really tried to give a sense to the idea that is trying to become a reality that in some places, and give it a more proper sense that is ours."

Despite the reference to Buen Vivir as a "political slogan" or a "marketing" spin for the government to achieve its contradictory neoextractivist aims, there is a clear role for governments, institutions, and policy that should be highlighted in a genuine attempt to connect policy with practice, and provide the essential structural support that endogenous practice needs. Let us start by taking a look at the role of government.

The role of government

When people spoke to me about practices of Buen Vivir at the institutional level – whether in general conversation with a taxi driver or in a formal interview with a key informant – they most often referred to government at the local level. Much more regard was given by the majority of key informants to local government as a key actor in realising Buen Vivir. Therefore, local government plays a central role in obtaining Buen Vivir, in parallel with communities because the government must provide the institutions, structures, and resources to implement Buen Vivir at the local level, manifesting as Vivir Bien. As Rafael states, "governments must help create the environment in which Buen Vivir can flourish." One of the ways in which they can do that is to allow for the endogenous identification of fundamental needs.

The exogenous identification and satisfaction of needs through a top-down approach puts limits on a community's self-determination. The exogenous approach is foundational in the traditional model of development, which has also supported the neoliberal economic model adopted throughout the West and has been promoted as "desired development" in countries in the periphery. Though, as this study finds, satisfying needs through self-determination and community capa-bilities is best practiced through direct participation in a participatory democracy. Giovannini (2012) argues that the SSE helps achieve self-determination "intended as Buen Vivir, in opposition to externally driven aid actions and development policies or projects, that are often imposed rather than collectively shared and approved by the concerned communities."

Full participation of the people is one of the core principles of Buen Vivir, but it is also a precondition and requires complete political will. Moreover, participa-tion is not only required for the implementation of Buen Vivir, but also for its definition at the local level (Cubillo-Guevara, Hidalgo-Capitán & García-Álvarez 2016). It is the community that defines what it means to them. As Joaquín says, "A democratic government must demonstrate, above all, greater humility and greater love for his community, his people, his society. Humility to say 'I alone cannot do it, I have to work with all of you together' because it is not a problem that I alone have created, and I do not have all of the solution." A democratic participatory approach to local development is therefore fundamental, Joaquín states:

> That's what I call participation, sharing the challenge of making positive democratic decisions. The issue, I think, is that it commits all citizens to be part of a team – stop being "me" to become "us." Our government has to be built and driven by all citizens. I would take care to strengthen the social capital that exists, human capital. I think the foundation is people, the community, and organisation.

This has been the aim of the Cotacachi Municipal Government since 1998. In Cotacachi, participation takes the form of a participatory democracy, applied through a participatory budget. A participatory democracy can be defined as considering "the opinions, criteria, and decisions of the people, and seeks consensus in order to achieve the social, economic, and environmental development of the community" (Saltos 2008). It is an effective way to harmonise institutional and bottom-up approaches. This mode of participation is more beneficial than traditional top-down participation because, as Giovannini (2015) states, it "has also an impact on the community as a whole, given that it facilitates both the identification of new needs emerging from the community and the implementation of strategies and the exploitation of resources, which are suitable to addressing these needs."

The participatory budgeting experience in Cotacachi has largely been a positive one in that it has been well received within communities and local government, with positive results for health, education, sanitation, equity, and general quality of life (Saltos 2008). It has also been awarded for internationally recognised best practice in citizens' participation and has served as a "true exercise of the rights and responsibilities of the citizens, and has strengthened the capacity of individuals, groups, and organizations to face their problems, defend their interests, and act as resolute, responsible, and active agents in the canton's democratic life" (Saltos 2008).

Participatory budgeting is designed by a participatory democracy governance model from the bottom-up. In the case of Cotacachi, the participatory budget is underlined by four principles: 1) Territorial, ethnic, and social participation; 2) budget transparency; 3) solidarity and self-determination; 4) a social and moral commitment to "unity in diversity" (Saltos 2008). The municipality is kept to account through a process of transparency which includes an evaluation forum for citizens and the Assembly for Cantonal Unity (AUC). The AUC was formed by local government and organised civil society with the objectives to collaborate, coordinate, and plan in a participatory manner, meeting annually and represented by the county's existing territorial, gender, generational, and thematic diversity (Saltos 2008).

The participatory budgeting cycle is an eight-step process: 1) Information and coordination with social actors from each territorial "zone;" 2) identification of works and projects with workshops held for and attended by all residents; 3) prioritisation of works and projects through workshops in each "zone;" 4) presentation of the proposal by a technical team; 5) coordination, where consensus is reached; 6) presentation of the final budget for approval by the local government; 7) execution of the works and projects; and 8) evaluation of the process through workshops held with social actors (Saltos 2008).

If used for consensus and dialogue a participatory budget can be understood as a tool for democracy, stimulating social capital (Cabannes 2004). Participatory budgeting is directly related to the SSE, questioning the relationship between the political and economic spheres, as procurers have more control over the direct benefits to the city or community (Cabannes 2004). Moreover, participatory budgeting has the potential to improve a community's wellbeing, because of a better understanding of actual needs and a "responsive government" to provide the resources, especially in areas with minimal public resources because citizens will "select projects that will best address their community's most demanding needs" (Boulding & Wampler 2010).

The advantage of participatory budgeting is that it can be replicated in any community or city, if the political will and structures exist, despite levels of economy; though they do require a "culture of participation" and "mobilised citizenry" for their success (Cabannes 2004). Cabannes examined 25 cases of successful participatory budgeting systems around the world and found that the annual budgets varied greatly from more than USD $2,200 per resident in St Denis and Bobbing in France, to less than USD $20 in Villa El Salvador, Peru (Cabannes 2004).

While in general it is held in good esteem, with some community members believing that it has greatly contributed to the wellbeing of the community, others are more sceptical that the process has started to become co-opted by certain interests. In one participatory budgeting workshop I attended, the element of mobilised citizenry was present, though some community members felt that their needs from the previous year were still not being met, mostly due to resources.

It has been a case of trial and error, says Leandro. When the participatory budget was first introduced there were conflicts over decisions; it was more of a process of representative participation. He recalls one meeting which he attended whereby community members did not feel their participation was respected, saying, "but why should we come to inaugurate [the new public works] – I did not even know they were going to do that." But, as he recounts, "it was in the budget and who made that budget? The leader of the neighbourhood. And the leader of the neighbourhood said, 'Oh, I saw that the neighbourhood was deteriorating so I requested it.' But there were other people that said no." Though, he continues, "there was a conflict and so the organisation went to work from the grassroots. That is, the people decide."

Participatory budgeting within a democratic participatory approach if undertaken effectively and with genuine intent addresses the dimension of "empowerment" within a Buen Vivir framework and could help dispel the sentiment of Buen Vivir being just a political slogan or an empty utopia. It could also be an effective method to enable communities to reflect on what Buen Vivir really means to them, which can in turn strengthen Vivir Bien and citizen responsibility, both individually and collectively.

The role of organisations

Civil society and the social organisation of communities is doubly vital for helping communities satisfy their fundamental needs, through associations and local organisations. It is also necessary for effective and democratic participation, as Joaquín explains:

> Where there is a diverse, pluralistic social fabric it is an important step in the governance of Cotacachi, the municipality of Cotacachi. If we build the concept of the organisation of urban, rural women rights, of children and youth to urban and rural areas, the organisation of farmers, the tourism sector, the artisanal sector, urban neighbourhoods; we contribute to that space for citizen participation that could only be much more effective in their demands and actions. [But] building the social fabric can be done when there is political will and when there is a vision of what you want to do. Because if it is to manipulate a group and give them food only, that is much easier. But that's populism, that's patronage.

Social organisation helps achieve change for the community, by the community. Laura uses the example of Cotacachi becoming Ecuador's first ecological county by decree, achieved through the will of the people: "Organisation played an important role. As with all organisations of Cotacachi – some more, some less – but they finally gathered together and proposed to the mayor saying, 'well, we want this, and we are all going to conceive that Cotacachi become an ecological canton.'"

The need for cooperation in the form of help also from external organisations was unanimously stated from all key informants, who see the value in working plurally with organisations to meet needs and achieve Buen Vivir. Diego states that this may be in the form of "support from the other institutions of advanced management to meet the needs that perhaps the same structure or policies of the parish [local government] cannot cover. At least the most unmet needs in the communities."

Cooperation, though, does not allude merely to financial aid with no consideration of the actual needs of the community. "Satellite cooperation" is not beneficial, as Joaquín argues, because it "means only leaving machines; (for instance) it does not contribute to capacity, the training of people in production, and so suddenly it does not meet its target. But if there is a much closer coordination, it is better taken advantage of." Gabriela similarly states that outside support is good, however: "It also pushes us to start working on, reflecting on what we want [as a community]. So, cooperation needs to work on the real needs of the community."

Fernando argues that the needs of the community and the sustainability of projects has not been a priority in the past with international cooperation. He says:

If it was sustainable or not often did not matter. And I think that cooperation must today cooperate in things that are sustainable in the long term. It must be a common goal of society. It has to be that they help to sow the seeds that people want. So, we believe that cooperation is fundamental to achieving [needs], at least in the COOTAD [Code for Territorial Organisation, Autonomy and Decentralisation] it gives us the authority to sign agreements and achieve goals and what we have to do is commit to cooperation but not to impose the implementation of projects and programs based on the objectives of cooperation. But cooperation based on the objectives of the community.

There have been cases in the past of cooperation in Cotacachi, notably in Intag, with international NGOs and development organisations that have exogenously imposed certain development projects and programs on various communities without taking into consideration the actual needs of that community. Most programs have been aimed at building the financial capacity and creating economic opportunities for women and youth, and although community members have appreciated the intention behind the programs, at the same time they have concerns that they have not contributed to satisfying their real needs, and ultimately once the organisation has left, the project fails.

Another area where organisations can assist is in the "plurality of knowledge" and technical abilities. In local hydroelectricity project HidroNangulvi, HidroIntag cooperated internationally through technical and financial support with Cuban sovereign energy institute CUBASOLAR, Ecuadorian engineers, the Central University of Ecuador, as well as hydropower professionals from France (*Hidronangulvi* 2016). Plurality of knowledge and technical abilities will ultimately be one of the most critical factors to help society overcome large-scale extractivism and move towards a post-extractive society. This will require plurally coordinating traditional, community, and Indigenous knowledge with Western technical knowledge. A move towards post-extractivism will enable communities to surmount one of the greatest challenges to achieving Buen Vivir. The following chapter looks at this and other challenges in greater detail.

Notes

1 The Diccionario Kichwa – Castellano / Runa Shimi – Ministerio de Educacion defines a *minga/minka* as "communal work." It generally entails Laboral work involving two or more people that benefits the community.
2 For the 2015–2019 period.

References

Acosta, A 2012, *The buen vivir: An opportunity to imagine another world, Inside a champion: An analysis of the Brazilian Development Model, Democracy*, Heinrich Böll Foundation, Berlin, Germany, <http://www.br.boell.org/downloads/Democracy_Inside _A_Champion.pdf#page=194>.

Actualizacion pdyot cotacachi 2015–2035, 2016, Md Cotacachi, Cotacachi, Ecuador.

Boulding, C & Wampler, B 2010, 'Voice, votes, and resources: Evaluating the effect of participatory democracy on well-being', *World Development*, vol. 38, no. 1, pp. 125–35. doi: 10.1016/j.worlddev.2009.05.002.

Cabannes, Y 2004, 'Participatory budgeting: A significant contribution to participatory democracy', *Environment and Urbanization*, vol. 16, no. 1, pp. 27–46. doi: 10.1630/095624704323026133.

Chassagne, N & Everingham, P 2019, 'Buen vivir: Degrowing extractivism and growing wellbeing through tourism', *Journal of Sustainable Tourism*, vol. 27, no. 12, pp. 1909–25. doi: 10.1080/09669582.2019.1660668.

Cubillo-Guevara, AP, Hidalgo-Capitán, AL & García-Álvarez, S 2016, 'El buen vivir como alternativa al desarrollo para américa latina', *Iberoamerican Journal of Development Studies*, vol. 5, no. 2 pp. 30–57.

Felipe, GO 2014, *Utopías en la era de la supervivencia. Una interpretación del buen vivir*, ITACA, Colonia del Mar.

Giovannini, M 2012, 'Social enterprises for development as *buen vivir*', *Journal of Enterprising Communities: People and Places in the Global Economy*, vol. 6, no. 3, pp. 284–99. doi: 10.1108/17506201211258432.

Giovannini, M 2015, 'Alternatives to development: The contribution of indigenous community enterprises in chiapas', *Journal of International Development* vol. 28, no. 7, pp. 1138–1154. doi: 10.1002/jid.3141.

HidroIntag 2009, *Sustainable hydroelectric generation system in the intag basin*, Cotacachi, Ecuador.

Hidronangulvi, 2016, Municipio de Cotacachi, Cotacachi, <http://www.cotacachi.gob.ec/index.php/component/phocadownload/category/59>.

Howard, J & Wheeler, J 2015, 'What community development and citizen participation should contribute to the new global framework for sustainable development', *Community Development Journal*, vol. 50, no. 4, pp. 552–70. doi: 10.1093/cdj/bsv033.

Olivera, R 2010, *Coffee in the clouds*, New Internationalist, <https://newint.org/features/2010/07/01/ecuador-copper-mining-local-protests>.

Rivera, J 2007, 'Foro promueve creación de más bosques protectores', *Periodico Intag*, p. 2.

Ruttenberg, T 2013, 'Wellbeing economics and buen vivir: Development alternatives for inclusive human security', *Fletcher Journal of Human Security*, vol. XXVIII, pp. 68–93. https://fletcher.tufts.edu/Praxis/~/media/Fletcher/Microsites/praxis/xxviii/article4_Ruttenberg_BuenVivir.pdf.

Saltos, T 2008, *The participatory budgeting experience cotacachi - Ecuador*, 2008/02, World Bank, Washington, DC, http://siteresources.worldbank.org/EXTSOCIALDEVELOPMENT/Resources/244362-1170428243464/3408356-1194298468208/4357878-1206561986056/TatyanaSaltosPaperSession3Day2.pdf.

SENPLADES 2013, *Plan nacional para el buen vivir 2013–2017*, Secretaría Nacional de Planificación y Desarrollo, Quito, Ecuador.

Zorrilla, C 2010, *Defensa y conservacion ecologica de intag*, DECOIN, viewed 02 September, <www.decoin.org/accomplishments/>.

6 Challenging the Good Life

Now that we have a more solid understanding of Buen Vivir, including what it looks like at the coalface and the role of the key actors, the discussion would be incomplete if we did not at least try to understand the main roadblocks to achieving it. Key informants were generally quite forward in offering their opinion on its challenges. After careful reflection of what Buen Vivir meant to them, a discussion on the challenges to achieving it followed at the end of the interview. In comparison to the many principles of Buen Vivir arising from the field or the literature, the list of challenges was relatively few, albeit significant.

The most pertinent challenge to Buen Vivir is creating a solid, coherent understanding of what it entails. In the words of local cooperative manager Luis, "First, above all else, it is having a qualified concept. When we know what Buen Vivir is, or at least being able to construct this Buen Vivir as a generalised idea, [this] is the first challenge. To know what the objective is." Now that we have built that knowledge, we can move to address the next most significant challenges.

The next most significant obstacle to achieving Buen Vivir is education – that is, both access to decent scholarly education, and the lack of education or awareness with regard to Buen Vivir. On the first aspect, Diego argues, "I believe that we need a specialised education, education of quality, an education that does not distinguish colour or nationality." In terms of education for Buen Vivir, Felipe explains, "Education [is] starting at home, with your examples of, you know, being conscious when you buy something. So, we need to change society, so people have a different vision of what they need to have this wellbeing." On that, it can also help society to distinguish between the "false" needs or desires and fundamental needs when it comes to building awareness and educating people on the principles of Buen Vivir. As Rafael explains:

> They tell you that you will be happy if you travel, if you have credit cards, if you buy this, if you have all these [material] values and [it] is not true. So, this needs to change, but it is a very complex task. You have to start with children, as Mujica says. Mujica says that the older generations, which includes us, are lost. We do not change our way of living. We have the discourse for this, but a way of living that does not agree with the discourse. Children possibly can grow to be real environmentalists.

Mateo argues that education is needed to change attitudes and behaviours, and governments play a hand in that through their development policies. "It all needs to change. In the same vein as work. Perhaps the government... can educate for cultural change, above all: our reality, education, values are based on consumerism. Everybody is trying to buy and to have and have [more]. But we do not know at what point to stop."

The next greatest challenge was precisely that of changing the culture of consumerism, prevalent in capitalist societies. Rafael explains, "The problem is that the idea of progress is to have more; the idea of development, developed countries are the most economically powerful, and wellbeing is more or less defined at the middle-class level of rich countries in the world. Not everyone can live like the middle class of the United States and Europe because the world would explode." Rafael also says that neoliberal media plays a defining role in driving consumerism, which must stop. "But the media, the internet, publicity... for me, the global cancer is called marketing. Marketing is destroying humanity. With marketing you create needs that are not needed."

According to Emanuel, "The first challenge is mental. We have to stop being slaves to [material] things." This challenge also rests on policy, changing the economic model of unbridled growth that supports and encourages consumerist behaviours. This model of development is unsustainable. Scientists state that the earth only has enough resources for each person to consume 1.8 "global hectares" of resources annually, which is the equivalent of what a person in Ghana or Guatemala consumes (Hickel 2015); yet the current model dictates that all societies should strive for Western levels of development. It is an oxymoron. Economist Peter Edwards argues, "We should look at societies where people live long and happy lives at relatively low levels of income and consumption not as basket cases that need to be developed towards western models, but as exemplars of efficient living" (Hickel 2015).

The extractivism dilemma

Our view of the role of natural resources and our perceived right to exploit them exponentially for consumerist desires is what holds up the current economic model. Implicated in this is the extractive industry. Extractivism poses a significant challenge to Buen Vivir. In the field, it was not always discussed as a direct challenge to Buen Vivir itself; rather it was often mentioned as having adverse impacts on the community, the environment, and wellbeing, which poses a significant indirect threat to Socio-Eco Wellbeing. In that sense Buen Vivir and extractivism are incompatible. Miguel argues, "never can you reach Sumak Kawsay with extractivism." Fernando further states, "It is contradictory. We exploit all the resources we have. We extract all the oil, mining and are over-indebted and -sold with these products, with these strategic sectors. We must be clear. We are a very consumerist society – that leads us to be extractivist." Development policy in Ecuador, like in much of Latin America, is underlined by extractivism. Extractivism refers to the extraction and removal of natural resources in large-scale to satisfy the market. This is not limited to mining and oil, but also includes large scale forestry, farming, and fishing (Acosta 2013).

Many scholars and economists alike argue that, in Latin America, an extractive-based model of development has failed to decrease inequality and has been at the root of many environmental and social problems. The current model of development and its derivatives, including Sustainable Development, emphasise individual wealth and wellbeing, and the use of natural resources as a commodity – the sustainability of which has often come into question by communities, organisations, and even governments and economists (Cerdán 2013; Esteva 2010; Guillen-Royo 2015; Morse 2008). However, the reality is that we are still very much in a global system that values extractivism (even neoextractivism), and the biocentrism of Buen Vivir struggles to thrive in this current context. Indeed, it challenges the delicate equilibrium of Buen Vivir which focuses on the importance of solidarity, environmental and communal wellbeing, and mutual respect between society and the environment.

The challenge exists on several levels. First, on the political level where the exploitation of natural resources on a large-scale has underlined global economic development policy for decades, but conflicts with action against climate change. Secondly, at the grassroots level, where communities are either directly suffering from the economic, environmental, and social impacts of extractivism or fighting to keep extractivism out of their communities. And lastly, at the environmental level, where impacts from large-scale activities have been attributed to causing climate change (IFRC 2010; IPCC 2015). This challenge must be at least confronted immediately and genuinely, if not resolved, if Buen Vivir is to be a viable and practical alternative.

The transition towards a post-extractive society is therefore necessary, as Buen Vivir can only be achieved in the absence of large-scale extractivism. Changes of attitudes and behaviours manifested in Vivir Bien can help achieve this transition. The extractivist challenge is thus also one of policy. As Emmanuel explains, beyond local government there is a push for extractivism, though participation supported by local governments can help communities' voices on this issue be heard. He states, "We have a political position that is putting the issue of extractivism on the table at the national level. [Through local participation] we are able at least to have a slightly higher voice heard a little better and to generate a more critical thinking on this issue."

Nonetheless, participation was also revealed as a major challenge. There are various participatory approaches used in neoliberal development by governments and development professionals. As an alternative to development, the full involvement of communities in decision-making is the most appropriate approach; and the only one suitable for Buen Vivir is "shared control." With shared control,

> Citizens become empowered by accepting increasing responsibility for developing and implementing action plans that are accountable to group members and for either creating or strengthening local institutions. The development professionals become facilitators of a locally driven process. Stakeholders

assume control and ownership of their component of the project or program and make decisions accordingly. At this level, local participation is most sustainable because the people concerned have a stake in maintaining structures or practices. Participatory monitoring – in which citizens, groups, or organizations assess their own actions using procedures and performance indicators they selected when finalizing their plans – reinforces empowerment and sustainability.

(Ondrik n.d.)

This can be a part of a pluralised democratic participatory approach, with participatory budgeting being one method for ensuring shared control. While full, grassroots-led participation has been identified as a key challenge, taking a shared control approach allows the community on the one hand to define Buen Vivir and implement Vivir Bien for themselves, and on the other hand meet local government expectations for participatory budgeting in a hybrid approach that allows the environment for Buen Vivir to flourish in a meaningful way.

Javier distinguishes between global challenges and local challenges, which further affirms the need to juxtapose local practices against policies of Buen Vivir within the broader aspirational or utopian goals for sustainability and wellbeing; because in the age of globalisation, no community lives in total isolation. He explains:

> Speaking of the global and the local. Globally, what is needed it is courage of our leaders to make decisions, for example we have the world summit COP21 in Paris on climate change.[1] Let's look at the decisions they make. Then in the local, first we need to seriously start recognising that the planet is already in danger. We need awareness. On all levels. At the governmental level, at the institutional level, at the family level, an awareness for people to say, "we need to change now!" What are we waiting for, that there's no petrol left? Or that we have exhausted all the copper and the world's resources? And then say, "now what do we do?" It will be too late.

Global action is vital to promoting change on a local level and local changes are necessary to achieving a broader, global change, and vice-versa. Only if these challenges are met both locally and globally, argues Javier, can we "have confidence in the creativity of man and civilisation, and of society, to do extraordinary things. But on the path towards Buen Vivir, not on the path of repeating the same errors that have led this planet to environmental saturation." This is precisely what the people of Cotacachi County are trying to achieve.

The Cotacachi experience

Communities in Cotacachi County highly value the natural environment in the Andes – one of the most pristine environments on earth. In the highlands of Ecuador, Intag is one of the world's most biodiverse and ecologically rich regions.

The region contains an internationally protected area, the Cotacachi-Cayapas Reserve, and is also home to two of the world's 35 internationally recognised bio-diversity hotspots:[2] The Tropical Andes and Tumbes-Choco-Magdalena. These are two of the most important ecological zones on earth, with a high degree of endemism of plant and animal species, 49 percent of all bird species in Ecuador, seven vegetation ecosystems with 13 percent of total species of Ecuador, and 28 endangered species including the mountain tapir, spectacled bear, and brown spider monkey and mantled howler monkey (Waldmüller 2015). However, many communities there fear their environment and values are threatened by the push to have their lands exploited for copper, gold, and other valuable minerals for the good of the global market and in the name of economic growth and development. Indeed, many of the region's endangered and vulnerable species are under threat from the deforestation and loss of habitat that extractivism would pose.

Not only do communities in Cotacachi have a strong affiliation with the idea of Buen Vivir, but they also have direct experience with extractivism. Furthermore, inherent in their interpretation of Buen Vivir are the principles of community, reciprocity, and the sustainable use of resources. The people of Cotacachi are highly embroiled in environmental activism and the promotion of Buen Vivir. Cotacachi County was the first declared an "Ecological County" by decree in Latin America. It has a population of approximately 40,036 habitants, 78 percent of whom live in a rural area (*Actualizacion pdyot cotacachi 2015–2035* 2016), and because of this rurality, Cotacacheños are highly susceptible to the impacts of extractivism in these areas – especially in the Intag region, which, as mentioned previously, has one of the world's highest rates of biodiversity.

Extractivism and its impacts are freely discussed in Cotacachi, from television and radio programs to everyday conversations on the street. This public sentiment at the community level is often heard in popular opinion. Riding in a taxi through the surrounding hills the Indigenous pueblo of Otavalo on a visit to the nationally protected Cotacachi-Cayapas Reserve, I noticed an abundance of graffiti. The taxi driver explains, "The issue is that there is an expansion of mining which negatively impacts communities, but fundamental needs are still going unmet. You can't have Buen Vivir if the government is exploiting petroleum. It damages the environment; that's not Buen Vivir."

The current situation in Cotacachi started in 1989 when Japanese company Bishi Metals started exploration in the area, mainly for copper. But after facing stern community opposition supported by the local government, the company left. The Environmental Impact Assessments conducted by Bishi Metals were made public to communities by research undertaken by DECOIN, who were consequently made aware of the impacts which included desertification from extensive deforestation of the area, heavy pollution of rivers including cyanide and arsenic from the dumping of waste materials, and the estimated displacement of 100 families (Stahler-Sholk, Vanden & Kuecker 2008). This increased mining resistance even further and led to locals burning down the mining camp after officials refused to meet with them. In recent times, mining opposition has been more pacific and strategic.

In 2004, the Ecuadorian government granted a mining contract to Canadian company Ascendant Copper based in the city of Junín, in the northern reach of the Intag Valley. Ascendant Copper focused years of effort on gaining a social licence from the surrounding communities, but later was severely undermined by unauthorised acts of violence committed by company employees and security forces on opposing community members (Rogge & Moreno 2008). Additionally, the county government took steps to undertake a case study of similar sorts of extractive activities in Chile to inform its communities of the impacts.

Once in office, the former Correa government then moved to expel the company from the territory in 2008. Since then mining resistance in this region has been led by local communities and supported by both local organisations and local governments in the pursuit of environment and social justice based on solidarity, community, and environment.[3] This move was welcomed in many communities. Extractive activities are seen as a threat to their ability to continue their livelihoods and meet the needs of future generations. As community president of Rio Verde Carmen Proaño stated, "We can't sell our children's future by letting a mining company come in and contaminate our beautiful river" (D'Amico 2011). This is not a minority, radical perception, but rather a sense of their reality, even reflected in local government policies, such as various ordinances for the care and protection of the environment.

Mayor of Cotacachi Auki Tituaña[4] worked with the communities to become an ecological county within which extractivism is banned (at the local government level) and local parish and county governments have worked with the communities to also establish economic alternatives to extractivism, providing support and resources. However, the past and current national governments clearly support a new policy of extractivism, resulting in a disconnect between local and national governments on the issues of extractivism and Buen Vivir ("Alcalde de cotacachi dice estar en desacuerdo con el gobierno" 2015).[5]

The social unrest and tensions that extractive exploration and concession have caused between communities and government (particularly national) have been significant. As Avci (2012) states, these types of socio-environmental conflicts are concerned with a conflict over material resources and are essentially manifestations of contested understandings of development between society and the state of a "desired society" (Bebbington & Bebbington 2009), involving greater demands for respect for culture, and a community's relation to their environment (Escobar 2006).

One of the most vocal environmental groups in the region, DECOIN, has been in direct attack from the government for its opposition to mining since 2013. In 2013, Amnesty International appealed for the safety of one of its founders, Carlos Zorrilla, after former President Correa accused Zorrilla and other individuals in Intag of defending foreign interests in a televised speech, and called on the Ecuadorians to react after several Intag community members blocked entry access of National Mining Agency employees.

In 2014, tensions in Cotacachi heightened when Javier Ramirez, a Junín community leader, was arrested in Intag for opposing the Llurimagua concession for copper mining in the region by state-run mining company ENAMI. He was held on charges of rebellion, terrorism, and sabotage. Some community members in the Intag Valley have said during conversation that, following his arrest, there were several people who went from being in opposition to extractivism to supporting it because of fear of persecution, and this has caused greater social fragmentation between communities and family members. Other community members told me of the conflict that has resulted between friends and family members between the supporters who have gone to work as fly-in-fly-out employees for the mine, and the resisters who have been working hard to keep extractivism out of the region. These factions have created fear and insecurity among communities and severely weakened social cohesion.

Starting in August 2015, Indigenous groups were in protest around the country during my time in the field. For much of his term in office, there was opposition against former President Correa for his contradictory policies. These protests were staged to start a social movement which would see the end of the Correa government.[6] One of the main driving forces behind it is the continued expansion of extractive projects in the country, especially in the Shuar and Achuar territories in the south, but with an overall concern for the granting of mining and petroleum concessions without genuine prior and informed consent from communities (Zorrilla 2015).

In the province of Imbabura, which includes Cotacachi County, the movement/protest involved most major Indigenous groups, as well as other community members and a transportation strike. On a local social media community page, the mobilisation continued in the name of "Ally Kawsay/Vivir Bien":

> The government wants to open up 50 thousand hectares of Cotacachi to mining, which will lead our land to destruction, to contamination, to pillage while displacing communities, oppressing innocent people, corrupting its public servants with crumbs and condemning us all, but above all future generations. The people of Intag have always been an example of dignity and struggle, but it affects us all, we need to defend ourselves to the death, it is time to do it from our suburbs, communities, colleges, associations, we are going to show the government that life cannot be sold and that they need to keep their criminal claws away from our land and our people and also from the rest of the communities threatened around the country.
>
> (Rubio 2016)

Despite ongoing local efforts, however, the situation in Cotacachi has not improved in recent years. By 2020, most of Intag is now under concession, with three main mining companies trying to expand into the area: Canadian Cornerstone (in association with Ecuador's state-owned ENAMI), Chile's CODELCO in association with ENAMI, and BHP Billiton's Cerro Quebrado subsidiary. With neoextractive intents evident, Chilean-run CODELCO and the Ecuadorian government's ENAMI have taken over the Llurimagua copper mine in Junín, which is now in pre-feasibility stage. The two companies are looking to extend the mining concession area another 701 hectares, extending the reach of impacts far beyond the community of Junín.

The region's biodiversity status was reaffirmed when, in 2018, researchers identified 279 endangered animal species in the region impacted by the Llurimagua project and included on the IUCN Red List – many of which are critically endangered (Zorrilla 2020a). Scientists have also recently found two endemic frog species within the mining concession that exist nowhere else in the world. An Environmental Impact Study prepared in 2018 for the expansion of the advanced exploration phase found an additional three critically endangered animal species (Zorrilla 2020a). The reports recognised the high risk of extinction of these critically endangered species if the projects were to go ahead.

There is a clear dislocation between the interest of the national government and that of the local government. The 2018 Environmental Impact Assessments found that the projects would violate the legally binding Cotacachi County Ecological Ordinance. In addition to the Ecological County Ordinance, in 2017, the Cotacachi County government approved a resolution to end metal mining within its territory. In 2018, a county-wide ordinance was then passed declaring all of Intag an Area for Conservation and Sustainable Use (Zorrilla 2019). Owing to its biological diversity status, the province of Imbabura (within which Cotacachi resides) was declared a Global Geopark by UNESCO in 2019. Global Geoparks are defined by UNESCO as a "single, unified geographical areas where sites and landscapes of international geological significance are managed with a holistic concept of protection, education and sustainable development" (*Unesco global geoparks*). UNESCO Global Geoparks do not have any legal status attached to them, but they do demand that any economic activity within their borders comply with Indigenous, local, and national laws to protect them. It is a community-led approach of combining conservation with sustainability by involving local communities, which appropriately supports a Buen Vivir approach.

The local communities are still very active in their opposition against extractivism. In between when my fieldwork was conducted, and at the time of writing, the expanding mining concessions in the area have meant that more communities will be directly impacted by these activities. In January 2020, 320 residents of 16 communities in the Intag Valley – along with elected officials from the Apuela, Cuellaje, and Plaza Gutiérrez parish governments, delegates from the Cotacachi mayor's office, and the president of Cotacachi's Assembly for County Unity – attended a community assembly to protest the impacts of the Cerro Quebrado mine on surrounding communities and their environment (Zorrilla 2020b). The assembly resulted in a number of resolutions, including:

- A request to the municipal government to apply the current environmental ordinances;
- A request to revoke all mining concessions in Intag for not carrying out constitutional rights for the Environmental Consultation of the communities (article 398);

- A request to local, sectional, and national governments to prioritise investments in agricultural and tourism activities, away from extractivism;
- A request to the municipal government to draft and approve an ordinance declaring the Cotacachi County free of metal mining;
- The creation of new tools to protect water resources, prioritising consumption for human use, and prohibiting it for the use of mining activities;
- A request for popular consultation at the county level, so that the people can decide if metal mining should be definitively prohibited, in all its phases, within the Cotacachi Canton;
- To undertake education and training programs on the impacts of mining; and
- To create an effective Intag-wide organisation to help in the search for alternatives to metallic mining (Zorrilla 2020b).

In addition, at the time of writing, the affected communities were in the middle of putting together a constitutional injunction against the Ecuadorian government for the violation of constitutional rights and the Rights of Nature.

The recent protests have been led by DECOIN, a grassroots organisation working with communities since 1995 to prevent large-scale extractivism from entering the region. DECOIN's members live and work in the region, and the organisation supports the communities' right to self-determination and to choosing their own path to wellbeing. While this movement is community-led, it still has local government support. Five of six local parish governments in the Intag region have affiliated with the political party opposed to mining. In March 2020, newly re-elected Mayor of Cotacachi Municipality Auki Tituaña sent an official letter to the national government objecting to mining activities being carried out within the county's territory.

These social movements are the expression of self-determination of the people, who are increasingly frustrated with the contradictions between Buen Vivir policy and government actions, as well as the vertical nature of the decisions that greatly affect their lives. Leandro explains: "You cannot minimise this issue because there have been things in Ecuador which come back to the needs of these people... The Indigenous movement leads us to that; they have brought us to that [matter] which I agree on, Sumak Kawsay. [They are saying], 'But look, we [just] want Sumak Kawsay.'"

The current situation especially highlights the need for political will at all levels for the achievement of Buen Vivir. Buen Vivir cannot be achieved and Socio-Eco Wellbeing realised in an extractive environment. Moncayo ("Patricio moncayo: 'Hablan de matriz productiva, pero recuerdan la devaluación'" 2015) affirms that policy for Buen Vivir cannot be conceived vertically, or from a more top-down process, simply because it involves not just government, but also society, organisations, and private enterprises. A more horizontal, democratic, and participatory process is necessary. In Cotacachi, this effort for more horizontal governance at the local level has resulted in more successful community opposition to extractivism as an economic and development policy and through these democratic participatory processes, this opposition has also gained local government support.

Laura argues that this verticality could be changed if the government acted as a facilitator:

> For example, health and education [reforms] have been a totally vertical thing… It is imposed. It is vertical in many areas [at the national level], in planning; and Buen Vivir, too, is vertical. So, what we have done in Cotacachi for a long time… is generating things from the people; that has been like that for a while.

This comes back to the role of government discussed in Chapter Five. Laura affirms: "The role of the government, I believe that it should be a facilitating role… because they say everything is done is for the benefit of the people; it is not true. But if we change the vertical role of government management, say, things could be done differently."

Neoextractivism, government, and communities: A fundamental tension

According to political and academic analyst Patricio Moncayo, the basis of the former Correa government's development model, "as with all models, is ideological. The right claims neoliberalism and the left [as with Correa] revokes the regulatory power of the State. There is a conceptual error. The debate is on the capacity of government, which permits it to successfully face problems which emerge like the current situation" ("Patricio moncayo: 'Hablan de matriz productiva, pero recuerdan la devaluación'" 2015). The situation which Moncayo speaks of is the social mobilisation in Ecuador fuelled by neoextractivism, which challenges the notion of Buen Vivir.

The Ecuadorian government's neoextractivist position in relation to Buen Vivir is contradictory to the aims of Buen Vivir; nonetheless, the former Correa government stated that the continuation of extractive activities is necessary for national fiscal revenue in the fight for poverty reduction (Guardiola & García-Quero 2014). Poverty reduction, it is argued, is a means to ensuring wellbeing, albeit with a decreased reliance on resource exports (SENPLADES, 2013). The government stresses that an endogenous model such as Buen Vivir has a higher cost structure and will first need to allow for new infrastructure and capacities to allow it (SENPLADES 2009), justifying its neoextractive approach.

The argument for the neoextractive model maintains that extractive activities can help alleviate poverty and affront the inequalities that traditional development has created. This increase of flow of revenue to the state from extractive activities is said to help the government implement the necessary social, environmental, and economic development agenda to achieve Buen Vivir (Arsel & Angel 2012). On the benefits of mining, former President Correa said, "Water is more valuable than gold, in principle… but this gold can serve us to control floods, for roads, schools, health and, in effect, we need water and copper to overcome poverty" ("Rafael correa reforzó el discurso minero en zamora" 2015). Gudynas (2013a) argues, "although extractivism veers away from social justice because of its high social and environmental impacts, the governments of the left are attempting to return to it through wealth distribution measures, especially benefit payments. But essentially this is an economic justice that is very manipulative and looks a lot like charity and benevolence." This creates a false dichotomy. As Gudynas asserts, "the myth of progress and development is maintained under a new cultural and political hybridity" (Acosta 2013).

Article 74 of the Constitution (Constitución de la república del ecuador 2008) states that "Persons, communities, peoples, and nations shall have the right to benefit from the environment and the natural wealth for Buen Vivir" and that "their production, delivery, use and development shall be regulated by the State." The contradiction is that the neoextractive policies deny any kind of management of natural resources by communities, reducing their self-determination and effectively entertaining the continuation of extractivism under a different name.

This is conflicting and, Laura states, it has helped form the tension between the government and the people, who initially believed in the good intentions behind Buen Vivir policy and the Rights of Nature:

> Then, the moment that it starts to diverge is when the question of Sumak Kawsay is maintained here [in the community] but others begin to violate it. That is, there are Rights of Nature that are violated under the pretext of achieving Buen Vivir. There are rights of the peoples and nationalities of the population in general that are violated under the pretext of attaining this other [conception of wellbeing]. So, this separation [between Buen Vivir policy and the Rights of Nature] that there is now is an explicit contradiction and it is why many people were quite critical when the constitution was approved.

If we consider Dryzek's categorisation of environmental discourses as "status quo," "reform" or "transformation," then neoextractive policies just straddle the line between status quo and reform because they seek to problem-solve through slight adjustments to the status quo (Dryzek 1997), in this case through the state and "administrative rationalism." It is taking the wealth derived from the extraction of natural resources and putting it back into the hands of the state, rather than multinationals based in another country. But it does not lead to the kind of transformation needed to fully realise Buen Vivir, which would involve greater local control and genuine political efforts towards a post-extractive economy.

In this part of Ecuador, and particularly in the Intag Valley, the opposition to extractivism runs deep, but many point to the way we use those resources which is the fundamental problem. Community activist Diego argues:

> Well, natural resources play an important role in the productive environment. There are things you need to generate, to attain Sumak or Ally Kawsay. They are important but should always be handled with extraordinary care. They must be handled prudently; we must not satiate [our own needs] with resources because we must also think about future generations.

Laura is concerned that by the time these policies allow for the complete departure from large-scale extractivism, it will be too late:

> The President [Correa] said that to achieve Buen Vivir we need housing, we need everything. Where do we get this? "From our natural resources," he said. And then there is the justification for mining and to continue to sell the oil blocks. But that does not sit well with me and it will never sit well with me as a pretext of extractivism. They have said one and a thousand times that to get out of extractivism we will continue extractivism, but only for 50 years, no more. Then they will have nothing more to extract.

In this political sentiment, Rafael justifies:

> *Nobody* likes extractivism, starting with [former] President Correa. The thing is that there are times when you have no alternative. I do not think anyone is happy that oil is being pulled out, not in Yasuní or anywhere.[7] But what happens in the world if we stop oil? The world disappears, companies disappear, products disappear... Everything is made of plastics: planes and cars, and everything. So, we have created a system in which it is not possible to live without oil.

This statement fails to acknowledge that in a plural economy where greener technologies are embraced, we are seeing more plastic alternatives being developed, moving us closer to a post-extractive society. Additionally, Emmanuel argues that the problem is the scale and capitalist nature in which we consume that dictate the need for large-scale extractivism:

> We have been cut off from the knowledge we had [before modern development]. Everything is multinational, so they need you to consume, no one but them – you do not need it. They need you to consume. Ultimately you can have food, housing, clothes without recourse to multinationals; you can. Here [in the region] there are seamstresses, there are people who produce, and there is a textile industry. People can dress, can eat, can inform themselves... you can have fun, you can build [a life] without resorting to multinationals.

A move towards post-extractivism for the objectives of Buen Vivir aligns with the need for Buen Vivir to be an endogenous-led but plural process: a conscious change at the community level and a higher political will to allow for those changes through policy and political structures. However, in the instance of Cotacachi, despite many community efforts, it is still a case of top-down policy enforcement from the national government versus local resistance. Despite the increasing social mobilisation, the national government has strengthened its neoextractive policies, evident in the expansion of mining projects such as state-run ENAMI and the Chilean-owned CODELCO's Llurimagua project. This neoextractive approach is therefore arguably even more vertically inclined than a traditional extractive approach because the impetus is coming directly from the top-down, from the state, rather than from exogenous actors such as multinationals.

For Leandro there is an inherent connection between the struggle for Buen Vivir and the inability to achieve it, and the social movements that have been driven by a policy of extractivism. And as head of a local organisation, Felipe states that, between the community and the government, the conflict ultimately rests on the fact that "there's different visions of development, of what wellbeing is. Completely different." Emmanuel argues that "what is not said is that this state of wellbeing has another face, which is the plunder and exploitation of the rest of the planet. They [the West] exploited South America, Africa had no state of wellbeing [according to them], I suppose [also] in Australia if they did not displace all the Indigenous there, there would have been no such state of wellbeing."

Besides the contradictions in policy, extractivism also severely disrupts the ability for communities to put the principles in practice through Vivir Bien. As Emmanuel states, "It is not enough to only have this utopian goal as a point of arrival 'one day in the future.' It needs to have actuality for people to be able to relate it to their daily lives." This is one shortcoming of sustainability: the reasons to act are often far removed from the majority of people's lives. Emmanuel continues, "We see that this [Buen Vivir] is not something that we are going to arrive at tomorrow, or the next day, or in five years. Rather we want to achieve something daily." The result is Socio-Eco Wellbeing.

Socio-Eco Wellbeing for the Good Life

Socio-Eco Wellbeing is not an endpoint, but rather a state of being. Many key informants, however, feel that their communities do not have an adequate level of social and environmental wellbeing because of the threats of extractivism and the environmental destruction on productive land that can come with these types of activities. In a national speech in Quito in September 2015, former President Correa argued that the petroleum boom in Ecuador led to greater social wellbeing ("Enlace ciudadano 440, desde quito" 2015), highlighting the tensions between policy and on-the-ground reality.

Local government employee Fernando states, "I could say one or two things about the central government and its policy of Buen Vivir applied to the territories. Well, there's no wellbeing, we are searching for wellbeing. My way of doing things is not only about chasing things built of cement because cement is not wellbeing."

Wellbeing is the holy grail of most conceptions of development; however, it is in the way wellbeing is defined and understood that is problematic in its own achievement. This is where Socio-Eco Wellbeing is different. First, Socio-Eco Wellbeing under Buen Vivir correlates to the wellbeing of a community, not an individual. Secondly, as opposed to the neoliberal concept of development which is anthropocentric – that is, that the needs of society come first and foremost – Buen Vivir is characteristically biocentric meaning that neither society nor the environment have dominion over one another but are interconnected and reciprocal in nature, and therefore the wellbeing of one is inherent in the other.

This biocentric focus makes ecological sustainability a core element of Buen Vivir. I call this environmental wellbeing because in Buen Vivir, both the political and cosmological conception is that nature is an actor, and thus its wellbeing is important for its survival and indeed consequently for human survival. Typically, in development the human dimension of wellbeing is considered paramount and wellbeing is thus elevated to a social concept. But this does not consider the reciprocal relationship between humans and their environment – the continuum between nature and society. When we consider environmental wellbeing, we also respect the Rights of Nature and the environmental needs that must be upheld to continue that relationship. Thus, if we have Socio-Eco Wellbeing, we have sustainability, which correlates the health of the environment to the wellbeing of society, and vice-versa.

The consequences of extractivism on wellbeing were revealed as: 1) the limits of natural resource use; 2) the impacts caused by large scale extractive activities; and 3) the need for alternatives to extractivism. This did not mean that all informants were against the act of extracting raw materials from natural resources; however, the consensus was that the activities should not be undertaken on such a large scale for commercial purposes, in areas with such high biodiversity, in protected areas,[8] and in close proximity to communities, in order to protect this fragile state of Socio-Eco Wellbeing.

There is a cultural nuance when it comes to understanding the meaning that the environment has for communities here. To better understand the ways in which key informants believed that extractivism challenges the ability to achieve Socio-Eco Wellbeing through Buen Vivir, it is necessary to delve into the meanings of environment and nature within the context of Buen Vivir – that is, the cultural and linguistic signification attached to both concepts, and how they impact the levels of wellbeing in society.

Meanings of environment and the Rights of Nature

To better understand the environmental aspect of Buen Vivir, key informants were asked to describe what the environment means to them. Depending on their responses they were also asked to signify what nature or Pachamama means, and what the differences are between the two. These responses contributed to the identification of the principles and they are an important aspect of understanding the connection of these meanings to the real or perceived impacts of extractivism on the Socio-Eco Wellbeing in these communities.

Primarily, humans and their environment cannot be separated. Fernando speaks of the totality of the environment: "The environment is everything around us – no. It is all around us from the common environment we live in, the community we live in, the water, the river that is all around us, the air and in itself, the whole biodiversity… it has to be a complete, whole environment. It has to be an environment where one coexists."

In Western society we tend to think of the environment as separate to human beings, and in English its connotations are as such. The Oxford Dictionary (Stevenson 2010) defines the term "environment" as "the surroundings or conditions in which a person, animal, or plant lives or operates," and "the natural world, as a whole or in a particular geographical area, especially as affected by human activity." These definitions imply an innate separation between living beings and their environment.

The key informants thus infer that the Spanish term, if used in its figurative meaning and not in its literal sense, includes not only all living beings and geophysical elements surrounding them, but also the relationship between them. Leandro says, "For us, in Ally Kawsay, the environmental issue is extremely important. That is, we want to live in harmony with nature… we are part of this whole ecosystem. We do not want to exclude ourselves [from it]."

Many prefer to use the terms "*naturaleza*" or "Pachamama" instead of "*medioambiente*" when talking about nature specifically, although one is often inherent in the other. Diego, for example, describes nature as being part of the environment: "It [the environment] is of extreme importance because without nature we would need to immigrate to another planet in order to survive. It is that which generates food, which generates health, which we can interact with, share. I consider it as intimately as our mother… it could be understood as the best legacy that we can leave to future generations." In Indigenous cosmovision, Pachamama has much more profound connotations that the English term "environment." Indigenous key informants speak of Pachamama as personified. Indigenous community leader David explains: "I mean that Pachamama is a person. So, a person with hair, etc." This conception is spiritually based and limited to Indigenous cosmology and cultural context and therefore cannot be readily transferred outside of that worldview, but it demonstrates the kind of respect that we must start to institute for our environment and nature.

The Kichwa term "Pachamama" can best be translated as "Mother Earth" in English, that is, "the source of all its living beings and natural features." This is closer to the understanding of "environment" by key informants as it is a holistic view of the earth as one connected whole, rather than separate hierarchically organised elements. Rodriguez explains that Mother Earth is fundamentally important to human survival and relates not only to current but also to future generations: "It means everything, everything because it is like the Mother, like the Father, we must look after it. We must always be in harmony with it. Never must we think only in terms of 50 or 80 years… because there will be generations coming after us."

Rodriguez explains the distinction between Pachamama and nature from his point of view: "The difference is that nature for me can be rebuilt if it is damaged or maintained if it is doing well or left it as it is. But Pachamama, the earth, the land for me is untouchable, it is unmovable. It is our shoes [it grounds us]." As a non-Indigenous *campesino* who works on the land, the distinction may be different or non-existent from that of an Indigenous person or a city-dweller. Nonetheless, in the context of Buen Vivir, Sumak Kawsay, or Vivir Bien, one cannot exist without the other in good health.

In that respect, nature is part of Mother Earth and therefore has a more profound connotation that the Western use of the term. It is for this reason that nature and her resources must be used sustainably with full consideration of the impacts of that use and the cyclical relationship with human beings. Driven by these meanings of "environment" and "nature," the environment becomes an actor, and thus is the holder of rights, as Luis explains: "For me it [the environment] is fundamental. The protection of the environment where we are sheltering, where we are living is our home. It's like taking care of and maintaining your home. It means starting to respect all rights, also those of nature."

These worldviews have also been reflected in policy. Ecuador's new constitution of 2008 was the first in the world to legally recognise the Rights of Nature. Chapter Seven of the constitution outlines those rights including entitlement and application, that nature has the right to restoration (art. 72), and that the state must use the precautionary principle with regards to activities that impact species, ecosystems, and natural cycles (art. 73). Article 71 states, "Nature or Pachamama, where life is reproduced and exists, has the right to exist, persist, maintain and regenerate its vital cycles, structure, functions and its processes in evolution." This article supports the unique biocentric view of nature promoted in Buen Vivir and gives agency to nature as a legal actor.

Luis says, "There is a new tendency in international law, that is precisely to promote the Rights to Nature, which for me this is fundamental. It is to achieve as a human collective the long term and to guarantee for generations [to come] a good environment. We do not need to use all the resources we have now in order to have a good quality of life."

As opposed to human rights and animal rights which prioritises the individual, the Rights of Nature take a collective approach, to ensure the wellbeing of nature, its ecosystems, and "other natural entities that are alive or sustain life" (Chapron, Epstein & López-Bao 2019). Therefore, to uphold these rights, a shift in mindset has to occur from the individual to the collective, and from perceiving nature as a commodity to acknowledging the cyclical relationship between humans and the earth. Buen Vivir and the Rights of Nature are thus complementary to one another.

While spiritual beliefs regarding Pachamama and nature espoused in Indigenous cosmology are culturally biased, the shift in thinking (both legally and morally) required to enact the Rights of Nature could lead to more ecologically sustainable outcomes than the current way of approaching Sustainable Development (Chapron, Epstein & López-Bao 2019). "As Einstein said, you can't solve a problem with the mentality that created it. The most radical shift we can envision is to consider nature as a person... and then to treat nature accordingly" (Kilvert 2019).

The sustainable use of resources

Although the Indigenous Sumak Kawsay heavily denounces the legacy that modernity has left on the state of the environment, the evolving concept of Buen Vivir seeks to embrace all epistemologies, but in a holistic way. This does not mean returning to the past (Gudynas 2011), but rather as the previous chapter suggests it requires new ways of thinking, based on fundamental needs rather than on satisfying desires for unbridled consumption and wealth creation through the exploitation and commercialisation of nature.

The Ecuadorian "Rights of Nature" do not imply a nature untouched, a "virgin nature" (Acosta 2010). Buen Vivir does not lead to an unrealistic conservation of natural resources; rather, their sustainable use allows for their regeneration for use by future generations – a key objective of sustainability. As Prada Alcoreza (2011) stresses:

> It is true that ancient societies, civilizations, world-systems have exploited also the land, domesticated plants, domesticated animals, domesticated the genomes, mined minerals, but did so to meet specific needs... [not] the satisfaction of profit.

When asked about how they think about their natural resources, key informants all spoke of them as necessary and indispensable, and part of their environment, and so respect must be shown. Diego says nature, with its resources, plays "a role of inconceivable meaning because it is linked absolutely everything that we need. It is the one that helps us to live, the one that helps us breathe. It is the role of the mother: the biological role, the role in which allows us to develop in our environment."

Likewise, Joaquín affirms that "water is critical, land is critical to survival and family development. Electric power too. Even better if it is with clean energies. Then it is a complement to life." However, many key informants discussed the fact that it is the way society uses these resources that puts a strain on the environment, and that we can meet our fundamental needs "without reducing the regeneration capacity that nature has," as Emmanuel says.

The way we conceive of our natural resources and the role of nature in modern society dictates the way we use them, which, as Laura argues, is fundamentally damaging in itself:

> [We think] a resource is something that you have and you readily take advantage of. That cannot continue like this because we are part of it [the environment]. At some point the forest is going to end, at some point the sources of water will dry up, if we continue as we are. But we have children and we are going to have grandchildren. They will no longer have what we are calling "resources."

Almost all the key informants believe that it is a question of respecting the biophysical limits of the environment, not upsetting the fragile balance which will destroy the earth's natural regeneration capacity. This balance is already being threatened by the impacts of climate change caused by human activity – both already underway and forecast to increase by climate scientists (IPCC 2015). However, key informants firmly argue that the key to overcoming these challenges is not to stop using natural resources altogether, but to use them in a more sustainable manner, to use only what is needed to meet fundamental needs, not for rampant consumerism and wealth creation and accumulation.

Indigenous leader Gabriela affirms that

> you should use what is necessary, and I believe that God or the Pachamama gives to us so that people can live but not to accumulate wealth, perhaps in a single family or a single company. I believe that everything is made for us to survive or live on this planet, but we also have to take only what is necessary.

Leandro explains the rationale behind the sustainable use of resources: "It is a direct relationship [between nature and society], it is a relationship in harmony, it is a relationship of 'you take this, and give me that.' So, it is not a relationship of 'I use you and it doesn't matter what happens to you.'" Yet the latter is precisely the approach neoliberal development has taken for decades.

There are two principal issues involving the use of natural resources: market consumerism, i.e. the consumption of products and goods; and energy production and consumption, i.e. the extraction, production, and end-use of natural resources for energy. Both rest on a lateral-scale change of behaviours and attitudes, but are sustained by the continuance of unbridled consumerism, and therefore without promising efficient energy and resource alternatives we cannot achieve positive change.

For Luis, the unsustainable use of natural resources not only involves mining and petroleum, but also extends to all extractive activities using renewable resources on a large scale, activities which have been promoted as solutions to Sustainable Development. He states:

> Natural resources provide us with everything human beings need. Unfortunately, there is a tendency to overexploit nature – extreme consumerism – [and] a transformation of natural resources into some kind of product. What happens in many places, and what I do not want to happen in my country, is that there are large plantations of sugar cane, of corn, a single monoculture, a single product to meet energy needs so that machineries can work. We are sacrificing a form of food to fuel machines. One can live a little more harmoniously with what we have. But this is what is happening and it is exploitation.

Transformation of the energy matrix in Ecuador has been supported in policy by both the Constitution and the Plan Nacional para el Buen Vivir. The Constitution (Constitución de la república del ecuador 2008) states:

> The State shall promote, in the public and private sectors, the use of environmentally clean technologies and non-polluting and low-impact alternative sources of energy. Energy sovereignty shall not be achieved to the detriment of food sovereignty, nor shall it affect the right to water.

(Article 15)

The State shall guarantee that the mechanisms for producing, consuming, and using natural resources and energy conserve and restore the cycles of nature and make it possible to have living conditions marked by dignity.

(Article 408)

Strategies such as those seek to maintain neoliberal development through the market via a "sustained economic growth" or, as the OECD describes it, "inclusive green growth" (*Inclusive green growth: For the future we want* 2012). While the extractivism of combustible renewables like those mentioned by Luis above is a much more positive step in the right direction, away from non-renewable extractivism, they still have major impacts on the environment and communities where production and extraction are present on a large scale.

In a policy paper on "Transforming the Energy Matrix," Dafermos et al. (2015) critique this model of renewable energy under a green growth strategy:

Although they are based on the use of renewable energy sources and are therefore supportive of the re-orientation of the mode of energy production in the direction of greater environmental sustainability and eco-friendliness, the logic of mass production of a commodity for a homogeneous, mass consumer market remains the organising principle of those infrastructures. As a result, they do not have the capacity to meet the increasingly more varied needs of energy users. Worse still, by keeping users in a state of passive consumerism and energy illiteracy, the underlying centralisation of the means of energy production constitutes a barrier to the emergence of a post-consumerist knowledge society.

Emmanuel also maintains that this must change: "Extractivism is an economic model which extracts natural resources to commercialise them and transform them into a product to obtain money. I think we should be able to develop an economic model which doesn't extract resources, but generates them." A viable and sustainable solution to resource use is to change behaviours and strive for the widespread reduction, reuse, and recycling of resources first and foremost, and then resort to renewable alternatives. Mindsets need to change.

Dafermos et al. (2015) suggest that "Proposing alternatives that harmonise energy needs with ecological sustainability requires a re-consideration of the concept of 'development' and a search for new evolutionary paradigms for society." In a strategy which combines "the promotion of efficient energy savings based on changing consumer habits, of new ways of exchanging goods and services, of territorial re-arrangement," the authors propose a model of energy production using "small-scale generation, consumer accessibility and end-user participation" – effectively organising natural resource use around the idea of "commons" rather than as a "commodity." The small-scale hydroelectric infrastructure being developed in Cotacachi County, discussed in the previous chapter, is one example of this approach.

Perceptions and impacts of extractivism:
The Buen Vivir–extractivism discord

In full consideration of local understandings of nature, the environment, and how communities believe resources should be used, we can better understand the concern for the impacts that extractivism brings and the perception of those impacts based on the above-mentioned experiences of conflict in Cotacachi. Key informants were asked the open-ended question: "What about mining, forestation, and other extraction – what do you think about what they are doing and why?" The overwhelming concern was on the impacts of extractive activities, particularly the social and environmental impacts that extractive activities have and could have on communities in the county. The most significant concerns in the findings were those adverse impacts on water, social repercussions, the wider environment, and human health. Interestingly, key informants did not mention any positive benefits. It is important to note that all the issues are all interlinked in some way, especially water quality, environmental contamination, and health issues. It must also be noted in contextually that the most problematic large-scale extractivism project in the Cotacachi County – Llurimagua – is situated in the city of Junín, approximately 2.5 hours north of the furthest community I visited within the county area. There are many temporary workers from within the county who travel in and out of Junín to work in the mines, which has caused a strain on the social fabric of communities. Some workers support the mining activity, and others less so but do it to earn more income for their families. The resultant impacts within Junín are well known to the surrounding communities due to lived experience, as well as environmental activism and advocacy.

Felipe, who has considerable lived experience with extractivism, particularly open-pit mining, says, "It's the most environmentally destructive economic activity besides war, which I consider an economic activity. It destroys not only the rivers and the forest and the topsoils and so forth, but it also destroys community." On the environmental impacts, Luis states, "the mining consequences there are in the places they are present are terrible. From contamination and water, a large mining company needs industrial quantities of water to obtain the metals they are after. What's more, the chemicals they have to use…" Mateo argues, "A mine, extractivism, will always have an environmental impact. It is something we cannot stop…" Speaking of the activities in Junín, he continues, "The impact is the strongest first of all in the surrounding territories and communities, because it is a change of life in its totality, from being in harmony with one's environment, with one's nature. [But] the impact to the landscape and the contamination of water sources are what is most affected."

Although there exist other forms of extractivism within the county, none evokes as much opposition as mineral mining. Therefore, the majority of opinions of key informants regarding the environmental impacts of extractivism[9] in this study are formed by perceptions of the impacts of mining, rather than the direct lived impacts of mining and other types of extractive activities.[10] This in no way seeks to undermine those opinions, but rather sheds light on the extent of the indirect damage of large-scale extractivism on the Socio-Eco Wellbeing of a community. It also creates a solid argument for why alternatives should be sought.

Perceptions and concerns in the community of Seís de Julio de Cuellaje, and other like communities, are founded on a looming reality because of its location downstream from Junín. Rodriguez states, "the mountain ranges of Junín are super close; we are adjoining neighbours. We are only two rivers away. We would be the first to be contaminated."

Often extractive activities cover various terrains, taking the resources from one place and transporting them to another, and if they are not exported as raw materials then they may also be treated in a separate location. This extends the impacts not only from the place of extraction, but in various locations. In one Indigenous community outside of Cotacachi city, limestone mining for cement production has had several social-, environmental-, and health-related impacts within the community. Maria explains, "These [impacts] from mining have affected us quite a lot because, for one thing, when the plant recently extended it was capped with dust and yellow. And this is what is happening: Last year I harvested seven to eight quintals of corn, and the following year production was already reduced." These impacts Maria tells, have disrupted fragile ecosystems: "All of this has changed our climate. Faced with all of this we have lost our agricultural production." Diego speaks of the destruction caused by another mine in the Parish of Selva Alegre: "It is an open-pit mine that is practically depredated; there is no responsible management of remediation. They say that we oppose everything. However, we want Ecuador to live a productivity that is not linked to damaging nature."

Limestone is often mined at the surface in large quarries, which leaves contaminants exposed to open air with the potential to contaminate the local environment. Additionally, vibrations and noise pollution from the activities are known to have adverse consequences on human health in surrounding communities (Tripathy & Patnaik 1994; Yeboah 2008). In 2010, several community members blockaded access to the mine, calling for it to be closed due to its environmental and social impacts. This protest was supported by local organisations and a member of the provincial government, but the national government moved to stop the protests and reopen the mine.

While extractivists will argue for the positive benefits of extractive activities like economic development, job creation, and overall wealth creation, the reality on the ground it seems, is not as black and white. Many scholars contend that the capacity to generate local employment opportunities through extractivism, which truly benefits local communities, is quite weak (Acosta 2013; Granoff et al. 2016), and the wealth distribution, even under a neoextractive model, is too uneven to bring wide-scale benefit.

In addition, the economic benefits of extractivism are obsolete once the activities cease in the small towns that have been built on the back of those activities. Even though companies are obliged to have closure plans which include the economic impacts of closure among the environmental remediation plans, many communities can never fully recover, losing their ability to diversify their production economies, and some even end up as "ghost towns." Indeed, the true "economic costs of the social, environmental and production-related impacts" are often not calculated but if they were taken into account, any economic benefits to the local economy and the state would be disregarded (Acosta 2013).

There is a suspicion among key informants that the positive benefits are often exaggerated on the part of the government or the companies seeking social licence. Diego states:

> [They] should have transparent accounts and tell the population with an abso-lute reality what it is exposed to. When social impacts of extractive projects are carried out, there is usually a lie. There will be no pollution, there will be no depredation of nature, there will be no socioeconomic and socio-cultural problems, and there will be work for most people.

Many point to the impacts that extractivism has on traditional or alternative liveli-hoods. One case in point is the Pacto Parish, whose main livelihood depends on the sustainable production, sale, and export of organic panela, but where mining activities were also present (Játiva 2004). Italy is one of its principal importers and in 2002 announced that unless mining stopped in the area, they would halt the importation of panela because it could not guarantee organic certification of the product. This would have been the end of Italian cooperation for the parish, which benefits 4,000 people in Pacto, directly employing 2,000 of them with an annual total of USD $50,000 (in 2004). Meanwhile, the mine only employed 20 locals on a monthly wage of USD $200.

Despite the majority opposition to extractivism, there were also a few key informants who believed that extractivism should be permitted, but conducted responsibly to limit the impacts. Similarly, I was told by both key informants and in informal discussions that there is some (limited) community support for extrac-tivism. The consequences of these "pro-mining"–"anti-mining" factions have been studied independently and included by the county government in the update of the Development Plan and Territorial Ordering of the Santa Ana de Cotacachi County 2015–2035 in its diagnostic for social cohesion in the county. In a report (*Íntag: Una sociedad que la violencia no puede minar. Informe psicosocial de las afectaciones en íntag provocadas por las empresas mineras y el estado en el proyecto llurimagua* 2015)[11] on the psychological damages caused by mining companies and the state in the Llurimagua project in Intag, it was stated:

> Although the resistance to the mining extraction process has strengthened certain sectors, has consolidated alternative sources of economic sustenance and has provided greater communal organization, the community division has created rupture among the members of the community itself, which has generated labelling and power relations: people who are in favour of the extractive process are labelled as "pro-mining" and people who are against the extractive process as "anti-mining." This labelling dynamic divides the community and creates a break in ties between friends and family.

It is evident that at times of the conflict there has been psychological damage, understood as "the damage suffered by a subject as a result of an injury to his / her psychophysical integrity or health, consisting in the reduction of the possibilities of developing his personality normally in the social environment (Massimo, 1994)". It is the consequence of a negative event that goes beyond the ability to cope and adapt to the new situation (Echeburúa, Corral y Amor, 2004).There is a situation of widespread insecurity that expresses feelings of fear, suffering and fear that mining companies continue with their activities and are rooted in the area so that the population must leave their territories and their homes. The Community of Junín is in a situation of police occupation and a "de facto state of emergency." In Intag, the national police restrict human rights such as freedom of movement, rights of participation, right to work, freedom of expression, freedom of thought and opinion, and freedom of association.

The police invasion as a control measure to the community has altered diverse dynamics... a logic of fear has been established: to leave their homes, their children and to be imprisoned. The intimidation and political violence exercised by public officials who should be in charge of providing protection is so intense that the population is in a situation of uncertainty about the sense of community, solidarity, social organization and justice, and has been violated. The strength and the trust that existed between the neighbours and families [is] generating serious psychosocial affectations.

The social impacts of extractivism can be severely detrimental to a community, its social cohesion, and solidarity, as demonstrated by the psychological report. While the social programs for wealth redistribution promoted under a neoextractive approach seek to "compensate some of the negative impacts... cushion social demands and pacify social protests" (Gudynas 2009) they can only go so far to mitigate social damage. Moreover, social conflicts such as those discussed in the context of Cotacachi aggravate the situation in light of extractivism and gravely undermine any positive impacts of neoextractive policies because the blows are felt on a deeper socio-physiological level among community members, and rather seek to act as an economic band-aid. This refers not just to enhancing quality of life economically, but also to the non-materialistic sense of community, family, cohesion, peace, and wellbeing, the "other" types of wealth pointed out by Felipe in Chapter Four.

Felipe argues that large-scale extractivism disturbs the social fabric of a community, which, he says, is harmful to Buen Vivir:

> Mining disrupts that. It contaminates people, people's idea of what happiness is, by introducing materialism, consumerism and – and strengthening the monetary economy, while harming the other types of wealth a community has: environmental wealth, cultural wealth, social wealth. That if it's not devastated, it's severely harmed. So that disrupts the whole idea of Sumak Kawsay. People may not say "mining will destroy our Sumak Kawsay,"

but when they fight, it's really what they're fighting for, so they can live in harmony.

Not only does it destroy social cohesion, but it also reduces quality of life for those who work in these activities. Luis says, "For example, the miner spends seven, eight hours *inside* the mine [per day]. They have illnesses. They are people who have a fairly low quality of life. Then, the social repercussion also extends to small cities around the mine, which mainly market alcohol and sex."

Then there is a fear of what legacy these impacts may leave for future generations. Gabriela tells that communities fear "all of the contamination and illness that comes with it." She explains, "In Intag there is a [protected] water reserve. We are conserving it for our grandchildren's grandchildren. But if we exploit all of this, according to what I have seen, it will become a desert. There will be no produce, no animals, no water, everything will be contaminated. There will be no life." There was a strong link between contamination, water, and human health in the key informants' responses. Valentina states, "If the environment is contaminated, we get sick. More than anything else [the most concerning impact] is the contamination of the environment [because] we can get ill. Catastrophic illnesses."

There was concern that the magnitude of the impacts of extractive activities are so strong that they risk changing the way of life completely. All the impacts combined risk a strong decline in quality of life, not only for communities affected, but also for surrounding communities. Between the impacts of extractive activities and the social fractures caused by different approaches to extractivism, and variances in opinion on the necessity for extractivism to satisfy needs, it is clear that the "extractivist logic" of the current development model is inherently detrimental to the attainment of Buen Vivir. Rafael affirms, "We talk about a healthy and balanced environment, that we should act so that contamination is not so devastating, that it doesn't destroy... I believe these types of activities can put the brakes on the processes of Buen Vivir." Buen Vivir and extractivism are simply incompatible.

Many of the participants cited how these impacts also subsequently hamper a community's Vivir Bien, the day-to-day Socio-Eco Wellbeing. "Social wellbeing, environmental wellbeing, no [we don't have it] because... our Pachamama, as we say Mother Earth, is sick because of the contamination from mining, the contamination of our water, and the cutting down of forests, of trees," affirms Maria. "For us, Indigenous people, to have Buen Vivir, our earth has to be in good health," argues David. Luis says that extractivism and Buen Vivir are incompatible: "It's a contradiction of the idea, which doesn't work." Even Rafael tells me "these types of things are impossible to be 100 percent compatible. We can talk about remediation [of the environment], but we can never recover the environment in its totality."

The greatest tension is between Vivir Bien and extractivism, since Vivir Bien is the daily practice of the principles of Buen Vivir that provides the conditions necessary to eventually achieve the utopian goal of Buen Vivir. Any activity, policy, or situation which has tangible negative impacts on a community will prevent said community from putting the principles of Buen Vivir into daily practice and hence behavioural change, which will ultimately hinder the Socio-Eco Wellbeing of that community, and therefore obstruct the long-term goal of Buen Vivir. Even if the impacts of extractivism cannot be resolved in the immediate, it is imperative to immediately start transitioning from mere reform to the total transformation of society and politics. Community attitudes, beliefs, practices, and behaviours manifested under a philosophy and practice of Vivir Bien will help to lead to the market and policy changes which will ultimately influence a post-extractive society. It is a virtuous cycle.

On that note, the search for alternatives to extractivism is a preoccupation in Cotacachi. Tourism[12] and small-scale or community-scale agriculture are the most popular locally practiced economic activities. These alternatives support the national government's political promotion of an SSE, but the support and structure at that level is lacking in practice.

Towards transformation: Post-extractivism and Buen Vivir

Keeping in mind the perceived impacts of extractivism and the resultant impacts on Socio-Eco Wellbeing, it is logical that Buen Vivir cannot be fully realised in an extractive (or neoextractive) economy. Many in Cotacachi were optimistic that society can find alternative solutions in time to prevent further catastrophic effects of climate change. Speaking on transforming to a post-extractive society, Javier uses the example of copper being extracted in Junín and asks,

> Why still come to extract copper? It may be one of the last deposits in the world, so what do we want? Extract the last bit. And then what? We must ask the question now, now when we still have time. If we ask that question, that would be the first thing we could do for Buen Vivir or Vivir Bien. And then, we can have confidence in the creativity of man and civilization and society to do *extraordinary* things, but on the way to Buen Vivir, not on the path of repeating the same mistakes and bringing the planet to [its] environmental saturation [point].

The community vision for Buen Vivir is really only achievable in a post-extractive economy that prioritises alternatives and seeks to reduce both citizens' and the state's dependency on extractive sectors. It is important to reiterate that post-extractivism emphasises being mindful of the earth's physical limits and reducing extractivism to using only what is needed. This means resizing some industries to reduce the economic dependence on extractive activities and abolishing the large-scale extractivism of non-renewable resources. This is compatible with Latouche's argument for degrowth in certain sectors, as discussed in Chapter Two. This will not happen overnight, but society must revaluate the resources that it uses and immediately start the transitions needed, supported by effective policy.

Gudynas (2013b) argues that this transition period is necessary and includes changes on various scales, from local, to national, to global. Because of the nature of extractivism as an economic activity, post-extractive proposals cannot be implemented purely at the community level, nor can it be implemented by one country alone; cooperation at all levels is required. That said, to be fully sustainable, proposals must emanate from the bottom-up, from the context within which change is to have the most impact.

In this aim, Gudynas (2013) identifies several phases in this transition at the policy level. The first is to move away from what he calls "predatory extractivism" to "sensible extractivism" defined by government policy and regulations to mitigate the social and environmental impacts of extractivism and allow governments to move away from a dependency on exports. Then the focus moves to "indispensable extractivism" whereby extractive activities operate only to satisfy fundamental needs in a sort of "dematerialism" of the economy. Although, as Gudynas (2013b) states, the persistence of "business-as-usual" development will prove a challenge to transitioning away from "predatory extractivism," alternatives must be pursued immediately, starting at the grassroots level.

Alternatives to extractivism

Despite a policy of neoextractivism, the former Correa government recognised the need to diversify the economy, in order to eventually find alternatives to extractivism and the export of primary resources. The Plan Nacional para el Buen Vivir (2009) identified these at the national level as "petrochemical, bioenergy and biofuel; metal-mechanic industry; biomedicine, pharmaceuticals and generics; biochemistry; hardware and software; and environmental services." With greater focus on the SSE, the government stated, "in addition, priority is placed on value-added generating activities with important effects on employment generation and the satisfaction of basic needs (with emphasis in social housing), food, small-scale fishing, crafts, community tourism, textiles, and shoe confection." Much of the latter is already being well developed at the local level in Cotacachi, manifested in practice, or Vivir Bien. This "sensible extractivism" is part of its strategy to "exit" from extractivism, as Laura mentioned earlier. Though in practice the Ecuadorian government has continually pursued a business-as-usual approach of large-scale "predatory extractivism" irrespective of the social and environmental impacts and community sentiment, albeit under the new name of "neoextractivism."

As outlined earlier in the chapter, through the will of the people the local government has enacted a range of policies with the aim of preventing mining from entering the communities in Cotacachi. This includes civil society-led "development" initiatives, supported by local governments, such as tourism as an "alternative to development"; activities for the protection of various assets as part of the Cotacachi-Cayapas Reserve; various ordinances for the care and protection of the environment; and the ordinance of the county as the first Ecological County in South America.

Many community members say these economic initiatives will empower them to be able to demonstrate that they do not need extractivism to meet their fundamental needs. It also helps families and communities become self-sufficient through SSE activities, providing economic return within communities. The communities feel like there are alternatives to extractivism, but there are three key challenges preventing these alternatives from being viable on a wider scale: 1) full governmental support at the national level; 2) financial resources; and 3) global consumerism that drives the need for extractivism.

The local government here has been promoting alternative economies to extractivism since late 1990s. In 2001 the Pachakutik Movement started to take hold in Ecuador, and in the Cotacachi county it was supported and promoted by Indigenous Mayor Auki Tituaña. The national newspaper "El Comercio" applauded the proposal for "an alternative and more profitable economic model" that is "not based on petroleum and the extraction of our non-renewable resources, but on agriculture, tourism and the protection of the environment" ("Entre el orgullo y el olvido" 2001).

Much of this is demonstrated in the turning of the backs of local communities on a globalised market economy and a strengthening of the SSE, and a determination to nurture traditional and local ways of doing things. Auki Tituaña, who is a trained economist, reinforced this commitment to "restoring and preserving the cultural traditions and ecological integrity of the area" (*Working with local people and governments to create "eco-cities"*) as a reaction to the threat of large-scale extractivism in the region. This renewal of local custom is part of the quest for Buen Vivir according to local Indigenous leader David. "One needs to value our production, our customs, our traditions to live Sumak Kawsay," he says.

There is evidence of this in both rural and urban societies. For example, on one Sunday morning in the community of Pucará on the edge of the Intag Valley a group of people gathered on the local volleyball court surrounded by their harvest of beans. After a small truck began running over the beans, back and forth, they began collecting them in large hessian bags. "*Buena Cosecha*?" ("good harvest?") my research assistant asked and was responded to with a resounding "yes." Further down the road was a panela producer, a local farmer. Many of the neighbours pass by to buy panela from him rather than the supermarket in town. Trade is often within the community, though in some communities where produce is more abundant, it is sometimes taken to Quito for trade. Yet it remains small-scale and thus more sustainable than large-scale extractive activities. Joaquín affirms, "the community are making efforts to develop agricultural practices, education, and culture for the benefit of all. In this regard the survival of communities is very relevant for us, owing to this communitarian system."

In the same light, "Buen Vivir" markets are often held around Cotacachi County in the ethos of the SSE, bringing together local artisan producers with the idea of promoting sovereignty and food security. There has been a push to maintain and strengthen the Indigenous custom of *el Truque*, which is a type of community barter market system.

Nowhere is this resistance against extractive activities more evident than in the development of the community and eco-tourism sectors within Cotacachi. Associations like AACRI (Artisans Association of Coffee Farmers of Rio Intag) also work cooperatively with other organisations for small-scale sustainable tourism (Chassagne & Everingham 2019). The aim is for a "different kind of tourism" that is an agricultural exchange (Bold 2007). Many key informants also believe that this kind of tourism helps sustain the environment and their culture. Youth leader Sofia says that communities have much to exchange with tourists: "We teach them how we work with the environment, how we sow plantations, how we recycle etc."

The municipal government has identified tourism as a "management instrument which contributes to the conservation of the National System of Natural Protected Areas, in the framework of impact assessments and with the participation of local populations in the operation of their activities and in the distribution of their benefits" (Block 2007). Eco-tourism is already well developed in Cotacachi County, with community-based tourism projects the next approach for the sustainable development of tourism activities. One of the most renowned eco-tourism sites is the Laguna Cuicocha. At just over 3,000 metres above sea level, Laguna Cuicocha is a 3.2 km wide natural high-altitude lake situated in the crater of the still-active Cuicocha volcano. The lake is the start of the nationally protected Cotacachi-Cayapas Ecological Reserve, one of Ecuador's 46 protected areas. The 243,638-hectare reserve encompasses many natural riches over three provinces, including the Cotacachi Volcano, Laguna de Piña, and an abundance of wildlife and plant species. Next to the Galapagos Islands and the Amazon, it is one of Ecuador's most visited eco-tourism attractions. The Cotacachi-Cayapas Reserve also borders much of the county, adding to the dilemma large-scale resource extraction brings to this territory.

At the cultural and natural heritage site of Nangulvi in Intag, a tourist centre has been set up by the Ecotourism Network of Intag, in cooperation with several local organisations for "Sustainable tourism as a development alternative" to bring together local tourism operators to strengthen the capacity as an alternative to extractivism in the region. Locals believe that tourism is one of the most viable economic activities that can help the country and the region move away from extractivism. At the entrance of the community of Pucará, like many others in the region, is a large sign that says, "Welcome to Pucará, a productive, ecological, touristic and solidarity community free from mining." Similarly, a sign that welcomes visitors to the region states, "Youth, work and development for an Intag free of contamination. No to Mining!" Diego argues, "we should be looking for alternatives, which work in conjunction with what [natural and cultural riches] we have."

Artisan production is also a way that many communities, especially Indigenous ones, are finding alternatives to extractivism. Although these types of handicrafts are unique to each community, there is evidence of the resurgence of "slow living" and crafts as ways to make a living, which include small-batch handicrafts, artisanal clothing production, gourmet foods such as traditional methods of cheese production, wines, distillery, and condiments. The Indigenous markets in Otavalo, one of the largest and most famous in South America, is a testimony to the opportunity to trade these products not only at the local level, but also with some exporting internationally. The turn towards these types of economic alternatives is gaining momentum globally.

In some communities, extractive activities such as petroleum production have threatened traditional artisan livelihoods with impacts on the land and the means of production for resources such as plants and wool. Consequently, producers who were unable to make ends meet were sold petroleum by-products which were substantially cheaper than traditional resources and allowed them to cater *en masse* to an international market such as for commercial tourists. Nowadays, there are many cooperatives and associations which represent producers who use traditional methods and means of production, but by consequence of representation, producers are able to sell their products to a global market, albeit still using small-scale production methods.

Currently, there are 34 groups, associations and organisations who support the sustainable development of the watershed of Rio Intag, creating a communal value around local agri and tourism resources with the principles of environmental conservation, equality, and encouraging local talent, participation, and social justice (*Hidronangulvi* 2016). They employ approximately 1,200 families across the seven Parishes of Intag. Products are exported in the fair trade markets in Europe and Japan, as well as locally and nationally (*Hidronangulvi* 2016).

AACRI is an example of such an association. Started in 1998 with the aid of local environmental organisation DECOIN in response to the social and environmental problems caused by mining in the region and to provide communities with the opportunity to create alternative livelihoods (Chassagne & Everingham 2019), AACRI aims to provide local coffee producers with a way to access the global market, while continuing small-batch, sustainable, and organic production. AACRI currently supplies coffee to several countries worldwide, but much of their coffee is produced on small-scale family farms in the Intag Valley. Luis, who works for AACRI, says, "The coffee that we cultivate is not monoculture, it's not large-scale coffee production that belongs to one person or group of people; rather it is small lots of production, or terrain where producers can have coffee along with traditionally cultivated crops such as frit, corn, beans, or flowers, for example." This alternative activity also provides producers with an advantage in a competitive neoliberal environment, Luis explains: "They realise that it is easier to work cooperatively for quality produce to later have produce that can compete and can be sold in a better way and can also represent where they come from."

These are but a few examples of how alternatives to extractivism are being sought in Cotacachi. As Gudynas asserts, in the transition to post-extractivism, it is necessary to offer direction and ideas for actual changes (Gudynas 2013b). In the pursuit of Buen Vivir, such alternatives are thus necessary for change towards a post-extractive society, and representative of the types of economic activities which can be replicated in other communities in a culturally and contextually appropriate manner. A transition to a post-extractive economy is necessary to fully realise the utopia of Buen Vivir, towards transformation. Practices of Vivir Bien, including implementing alternatives at the community level, can help achieve that by reinforcing behaviours and changing attitudes and practices that will positively shift both the market and policy in a positive direction. It is a virtuous cycle.

Mutual respect for a healthy environment and strong communities are the basis of Buen Vivir. The impacts that large-scale extractivism have on communities challenge their social and environmental wellbeing and any ability to achieve Buen Vivir in the future, especially in Indigenous communities where there is a strong attachment to the land and its resources and a great reciprocal respect for it.

It is clear by the local discourses that each sector of society has a role to play. Particularly important is the role of community in changing attitudes, behaviours, values, and beliefs in consumerism and environmental practices, but also of governments in managing a transition towards post-extractivism through policy, regulations, and offering the spaces and structures for communities to drive change, such as though an SSE. After all, as reiterated by Delgado et al. (2010), "if communities could create Buen Vivir for themselves entirely, it would have already been done." The first challenge is a conceptual and psychological one.

With regards to Buen Vivir within the current context of (neo)extractivism there are two key factors. Firstly, a change at the community level leading to less consumerism will necessitate less extractivism. This is not limited to communities at the field site, but (arguably) even more so in countries in the core, whose consumer habits drive the necessity for natural resource consumption and in turn influence policies of extractivism for development in countries in the periphery. Extractivism is market-driven so a Vivir Bien approach will influence the future of natural resource use. Secondly, we may not be able to change the global economic system overnight, nor should we attempt to because radical opposition does not lead to long-term change. But governments in a democratic society are forced to be responsive to their citizens. If global consumer habits influence changes in the international market then governments will be forced to find and embrace alternatives to large-scale extractivism, for example social economies, alternative economies, and so forth.

Extraction and use of natural resources should be limited to meeting fundamental needs, not growth, and the diversification of alternatives should be promoted to achieve Socio-Eco Wellbeing through economic sufficiency (not growth) and construct the path towards post-extractivism.

Politically, transition should start in the immediate, with clear commitments. This involves governments of all levels taking solid steps towards alternate routes, rather than a simple "reformist departure" of the status quo. The Cotacachi government has made good headway but requires the support of the national government also, and the gap between policy and practice is still very wide.

As Acosta (2013) argues, "This double curse of natural resources and ideology is not inevitable and can be overcome." In terms of energy use, the type of strategy discussed by Dafermos et al. (2015) and supported by the views of the key informants is more consistent with the principles of Buen Vivir. At the same time, while it challenges the status quo beyond the dominant development model, it does not radically oppose it in rhetorical discourse, but rather suggests alternative solutions that can lead to transformation. The need to turn towards community-led alternative solutions is necessary if society is to take the direction outlined in the SDGs for a more "people-centred" approach (UNGA 2015). It suggests that a plural cooperation to transformation is required for the achievement of Buen Vivir. It would therefore require embracing local priorities over global markets and transitioning to transformation through the scaling-up of community-led change. Therefore, the role of communities is to monitor and/or change their own individual and community practices around natural resource use as well as the global consumption of products. Natural resources should be used in a sustainable manner, using only what is needed, not for economic growth and wealth creation under the guise of "development." Extractivism and consumption are a vicious cycle, as one encourages the other in a global market. As voiced to me, extractivism and its drivers have not created the freedoms we think we have. "We are slaves. Slaves to this concept of growth and development." The less focus there is on individual consumption and wealth, the greater emphasis is put on community values, encouraging solidarity and social cohesion, and true liberty.

Although the case focuses on Cotacachi County, the dilemma not only affects the reality of those communities touched by extractivism in those communities, but as we see with climate change and social justice issues, it has global repercussions. However, where once capitalism was king on a global scale, small pockets of alternative ways of doing things are popping up everywhere. These are not just in the Ecuadorian highlands, but this chapter has sought to provide examples of this type of determination. It is now not such a radical idea to think and strive for a post-extractive world. As Emmanuel told me, "The first challenge is mental. Of course, there will always be [some sort of] mining, but we have to stop being slaves and construct another society." And if we can achieve this transformation, Buen Vivir will be a viable alternative to Sustainable Development in the pursuit of Socio-Eco Wellbeing.

Notes

1 COP21 took place on in Paris in December 2015. The outcome of which was the Paris Agreement, opened for signature on 22 April 2016, whereby the 196 nations in attendance agreed to limit the global temperature increase to 1.5 degrees Celsius above pre-industrial levels; requiring governments to report on their progress. As of 7 September 2016, there were 180 signatories to the Paris Agreement, with 27 of those having deposited their instruments of ratification, acceptance, or approval accounting in total for 39.08% of the total global greenhouse gas emissions. In accordance with article 21, the agreement enters into force "on the thirtieth day after the date on which at least 55 Parties to the Convention accounting in total for at least an estimated 55% of the total global greenhouse gas emissions have deposited their instruments of ratification, acceptance, approval or accession with the Depositary"(*The paris agreement – status of ratification* 2016). It nonetheless remains unbinding.
2 To qualify as a hotspot, a region must contain at least 1,500 native species of vascular plants (> 0.5 percent of the world's total), and it has to have lost at least 70 percent of its original habitat. Collectively, hotspot areas support 44 percent of the world's plants and 35 percent of terrestrial vertebrates in an area that formerly

covered only 11.8 percent of the planet's land surface. The habitat extent of this land area had been reduced by 87.8 percent of its original extent, such that this wealth of biodiversity was restricted to only 1.4 percent of Earth's land surface: www.biodive rsityhotspots.org.

3 While most local governments support a resistance to developing extractivism within their territories, it must be noted that there also exists an internal conflict between local parish governments. While the municipal government openly supports the resistance to mining, there are a few parish governments who do not support the resistance, and according to some community members there have been public officials who have in fact supported mining, which has added to the factions between community members.

4 At the time of research, Auki Tituaña was no longer Mayor of Cotacachi County. Having served three previous terms between 1996 and 2009, he was re-elected in 2019. During his previous terms, Mayor Tituaña was one of the country's first Indigenous Mayor's and the recipient of several international prizes, including the UNESCO Cities of Peace Prize.

5 More information on the points of conflict between Cotacachi and National Governments can be found in "Alcalde de cotacachi dice estar en desacuerdo con el gobierno" (2015) and Tituaña (2004).

6 Former President Correa did not stand for re-election in 2017, though his political party attempted to push for constitutional changes to allow for indefinite re-election of former presidents (meaning he could stand again in 2021), these changes were quashed by 64.2 per cent in the public referendum and public consult of 4 February 2018 held by President Moreno (*Consulta 2018: Resultados a nivel nacional* 2018).

7 Former President Correa had contentiously allowed the drilling of Yasuni. The referendum and public consult of 4 February 2018 held under the Moreno government asked the question: Do you agree to increase the intangible zone by at least 50,000 hectares and reduce the area of oil exploitation authorized by the National Assembly in the Yasuni National Park from 1,030 hectares to 300? (*Consulta 2018: Resultados a nivel nacional* 2018) It resulted in a 67.31 percent "yes" vote; however, the question was part of the public consult, not the referendum, meaning that it does not result in changes to the constitution as an effect.

8 The referendum and public consult of 4 February 2018 asked citizens: Do you agree to amend the Constitution of the Republic of Ecuador to prohibit metallic mining in all its stages, in protected areas, in intangible zones, and urban centres, according to Annex 5? Annex 5: Add a second paragraph to article 407 of the Constitution of the Republic of Ecuador with the following text:
"All types of metallic mining are prohibited in any of its phases in protected areas, urban centers, intangible zones."
Replace Article 54 of the Organic Environmental Code with the following text:
"From the prohibition of extractive activities in protected areas intangible zones. The extractive activities of non-metallic mining hydrocarbons are prohibited within the National System of Protected Areas and in areas declared as intangible, including forestry exploitation, except for the exception provided in the Constitution, in which case the relevant provisions of this Code will apply. All types of metallic mining are prohibited in any of its phases in protected areas, urban centers, intangible zones" ("Cuáles son las siete preguntas de la consulta popular y el referéndum en ecuador?" 2017).
The people voted "yes" by 68.2 percent. It is unclear yet how this will play out in reality for Cotacachi with areas of high biodiversity value and protected areas such as the Cotacachi-Cayapas Reserve, although in the current situation, it is clear that the will of the people is not being upheld.

9 There are several key informants who, by their association, have experienced the environmental impacts of mining firsthand, but no details as to their association and experience can be divulged in order to protect their identities.

10 For more on the community views of the Environmental Impacts Studies carried out, see Zorrilla, C (2011) Mining Paradise: The new mining threat in Intag, 28 March, available at http://www.decoin.org/2011/03/mining-paradise-the-new-mining-threat-in -intag/.
11 See "Alcalde de cotacachi dice estar en desacuerdo con el gobierno" (2015).
12 See Chassagne & Everingham (2019).

References

Acosta, A 2010, 'Toward the universal declaration of rights of nature. Thoughts for action', *AFESE Journal*, vol. 24, pp. 1–17.
Acosta, A 2013, 'Extractivism and neoextractivism: Two sides of the same coin', in M. Lang & D. Mokrani (eds.), *Beyond development: Alternative visions from latin America*, Fundacion Rosa Lumxemburg, Quito, Ecuador.
Actualizacion pdyot cotacachi 2015–2035, 2016, Municipio deCotacachi, Cotacachi, Ecuador.
'Alcalde de cotacachi dice estar en desacuerdo con el gobierno', 2015, *La Hora Nacional*, 21 August 2015.
Arsel, M & Angel, NA 2012, '"Stating" nature's role in ecuadorian development: Civil society and the yasuni-itt initiative', *Journal of Developing Societies*, vol. 28, no. 2, pp. 203–27. doi: 10.1177/0169796x12448758.
Avci, D 2012, 'Politics of resistence against mining: A comparative study of conflicts in Intag, Ecuador and Ida, Turkey', International Institute of Social Sciences, ISS PhD Theses. Erasmus University Rotterdam.
Bebbington, A & Bebbington, DH 2009, 'Actores y ambientalismos: Conflictos socio-ambientales en perú1', *ÍCONOS*, vol. 35, pp. 117–28.
Block, P 2007, *Civic engagement and the restoration of community: Changing the nature of the conversation*, A Small Group, <http://www.asmallgroup.net/pages/images/pages /CES_jan2007.pdf>.
Bold, V 2007, 'Cotacachi actualiza su plan cantonal de turismo', *Periódico Intag*, October/ November, p. 40.
Cerdán, P 2013, 'Post-development and buen vivir: An approach to development from latin-America', *International Letters of Social and Humanistic Sciences*, vol. 10, pp. 15–24. doi: 10.18052/www.scipress.com/ILSHS.10.15.
Chapron, G, Epstein, Y & López-Bao, JV 2019, 'A rights revolution for nature', *Science*, vol. 363, no. 6434, pp. 1392–3. doi: 10.1126/science.aav5601.
Chassagne, N & Everingham, P 2019, 'Buen vivir: Degrowing extractivism and growing wellbeing through tourism', *Journal of Sustainable Tourism*, vol. 27, no. 12, pp. 1909–25. doi: 10.1080/09669582.2019.1660668.
Constitución de la república del ecuador 2008, Registro oficial 449, 20 October 2008, Quito.
Consulta 2018: Resultados a nivel nacional, 2018, viewed <https://www.eluniverso.com/ resultados-consulta-popular-2018-ecuador>.
'Cuáles son las siete preguntas de la consulta popular y el referéndum en ecuador?', 2017, *El Universo*, 3 October 2017.
D'Amico, L 2011, '"El Agua es Vida/Water Is Life': Community Watershed Reserves in Intag, Ecuador, and Emerging Ecological Identities', in BR Johnston, L Hiwasaki & IJ Klaver, eds, *Water, cultural diversity, and grlobal Environmental Change*) Springer, Dordrecht.

Dafermos, G, Kotsampopoulos, P, Latoufis, K, Margaris, I, Rivela, B, Washima, FP, Ariza-Montobbio, P & López, J 2015, 'Transforming the energy matrix: Transition policies for the development of the distributed energy model', *Journal of Peer Production*, vol. 7. <http://peerproduction.net/issues/issue-7-policies-for-the-commons/peer-reviewed-papers/transforming-the-energy-matrix/>.

Delgado, F, Rist, S & Escobar, C 2010, *El desarrollo endógeno sustentable como interfaz para implementar el vivir bien en la gestión pública boliviana*, Plural, La Paz.

Dryzek, JS 1997, *The politics of the earth: Environmental discourses*, Oxford University Press, Oxford.

'Enlace ciudadano 440, desde quito', 2015, *El Comercio*, 7 September 2015.

'Entre el orgullo y el olvido', 2001, *Periódico Intag*, February/March, p. 20.

Escobar, A 2006, 'Difference and conflict in the struggle over natural resources: A political ecology framework', *Development*, vol. 49, no. 3, pp. 6–13. doi: 10.1057/palgrave.development.1100267.

Esteva, G 2010, 'Development', in W Sachs, ed., *The development dictionary*, Zed Books, London.

Granoff, I, Hogarth, JR, Wykes, S & Doig, A 2016, *Beyond coal: Scaling up clean energy to fight global poverty*, Overseas Development Institute, London.

Guardiola, J & García-Quero, F 2014, 'Nature & buen vivir in ecuador: The battle between conservation and extraction', *Alternautas, (Re)Searching Development: The Abya Yala Chapter*, 3 December, <http://www.alternautas.net/blog/2014/12/1/nature-buen-vivir-in-ecuador-the-battle-between-conservation-and-extraction>.

Gudynas, E 2009, 'Diez tesis urgentes sobre el nuevo extractivismo', *Extractivismo, política y sociedad*, pp. 187–225, CLAES, Montevideo.

Gudynas, E 2011, 'Buen vivir: Today's tomorrow', *Development*, vol. 54, no. 4, pp. 441–7. doi: 10.1057/dev.2011.86.

Gudynas, E 2013a, 'Debates on development and its alternatives in latin America: A brief heterodox guide', in Lang M and Mokrani D, eds, *Beyond development*, Rosa Luxemburg Foundation, Quito, Ecuador.

Gudynas, E 2013b, 'Transitions to post-extractivism: Directions, options and areas of action', in in Lang M and Mokrani D, eds, *Beyond development: Alternative visions from latin America*, Fundacion Rosa Luxemburg, Quito, Ecuador.

Guillen-Royo, M 2015, *Sustainability and wellbeing: Human-scale development in practice*, Routledge, London.

Hickel, J 2015, *Forget 'developing' poor countries, it's time to 'de-develop' rich countries*, The Guardian, viewed 7 October 2015, <http://www.theguardian.com/global-development-professionals-network/2015/sep/23/developing-poor-countries-de-develop-rich-countries-sdgs>.

Hidronangulvi, 2016, Municipio de Cotacachi, Cotacachi, <http://www.cotacachi.gob.ec/index.php/component/phocadownload/category/59>.

IFRC 2010, *Climate change facts and figures*, COP16, International Federation of Red Cross and Red Cresent Societies, Cancun, <http://www.climatecentre.org/downloads/files/conferences/COP-16/Fact%20and%20Figures.pdf>.

Inclusive green growth: For the future we want, 2012, OECD, Paris, France, https://www.oecd.org/greengrowth/Rio+20%20brochure%20FINAL%20ENGLISH%20web%202.pdf.

Íntag: Una sociedad que la violencia no puede minar. Informe psicosocial de las afectaciones en íntag provocadas por las empresas mineras y el estado en el proyecto llurimagua, 2015, Colectivo de Investigación y Acción Psicosocial, Intag, Ecuador.

IPCC 2015, *Climate change 2014 synthesis report*, Intergovernmental Panel on Climate Change, Geneva, <https://www.ipcc.ch/pdf/assessment-report/ar5/syr/AR5_SYR_FI NAL_All_Topics.pdf>.

Játiva, E 2004, 'Organizaciones ambientalistas y communidades luchan juntas contra el problema minero en pacto', *Periódico Intag*, January, p. 24.

Kilvert, N 2019, 'There's a growing push to give nature legal rights, but what would that mean?', *ABC*, 16 March 2019.

Morse, S 2008, 'Post-sustainable development', *Sustainable Development*, vol. 16, no. 5, pp. 341–52.

Ondrik, RS n.d., *Participatory approaches to national development planning*, Asian Development Bank, Manila, <http://siteresources.worldbank.org/INTEASTASIAPACI FIC/Resources/226262-1143156545724/Brief_ADB.pdf>.

The Paris agreement - status of ratification, 2016, United Nations Framework Convention on Climate Change, viewed 13 September, <http://unfccc.int/paris_agreement/items/ 9444.php>.

'Patricio moncayo: 'Hablan de matriz productiva, pero recuerdan la devaluación'', 2015, http://www.elcomercio.com/actualidad/entrevista-patriciomoncayo-matrizproductiva -devaluacion-economia.html.

Prada, R 2011, 'La revolución mundial del vivir bien', *Aportes Andinos*, vol. 28, no. January 2011, pp. 1–3. http://repositorio.uasb.edu.ec/handle/10644/2790.

'Rafael correa reforzó el discurso minero en zamora', 2015, *El Comercio*, 6 October 2015.

Rogge, M & Moreno, E, *Under rich earth 2008*, Rye Cinema, Toronto, ON.

Rubio, G 2016, 'Movemiento ally kawsay', *Facebook*, 17 May, <https://www.facebook .com/photo.php?fbid=1599985880329638&set=a.1448400398821521.1073741828.1 00009547255193&type=3>.

SENPLADES 2009, *Plan nacional para el buen vivir 2009–2013 : Construyendo un estado plurinacional e intercultural*, Secretaría Nacional de Planificación y Desarrollo, Quito, Ecuador.

Stahler-Sholk, R, Vanden, HE & Kuecker, GD 2008, *Latin American social movements in the twenty-first century: Resistance, power, and democracy*, Rowman & Littlefield Publishing Group, Lanham.

Stevenson, A 2010, *Oxford dictionary of English*, Oxford University Press, US.

Tituaña, A 2004, *Carta del alcalde de cotacachi, auki tituaña, manifestando su rechazo frontal contra actividades mineras en zona de intag, canton de cotacachi*, Mining Watch Canada, viewed <http://miningwatch.ca/es/blog/2004/12/15/carta-del-alcalde-d e-cotacachi-auki-titua-manifestando-su-rechazo-frontal-contra>.

Tripathy, DP & Patnaik, NK 1994, *Noise pollution in opencast mines - its impact on human environment*, AA Balkema, Rotterdam, The Netherlands.

Unesco global geoparks 2016?, UNESCO, viewed <http://www.unesco.org/new/en/natura l-sciences/environment/earth-sciences/unesco-global-geoparks/>.

United Nations General Assembly 2015, *Transforming our world*, Resolution A/Res/70/1, United Nations/New York. https://www.un.org/ga/search/view_doc.asp?symbol=A/ RES/70/1&Lang=E.

Waldmüller, J 2015, 'Analysing the spill-over matrix of extractivism: Para-legality, separation and violence to integral health in the ecuadorian íntag', *Alternautas*, 20 August 2015, <http://www.alternautas.net/blog/2015/3/20/analyzing-the-spill-over -matrix-of-extractivism-from-para-legality-separation-and-violence-to-integral-health -in-the-ecuadorian-ntag>.

Working with local people and governments to create 'eco-cities' 2000?, Rainforest Information Centre, viewed 2 April 2018, <http://www.rainforestinfo.org.au/projects /anja/anjacoto.htm>.

Yeboah, JY 2008, *Environmental and health impact of mining on surrounding communities: A case study of anglogold ashanti in obuasi*, thesis, Department of Geography and Rural Development, Kwame Nkrumah University of Science and Technology.

Zorrilla, C 2015, 'Ecuador: Widespread protests from left and indigenous sectors demand progressive changes', *Upside Down World*, 25 August <http://upsidedownworld.org /archives/ecuador/ecuador-widespread-protests-from-left-and-indigenous-sectors-d emand-progressive-changes/>.

Zorrilla, C 2019, 'Twenty-three reasons why not to mine in the forests of ecuador's intag region', *DECOIN*, 23 April 14 November 2019, <https://www.decoin.org/>.

Zorrilla, C 2020a, 'Codelco about to finance catastrophic mine in ecuador', *DECOIN*, 28 February, viewed 5 May, <https://www.decoin.org/>.

Zorrilla, C 2020b, 'Community assembly makes it clear that residents will not allow any more mining company presence in intag', *DECOIN*, 22 January 2020, viewed 23 April 2020, <https://www.decoin.org/>.

7 Rethinking sustainability
Making the global align with the local

Going beyond the discourse critique of post-development calls for alternatives to development; this book proposes Buen Vivir as a plural alternative to Sustainable Development, and as a practical tool for communities with which to achieve sustainable Socio-Eco Wellbeing. The previous three chapters have empirically demonstrated the viability of Buen Vivir as a practical alternative (if several conditions are met) by looking at its principles identified by understandings and practices of Buen Vivir. Chapters Four to Six argued that for Buen Vivir to be viable, transformation (politically and practically) is required. Those chapters discussed the *practical* implications of Buen Vivir.

This transformation is conditional upon several factors: 1) That Buen Vivir is a plural approach to change, requiring cooperation from all actors; 2) that it nonetheless remains an endogenous, community-led approach to change with real democratic participatory processes to achieve it; and 3) the ability to fully achieve Buen Vivir hinges on an immediate transition to a post-extractive society, with full respect for the environment and our relationship to it. These factors are all dependant on political will. This chapter will thus discuss the *political* implications of Buen Vivir as an alternative to Sustainable Development and examine how it may allow governments to position themselves to meet their global sustainability commitments and responsibilities – to rethink sustainability.

Status quo or transformation? The political justification for Buen Vivir

Despite the contestability of Sustainable Development, in practice it has commonly been articulated within a neoliberal agenda, and therefore distilled into a singular definition. The most widely cited definition of Sustainable Development is found in the Brundtland Report, to meet "the needs of the present without compromising the ability of future generations to meet their own needs." This is the mainstream, dominant interpretation of Sustainable Development, widely embraced at a global policy level. Yet, this universal, singular notion of Sustainable Development has failed to achieve its social and environmental aims.

In the light of critiques of past failed attempts to secure a global sustainable future, the recent Post-2015 SDGs are, like their predecessor global commitments, aspiring, but not necessarily focused enough to achieve the transformation desired or indeed required for transformation. We cannot achieve Socio-Eco Wellbeing by continuing with the status quo. On that path, "there is a risk that the discourse of Sustainable Development be the perfect excuse for watering down the models of unbridled growth and hiding inequalities behind generic promises of unreal change" (José Gutiérrez Pérez 2006).

While we need global commitments for sustainability such as international treaties, declarations, and conferences, history tells us that these are good as a guide, but fail to achieve the drastic, everlasting change required for the transformation discussed in previous chapters: That is, at the political level, a policy of post-extractivism and the structure and spaces needed for a shift in power to provide communities with the opportunity to decide their own development needs not "desires" based on economic progress; and, at the community level, a global change in attitudes and behaviours towards more environmentally and socially sustainable practices, while proactively assuming a participatory role in the community.

However, as Bullard (2011) asserts, "What we lack is the imagination to think about how to live differently, how to unravel the power structures that obstruct change, and how to rethink 'development.'" Beyond development, it is time to rethink sustainability and how we can seek to achieve genuine Socio-Eco Wellbeing. This considers the wellbeing of both human and environmental needs equally, with the acknowledgement of the relationship between humans and our environment as inseparable and reciprocal. As anthropologist Jason Hickel (2015a) states, "This is not about giving anything up. And it's certainly not about living a life of voluntary misery or imposing harsh limits on human potential. On the contrary, it's about reaching a higher level of understanding and consciousness about what we're doing here and why."

Buen Vivir deconstructs old worldviews of sustainability and wellbeing and offers new ways of thinking. It offers the opportunity to rethink the way sustainability and wellbeing are currently approached in development (and particularly in the West). And contrary to neoliberal Sustainable Development, Buen Vivir's contested definition signifies a type of flexibility which allows it to be adapted differently to different contexts that have different realities, values, and needs, rather than one universal application based on Western values. It is therefore contextual with a core set of principles that promise to address the original fundament of Sustainable Development, which has been lost through misuse and misinterpretation by the status quo, and help communities identify and meet their fundamental needs.

As Chapter Four identified, Buen Vivir is a hybrid practice–policy (Vivir Bien–Buen Vivir) approach to achieving Socio-Eco Wellbeing, which is stimulated from the bottom-up, *not* top-down. That is, it shows promise in providing concrete practical pathways to Socio-Eco Wellbeing endogenously, while having profound policy implications. To that end, I re-emphasise that Buen Vivir should be considered a plural alternative in the form of a community tool whereby all key actors have a role to play: Communities, in changing behaviours, attitudes, and practices, and in practising their rights and responsibilities under Buen Vivir; governments, in providing the necessary structures and processes for change to be achieved at the community level, listening to and allowing communities to define their own path endogenously; and organisations, in facilitating change at the local level, acting as mediators or brokers between governments and communities to ensure that the change processes remain endogenous and are not co-opted for political gain. This necessitates cooperation and dialogue between the key actors (2013; 2002). In practice at the community level, it is referred to as "Vivir Bien," the behaviour and daily practice of communal social and environmental wellbeing. In policy it is referred to as "Buen Vivir." Both provoke change by the way the role of nature is perceived and by changing our relationship to our environment and our communities. Buen Vivir has the potential to change the way of knowing and doing entirely in practice, but in doing so to address policy around global commitments to encourage a forward momentum. Given the critiques of the rehashed and again revitalised neoliberal universal approach to Sustainable Development, a change in method for the practical application of Socio-Eco Wellbeing may be a beneficial solution.

While Buen Vivir as an alternative originates from post-development theory, it goes beyond that, because, as Gudynas (2013) argues, post-development fails to offer any concrete solutions and mainly focuses on a critique of the discourse. Moreover, critics of post-development argue that "they romanticized local traditions and local social movements, ignoring that the local is also embedded in global power relations" (Escobar 2000). Kiely (1999) notes, "When Rahnema (1997) argues that the end of development 'represents a call to the "good people" everywhere to think and work together,' we are left with the vacuous politics of USA for Africa's 'We are the World.' Instead of a politics which critically engages with material inequalities, we have a post-development era where 'people should be nicer to each other.'" It is not enough to appeal only to a moral obligation; change must also be addressed structurally. This is pertinent to the plural approach I have argued so far, which by no means alludes to an "uncritical, romantic celebration of the local" (Kiely 1999).

The approach I propose takes elements from post-developmentalism without causing an unworkable and radical juxtaposition which threatens to impede any proposed change. This approach embraces the importance of an endogenous approach, and aims for widespread change, starting at the local level and scaling it up to work cooperatively with the global agenda for sustainability and wellbeing. This is because no single approach could prove viable by ignoring wider political processes and by waging an outright attack on the dominant hegemonic ideology. With that aim, this chapter is concerned with how the local interfaces with the global. By starting local with a recognition of the political implications that global power relations can have on any endogenous approach, Buen Vivir seeks to provide communities with the tools to change their own reality whilst addressing the fact that the world is globally connected and thus all actions have wider political implications.

Enter the Sustainable Development Goals: What are the risks?

The ability for Sustainable Development's original objectives to be attained has been duly criticised, especially in recent times with growing inequalities and increasing impacts of climate change globally. Victor (2006) argues that "instead of bringing together nature, the economy, and social justice, sustainable development has spawned overspecialized and largely meaningless checklists and targets. Particularly harmful has been a series of consensus-driven UN summits that have yielded broad and incoherent documents and policies." The SDGs have been the global community's attempt to overcome that through advocating "transformative change" (Hujo et al. 2016; UNGA 2015). But just how transformative are they in themselves?

The SDGs came into effect on 1 January 2016 and include 17 goals and 169 targets, which are to be implemented by governments universally, regardless of local context. They provide an overarching perspective of how to measure progress to the global Sustainable Development agenda – hence their universality. The objective of the goals is to directly tackle the global challenges that threaten sustainability, such as poverty, climate change, unsustainable growth, migration and displacement, public health epidemics, inequality, social inclusion, lack of decent work, political instability, and violent conflict (Hujo et al. 2016).

With such an ambitious global ambit, and momentum towards a sustainable future, we should by now be living sustainability, and globally social inequality and injustice should be declining, if not halted. Yet the situation is precisely the contrary. So, what went wrong in the past and what are the future risks for Socio-Eco Wellbeing under the SDGs? I argue that three critical aspects of Sustainable Development may have contributed to its failure thus far: 1) Universality; 2) the focus on economic growth as a solution; and 3) the continuing anthropocentric nature of neoliberal Sustainable Development, which disregards the cause and effect of humans' relationship with nature. In trying to include all manner of voices to make Sustainable Development universal, it has turned it more into an aspirational ideal than a practical solution. Therefore, if not approached differently, the Sustainable Development Goals are not just inadequate, they are dangerous, locking us into "a failing economic model that requires urgent and deep structural changes" (Hickel 2015b). And as Villacís et al. (2015) state, "It needs to be clear that although goals are universal, and they help the world to have hope and to work together towards a sustainable future, it is crucial to consider different realities… Nature has no political limits."

The SDGs have been praised politically as a game changer because while the failed Millennium Development Goals applied to countries in the South, the SDGs apply universally to all. This last point is important because it means that they do not allow for the consideration of different realities. Goal 17 on partnerships, for example, emphasises economic partnerships and privileges the role the World Trade Organisation is to play in the implementation of the goals; in particular, debt relief and financing and strengthening the multilateral trading system through free trade. These ideas perpetuated by neoliberal development have been criticised for being at the root of global inequality in the first place.

Unless an approach draws on the social context from which it derives, it cannot be a viable solution to that community's needs. It is important to take into account unmeasurable "social variables" and to include "'interculturality' and 'traditional knowledges' [which] will help to understand and build sustainable societies according to their culture and world view" (2015). In that respect, the SDGs can only be successful in achieving transformative shifts towards Socio-Eco Wellbeing if the goals are viewed as a global guide, but the substantive and substantial change happens at the local level, driven by communities.

"Transforming our World," the 2030 Agenda for Sustainable Development that guides the implementation of the SDGs, resolves in the preamble to "take the bold and transformative steps which are urgently needed to shift the world on a sustainable and resilient path" (UNGA 2015); and the UN affirms that transformation must address the root causes of the environmental and social problems at stake, and that they can no longer be ignored (Hujo et al. 2016). This latter point demonstrates that even within the global discourse on the SDGs contradictions are starting to emerge that, if not kept in check, will lead the SDGs down the same failed path as Sustainable Development. So far, the business-as-usual approach to "transformation" will lead us to anything but that. Howard and Wheeler (2015) rightly ask, if business-as-usual is failing, how "is it possible for the new framework to be meaningful and accountable to the people it is designed to benefit?"

One of the greatest critiques of neoliberal development, and subsequently Sustainable Development, is this notion of developing countries seeking Western-style exponential growth fuelled by the exploitation of natural resources – be they renewable or not (Gupta & Vegelin 2016). The original aims of Sustainable Development emphasised needs rather than growth. However, since its conception, the needs aspect has been appropriated for consumption, fuelling growth akin to the countries in the Global North.

On the one hand, the UN Report of the High-Level Panel (HLP) of Eminent Persons on the Post-2015 Development Agenda stated that developed countries need to "re-imagine their growth models" (*A new global partnership: Eradicate poverty and transform economies through sustainable development* 2013). On the other hand, Goal 8 of the SDGs is devoted to increasing economic growth akin to neoliberal development. Target 8.1, for example, calls for "at least 7 percent gross domestic product growth per annum in the least developed countries" (UNGA 2015). This is the mortal flaw at the heart of the SDGs, relying on old models for growth, which are fuelled by policies of extractivism: "And not just a little bit of growth… How can they be calling for both less and more at the same time?" (Hickel 2015b). These visions that are based on linear progress are nonsensical. As Bullard (2011) asserts, "Sustainability is circular, complex; it is about harmony, relationships and rhythms. It is not an accounting exercise for rationing how we use the Earth's resources." Approaches like Buen Vivir that seek to live in harmony with nature emphasise this.

What would be more effective to reduce global inequality under Goal 8 would be targets for more effective wealth distribution. In addition, shifting the focus from economic growth to Socio-Eco Wellbeing would change the political outlook, but if done effectively, the policy implications are not likely to have any negative impact on quality of life. The argument to continue a growth trajectory for the sake of human wellbeing does not stand up. In fact, "effectively designed policies" aimed at reducing consumption while enhancing measures for protecting people and the planet would rather increase Socio-Eco Wellbeing (Howarth 2012).

On maintaining economic growth and consumption, one of the most concerning issues with the current model of Sustainable Development is the physical limitations of the environment. As set out in the Brundtland Report (*Our common future* 1987), "The concept of Sustainable Development does imply limits – not absolute limits but limitations imposed by the present state of technology and social organization on environmental resources and by the ability of the biosphere to absorb the effects of human activities." This anthropocentric view of how the world works also ignores the nature–society continuum which has more profound impacts on wellbeing than GDP. Higher GDP does not necessarily translate into an increase in quality of life in communities where basic needs are met; and in more affluent societies it speaks rather to fulfilling desires, translating into greater consumption and therefore more exploitation of natural resources in a paradoxical situation whereby society places mounting pressures on people to maintain wealth and consumption, in order to "keep up with the Joneses."

Moreover, this inherently anthropocentric process did not acknowledge the rights and needs of the environment to allow ecosystems to continue functioning. While there is nothing fundamentally wrong with the original *aims* of Sustainable Development (economic and social justice and needs satisfaction; environmental protection), the problem lies in the processes by which these aims have been pursued since being incorporated into mainstream neoliberal arguments. These processes continue with the SDGs. The approach now needs to be rethought to allow for any chance of transformation for Socio-Eco Wellbeing.

The local cooperating with the global

> Sustainability may yet be possible if sufficient numbers of scholars, practitioners and political actors embrace a plurality of approaches to and perspectives on sustainability, accept multiple interpretations and practices associated with an evolving concept of "development," and support a further opening up of local-to-global public spaces to debate and enact a politics of sustainability.
>
> (Sneddon, Howarth & Norgaard 2006)

Where the universal nature of Sustainable Development is criticised, Buen Vivir offers the opportunity for communities to determine their own version of the concept, speaking to their unsatisfied fundamental needs, albeit within a core set of principles. The SDGs, whose target 7b, as a brief example, ensures access to affordable, reliable, sustainable, and modern energy for all (Goal 7), stipulates that by 2030 the expansion of infrastructure and upgrade of technology for supplying modern and sustainable energy services for all in developing countries must be attained (UNGA 2015); the community in question can determine its own sustainable energy needs, aligned with the principles of Buen Vivir. It does not negate the need to find sustainable energy sources for all, but as Patterson et al. (2015) ask, "How do governments, the private sector, and communities interact in deciding on appropriate and sustainable energy systems, and how does this differ in different contexts?" Recognition of the cultural, geographic, and socio-economic context is crucial. It should not be determined exogenously; rather these needs should be determined on the ground and implemented in plural cooperation with the different actors. This is the point at which Sustainable Development and Buen Vivir have the potential to converge, given that the SDGs appeal for a more citizen-empowered approach to achieving sustainability in the plan for "people, planet and prosperity"; even though the goals and targets have so far left out any reference to "people" in their capacity to achieve sustainability and are designed to be "universal" in scope.

Participation as a condition in Buen Vivir policy aims to link policy with communities' experiences on the ground, further empowering a grassroots approach. In Cotacachi, this has been manifested in the democratic participatory approach discussed in Chapter Five. While there is no scope here to analyse its success thus far, it demonstrates ways in which Buen Vivir policy seeks to align itself with endogenous processes. Nonetheless, these processes must be examined with caution, because of the risk of the co-option of community interests for a "business-as-usual" Sustainable Development agenda (Howard & Wheeler 2015).

An endogenous biocentric approach that, in practice, reduces consumption, consumerism, and consequently natural resource use will have a significant impact on national and international policy. This necessarily has flow-on effects in the global market, which will stimulate the need to consider an alternative to the growth model. This is where the Social and Solidarity Economy (SSE) comes in. Giovannini (2014) argues that the SSE "encourages sobriety [in consumption] and respect for the environment." In that respect, sustainable degrowth or "A-growth" becomes an outcome of a Buen Vivir approach, and one that has positive effects on Socio-Eco Wellbeing. Eventually the argument for unsustained economic growth and a one-size-fits-all approach to needs satisfaction will not hold and the focus will be forced to shift, reducing the risk of co-optation in the argument for the status quo.

This is not to say that this approach calls for a direct attack on Sustainable Development, nor that it seeks to morph into a neoliberal approach couched in alternative language. To the contrary, a Buen Vivir approach is one that cooperates with the current paradigm in a plural system so that it may stimulate systematic change from the bottom-up – transfiguring the status quo towards real *transformation*. After all, as I argued in Part I, an attack on the current model will not result in the practical transformation needed for Socio-Eco Wellbeing, but instead will see it relegated to an ideological discourse. Cooperation is imperative: Cooperation to understand how the Buen Vivir approach suggested by this research fits in the current paradigm so it can be embraced and not rejected, and cooperation between actors with everyone playing their role.

Differences and synergies between Buen Vivir and the SDGs

As opposed to Sustainable Development which has an accepted definition but contested principles, Buen Vivir is contested by its definition but has a set of core principles. The metanarrative of Sustainable Development articulated through international frameworks such as the SDGs is very prescriptive, despite goals that are deemed "nationally appropriate" because the overall vision is still a very Eurocentric neoliberal approach. The problem is that there is no one-size-fits-all solution to transformative change. It depends on many contextual, geographical, socio-economic, and cultural factors. In that way, it cannot be prescribed from above. Buen Vivir on the other hand provides a descriptive approach to achieving Socio-Eco Wellbeing, which sets out principles and the direction for change but leaves the prescriptive elements up to the community itself. This allows the community to identify its own needs, rather than catering to those that satisfy a global development agenda; and it also creates greater accountability for the social and environmental consequences of decision-making within a community. The consequence is that as people have a more active and central role in their own development, they feel a greater sense of responsibility and connection to their own environments and communities.

In Chapter Three, I identified two key differences between Buen Vivir and Sustainable Development, which were that 1) Sustainable Development is a universal, top-down approach, compared to the endogenous, community-led approach to change under Buen Vivir; and 2) Sustainable Development's hierarchical anthropological nature puts human needs and wellbeing above all else, whereas Buen Vivir emphasises the importance of the reciprocal nature–society relationship in meeting needs. In the same light, the SDGs are universal. The problem is that this disallows for contextual differences in realities on the ground. Buen Vivir on the other hand depends on contextual differences by the community identification and satisfaction (with cooperation) of needs aligned through a set of (descriptive) core principles which allows communities themselves to decide how to (prescriptively) interpret them.

So, in other words, while there is a set of core principles for Buen Vivir, these are by no means universal goals linked to set global indicators; rather, they allow for communities to tailor their needs to their own realities. At the same time, the 2030 Agenda (UNGA 2015) states:

> We recognise that there are different approaches, visions, models and tools available to each country, in accordance with its national circumstances and priorities, to achieve sustainable development; and we reaffirm that planet Earth and its ecosystems are our common home and that "Mother Earth" is a common expression in a number of countries and regions.

Although the perspectives are different, this acknowledgement means that there is scope for Buen Vivir as a community "tool" and an alternative to Sustainable Development to be recognised as such in a global framework in a plural and cooperative way.

Another key point of difference, as briefly mentioned earlier, is the emphasis in Sustainable Development on economic growth. Although the growth model has been criticised and recognised as an obstacle to achieving social justice and environmental sustainability by some policy-makers and economists alike, it still prevails in the SDGs. The growth aspect of Sustainable Development not only makes ecological conservation difficult, but also threatens human wellbeing, because there is no evidence that the economic benefits "trickle down" to those at the bottom (Guillen-Royo 2015).

Sustainable Development, as an alternative development paradigm, seeks to address the lack of popular participation in mainstream development (Pieterse 2000). Both Buen Vivir as an alternative to development and Sustainable Development as alternative development have that in common. Participation is key for both approaches, although for Sustainable Development it is still very much reliant on the sort of top-down model of participation in which the people's needs are dictated by a higher political agenda. Altieri and Masera (1993) state that "Conventional 'top-down' development strategies have proved fundamentally limited in their ability to promote equitable and environmentally sustainable development." In contrast, Buen Vivir focuses on the democratic participation of the people whereby the people themselves drive the agenda and identify their own needs, most effectively through local participatory processes. Although there have been efforts under the new global framework to include voices and perspectives of the people, the extent to which local and marginalised communities can participate in the global policy process is limited (Howard & Wheeler 2015). The "transformative change" for participation defined by the SDGs "also means changing norms and institutions, both formal and informal, that shape the behaviour of people and organizations in the social, economic, environmental and political spheres" (Hujo et al. 2016), shifting power relations.

In the implementation of the goals, the 2030 Agenda has recalled the Global Partnership for Sustainable Development as an inclusive, multi-stakeholder partnership between governments, the private sector, and civil society, which nonetheless places the state at the centre of implementation. While the SDGs call for a revitalisation of the Global Partnership, Buen Vivir focuses on cooperation between actors, with communities taking the lead, governments facilitating the processes and guiding the private sector through regulations and laws, and organisations playing a mediating role for communities. The difference between the two is that the former, despite the language of "partnership," is still hierarchical and top-down, having greater risk for the co-optation of these processes than the latter which provides communities with greater empowerment and capacity-building.

The SDGs very much remain an alternative *for* development, whereas Buen Vivir is considered an alternative *to* development – an important distinction because while it is advocating a new paradigm, it is also one that can work plurally within a global system. As Villacís et al. (2015) assert, it is "unrealistic" to think of a model which can work completely outside of the current global system, as communities do not exist in political isolation – recalling the plurality of Buen Vivir. Kothari et al. (2014) believe that comparing similarities between the two means that the original meaning of Buen Vivir has been distorted "and/or clubbed with other contradictory concepts," co-opting "the voices and language of those advocating radical alternatives."

By no means do I advocate co-opting the voices of Buen Vivir; to the contrary, I argue that the way to make these voices heard without co-optation is by demonstrating how grassroots change can work within a wider system. While it is vital to radically change the ways of thinking and doing towards transformation and away from the status quo, I also recall the earlier point of the dangers of summoning radical discourses as opposed to plural and practical solutions if effective change is to be achieved, because, so far, no outright assault on the dominant paradigm has been successful in achieving the widespread practical transformation necessary for Socio-Eco Wellbeing. But, by taking a Buen Vivir approach, the aforementioned problems with mainstream Sustainable Development can be addressed by local communities living in local environments. This alignment can help governments understand where the principles for Buen Vivir can allow them to meet global sustainability commitments. "Think globally, act locally" is a well-known motto in this context. And changing the focus to biocentric, endogenous, and needs-based, rather than anthropocentric, exogenous, and growth-based, will help achieve the transformation needed.

Based on the fundamental differences and parallels between Buen Vivir and Sustainable Development discussed above and the discussion of the principles in Chapter Four, in analysing Buen Vivir as an alternative approach to Sustainable Development, it is important to acknowledge how its principles can cooperate with the 17 SDGs for a cooperative, plural, and practical approach to change. My aim is not to analyse if or how Buen Vivir can politically seek to meet the targets of the SDGs, nor is there interest in *aligning* Buen Vivir with the targets because while the broad-based universal goals evoke the common aims for sustainability and wellbeing, the prescriptive one-size-fits-all nature of the targets sustains the same criticisms of traditional development. Rather, I focus on cooperation with the broader Goals.[1] This is important because the goals demonstrate somewhat similar aims to sustainability and wellbeing as Buen Vivir. They demonstrate that transformative change is still possible. Yet the targets are still anchored in the status quo – the neoliberal model of development – which ultimately contradict the SDGs' acknowledgement of different approaches, visions, models, and tools for sustainability. And as former EU President Barroso said, "We cannot face the challenges of the future with the tools of the past" (Van den Bergh 2011).

Table 7.1 is the result of this comparative analysis between the 17 SDGs and the principles of Buen Vivir. As the principles of Buen Vivir will look different depending on context, the purpose here is analytical – that is, demonstrating that the local can cooperate with the global.

The aim of Table 7.1 is to support a community-led implementation of Buen Vivir over a global, universal approach. What the former might look like is the subject of the following chapter. This analysis completes the conceptual puzzle of Buen Vivir as an alternative to Sustainable Development, which cannot

Table 7.1 Comparison between Sustainable Development Goals and Buen Vivir principles

SDGs	Buen Vivir principles
Goal 1: End poverty in all its forms everywhere	All principles
Goal 2: End hunger, achieve food security and improved nutrition and promote sustainable agriculture	Food security
	Healthy environment
	SSE
Goal 3: Ensure healthy lives and promote wellbeing for all at all ages	Good health
	Community
	Harmony
	Healthy environment
	Reciprocity
	Culture
	Leisure Time
	Decent work
Goal 4: Ensure inclusive and equitable quality education and promote lifelong learning opportunities for all	Education
	Equality
	Holistic rights
	Culture
Goal 5: Achieve gender equality and empower all women and girls	Equality
	Respect
	Democratic participation
	Holistic rights
Goal 6: Ensure availability and sustainable management of water and sanitation for all	Reciprocity
	Healthy environment
	Self-determination
	Holistic rights
Goal 7: Ensure access to affordable, reliable, sustainable, and modern energy for all	Healthy environment
	Reciprocity
	Equality
	Self-determination
Goal 8: Promote sustained, inclusive, and sustainable economic growth, full and productive employment, and decent work for all	Reciprocity
	Self-determination
	SSE
	Decent work
	Leisure time
Goal 9: Build resilient infrastructure, promote inclusive and sustainable industrialisation and foster innovation	Decent work
	SSE
	Reciprocity
Goal 10: Reduce inequality within and among countries	Equality
	SSE
	Self-determination
Goal 11: Make cities and human settlements inclusive, safe, resilient, and sustainable	Community
	Harmony
	SSE
	Healthy environment
	Democratic participation
	Food security
Goal 12: Ensure sustainable consumption and production patterns	SSE
	Reciprocity

(*Continued*)

Table 7.1 Continued

SDGs	Buen Vivir principles
Goal 13: Take urgent action to combat climate change and its impacts	Healthy environment Reciprocity Self-determination
Goal 14: Conserve and sustainably use the oceans, seas, and marine resources for sustainable development	Reciprocity Healthy environment Self-determination Food security
Goal 15: Protect, restore, and promote sustainable use of terrestrial ecosystems, sustainably managed forests, combat desertification, and halt and reverse land degradation and halt biodiversity loss.	Reciprocity Healthy environment Self-determination Food security
Goal 16: Promote peaceful and inclusive societies for sustainable development, provide access to justice for all and build effective, accountable, and inclusive institutions at all levels	Community Solidarity Harmony Democratic participation Respect Self-determination
Goal 17: Strengthen the means of implementation and revitalise the Global Partnership for Sustainable Development	Democratic participation Self-determination Solidarity

be explained without contrasting (Pennings, Keman & Kleinnijenhuis 2006) the framework for Buen Vivir with the global framework for Sustainable Development implementation. After all, how can we advocate for an alternative without an analysis of what we are seeking to change? It is about challenging the vertical nature of sustainability and wellbeing and promoting more lateral thinking beyond "development," extending a horizontal understanding of the issues relating to environmental and social wellbeing.

Now that this conceptualisation is complete, and the political implications are understood, more needs to be said about the practical implications, so let us move on to the implementation of Buen Vivir, based on the empirical fieldwork findings.

Note

1 For a policy comparison between the MDGs, the SDGs, and the Ecuadorian government targets for Buen Vivir outlined in the PNBV, see Alternatives FOR Development or Alternatives TO Development (Villacís, Mora & López 2015).

References

Altieri, MA & Masera, O 1993, 'Sustainable rural development in latin America - building from the bottom up', *Ecological Economics*, vol. 7, no. 2, pp. 93–121. doi: 10.1016/0921-8009(93)90049-c.

Bullard, N 2011, 'It's too late for sustainability. What we need is system change', *Development*, vol. 54, no. 2, pp. 141–2.

Escobar, A 2000, 'Beyond the search for a paradigm? Post-development and beyond', *Development*, vol. 43, no. 4, pp. 11–4. doi: 10.1057/palgrave.development.1110188.

Giovannini, M 2014, *Indigenous peoples and self-determined development: The case of community enterprises in chiapas*, thesis, University of Trento.

Gudynas, E 2013, 'Debates on development and its alternatives in latin America: A brief heterodox guide', in Lang M and Mokrani D, eds, *Beyond development*, Rosa Luxemburg Foundation, Quito, Ecuador.

Guillen-Royo, M 2015, *Sustainability and wellbeing: Human-scale development in practice*, Routledge, London.

Gupta, J & Vegelin, C 2016, 'Sustainable development goals and inclusive development', *International Environmental Agreements: Politics, Law and Economics*, vol. 16, pp. 433–448 .

Hickel, J 2015a, *Forget 'developing' poor countries, it's time to 'de-develop' rich countries*, The Guardian, viewed 7 October 2015, <http://www.theguardian.com/glo bal-development-professionals-network/2015/sep/23/developing-poor-countries-de-de velop-rich-countries-sdgs>.

Hickel, J 2015b, 'The problem with saving the world. The un's new sustainable development goals aim to save the world without transforming it', *Jacobin Magazine*. https://jacobin mag.com/2015/08/global-poverty-climate-change-sdgs.

Howard, J & Wheeler, J 2015, 'What community development and citizen participation should contribute to the new global framework for sustainable development', *Community Development Journal*, vol. 50, no. 4, pp. 552–70. doi: 10.1093/cdj/bsv033.

Howarth, RB 2012, 'Sustainability, well-being, and economic growth', *Journal Center for Humans & Nature*, vol. 5, no. 2, pp. 32–9.

Hujo, K, Braumann, H, Esquivel, V, van Griethuysen, P, Krause, D, Utting, P & Yi, I 2016, *Policy innovations for transformative change: Implementing the 2030 agenda for sustainable development*, UNRISD Flagship Report 2016, UNRISD, Geneva, Switerland.

José Gutiérrez Pérez, MTPL 2006, 'Using qualitative indicators of sustainability in iberoamerican environmental research', *Forum Qualitative Sozialforschung/Forum: Qualitative Social Research*, vol. 7, no. 4. http://www.qualitative-research.net/index .php/fqs/article/view/172/2734.

Kiely, R 1999, 'The last refuge of the noble savage? A critical assessment of post-development theory', *The European Journal of Development Research*, vol. 11, no. 1, pp. 30–55. doi: 10.1080/09578819908426726.

Kothari, A, Demaria, F & Acosta, A 2014, 'Buen vivir, degrowth and ecological swaraj: Alternatives to sustainable development and the green economy', *Development*, vol. 57, pp. 362–75.

A new global partnership: Eradicate poverty and transform economies through sustainable development, 2013, High-Level Panel (HLP) of Eminent Persons on the Post-2015 Development Agenda United Nations, New York.

World Commission on Environment and Development (WCED) 1987, *Our Common Future*, Oxford University Press, Oxford and New York.

Patterson, J, Koch, F & Bowen, K 2015, 'How can we prevent the un's sustainable development goals from failing?', *The Conversation*, 30 July.

Pennings, P, Keman, H & Kleinnijenhuis, J 2006, *Doing research in political science*, SAGE Publications Ltd, London. doi: 10.4135/9781849209038.

Pieterse, JN 2000, 'After post-development', *Third World Quarterly*, vol. 21, no. 2, pp. 175–91. doi: 10.2307/3993415.

Rahnema, M & Bawtree, V, eds, 1997, *The post-development reader*, Zed Books, London.

Sneddon, C, Howarth, RB & Norgaard, RB 2006, 'Sustainable development in a post-brundtland world', *Ecological Economics*, vol. 57, no. 2, pp. 253–68. doi: 10.1016/j.ecolecon.2005.04.013.

UNGA 2015, in *A/Res/70/1* (ed UNG Assembly) United Nations, New York.

Van den Bergh, JC 2011, 'Environment versus growth—a criticism of "degrowth" and a plea for "a-growth"', *Ecological economics*, vol. 70, no. 5, pp. 881–90.

Victor, DG 2006, 'Recovering sustainable development', *Foreign Affairs*, vol. 85, no. 1, pp. 91–103. <http://ezproxy.lib.swin.edu.au/login?url=http://search.ebscohost.com/login.aspx?direct=true&db=a9h&AN=19250183&site=ehost-live&scope=site>.

Villacís, MA, Mora, MF & López, R 2015, *Alternatives for development or alternatives to development?*, Southern voice on post-MDG international development goals, Occasional paper series 23, Centre for Policy Dialogue, Dakah, Bangladesh.

8 Implementing Buen Vivir
The practical pathway to transformation

Implementing Buen Vivir at the local level can help achieve practical transformative change which also dialogues with the global discourse, provided there is support from government, and a promotion of its principles at grassroots through education, awareness, and a Vivir Bien philosophical outlook. It starts with a recognition that communities of all contexts have "agency and the capacity to identify solutions themselves" (Howard & Wheeler 2015). This community-led change has wider implications because it sets in motion a series of similar movements which eventually have an influence and effect on global policy, and it shows the importance of linking community-based alternative approaches to wider policy spaces. Felipe uses Cotacachi as an example:

> It needs to start from the bottom up. Here in Cotacachi County, we [the people] actually managed to pass an ecological ordinance. And that was the idea really, to start changing things around. It's happening all around the world where cities in the US, Australia and everywhere are not waiting for the national government to impose CO_2 controls, [for example]. In our case… the idea of this ordinance, with all its faults, is not perfect by any means, but it came from the grassroots. We convinced the local government and then if you can convince the provincial government, and… well [its] decentralising [decision-making], but also creating these positive examples of development and wellbeing.

Though as Howard and Wheeler (2015) state, a community, grassroots approach, "does not mean leaving communities to find their own solutions while the state retreats"; but it means long-term, meaningful support from institutions to create spaces for communities to increase their own capacity and self-reliance. Effective co-construction also requires political will and genuine commitment also dependant on resources and capacity at all levels of government (2015). Thus, the hybrid convergence of practice and policy is important for the implementation of Buen Vivir.

This type of approach allows communities to take hold of the processes and promote local knowledges while embracing the plurality of knowledges necessary to allow Buen Vivir to flourish. This is where organisations as mediators can step in. Eversole (2014) identifies "knowledge partnering" as a new kind of development partnership for development practice. "A knowledge partnership can be defined as a relationship in which individuals, groups, and organizations share their knowledge in order to create innovative solutions" (Eversole 2014). Although, as discussed throughout this research while cooperation is essential, local knowledge and an endogenous approach takes precedence.

This chapter therefore analyses the ways in which key actors can cooperate in the achievement of Buen Vivir, continuing on the trajectory of wider political commitments to ecological sustainability and wellbeing and drawing from the discussion in Chapter Five regarding the different roles of the key actors to discuss how its plurality can be practically implemented.

Within a political context and especially through a global lens, how we can measure whether Buen Vivir meets its aims becomes an issue to be broached. In this chapter, I will examine the issue of measurement in Buen Vivir, discussing if it is feasible or even appropriate. I conclude the chapter with a look at how a framework for implementation could 1) provide communities with a practical tool to move forward; and 2) provide governments with ways to plurally align national and global policy objectives for sustainability with local processes while allowing communities direct their own path to Socio-Eco Wellbeing and, ultimately, Buen Vivir.

The plurality of community-led implementation: A hybrid approach

The most effective way to achieve this hybrid, plural implementation is through true democratic participation, also a condition for achieving Buen Vivir. The SDGs identify that "forums that facilitate and institutionalise participation need to be created and strengthened to ensure that policy design and implementation foster transformative outcomes" (Hujo et al. 2016). This cannot be business-as-usual top-down participation as societies and economies cannot reach transformation by imposition. The type of participation in itself must be transformative and contribute to Socio-Eco Wellbeing. This supports the democratic participatory approach, reinforced through participatory budget processes and collective local management of resources and outlined as a priority for the achievement of Buen Vivir in Chapter Five.

Organisations both local and external to the community have a key role to play in ensuring that such democratic participation links communities with policy in spaces which allow communities to challenge any political decisions that are not in their interest (Howard & Wheeler 2015). In that respect, organisations work as mediators or intermediaries to keep governments to account and minimalise the risk of co-optation through these processes by helping communities represent themselves in policy decisions and by knowledge-partnering with communities when necessary. It also helps link local issues and needs to national and global policies and frameworks through dialogue (Howard & Wheeler 2015).

This follows the views of key informants that cooperation between actors is needed to fully achieve a plural Buen Vivir – it cannot be a sole effort on behalf of the communities, yet it is first and foremost local. Leandro says it is

> Collective work from the grassroots. The work has to be there first. I cannot, as a leader or as a member of the community, start cooperating with others without the knowledge of the people in my community. I must first come together with the people of my community and then build networks to continue working.

The importance of organisations to mediate between community needs and political decisions was noted by Luis, who states, "a community can do wonders with all the people who work in joint projects, but if tomorrow the state comes and only for economic interests establishes a mine, that will totally change the work of *all* the community for generations." The intention of the cooperating organisation also must be genuinely in support of grassroots processes by connecting "engagement and advocacy in formal spaces with broader social mobilization and coalition building efforts, rather than merely serving to reinforce the status quo" (Howard & Wheeler 2015). In that respect it is also important to reiterate again the role of the community in changing its practices, attitudes, and behaviours in line with the Buen Vivir principles. Vivir Bien is a crucial element in achieving ongoing change for Socio-Eco Wellbeing within a community with the long-term goal of Buen Vivir. Assuming the conditions and structures are in place politically for a community to strive for Buen Vivir, the role of the community in its daily practices is a fundamental condition of meeting the principles.

The core principles underlie practice and equally communities can draw on practices to promote the principles, for example by:

- Adopting a reciprocal approach to our relationship with nature;
- Public participation and enabling decision-making in a manner that honours that reciprocity;
- Fostering solidarity and harmony through an environment of community;
- Ensuring equity in participation in public decision-making;
- Manifesting a responsibility to participate in decision-making;
- Educating future generations on the principles of Buen Vivir;
- Participating in economic life;
- Understanding their fundamental rights and responsibilities, including those of the environment;
- Exercising those rights;
- Promoting and protecting cultural values and practices;
- Valuing the role of health in a community.

These practices, guided by the principles of Buen Vivir, can feed back into a policy framework for Buen Vivir, which in turn with the above analysis helps to demonstrate how the local interfaces with the global. Cooperation is a vital factor in practice. For many, the cooperation of organisations and the state helps bring resources and finance to help capacitate and meet the fundamental needs of a community. This cooperation, however, is not only economic, but also in terms of knowledge. It arms communities with the capacity to be critical against policy decisions; as Leandro says, what is needed is to

> Work with the people so that the population is critical, so that the population has the capacity to discern, capacity to debate, to have informed criterion based on something. Then through that we would achieve richer consensus, ideas would be richer, and participation would [also] be richer.

A cooperative hybrid Buen Vivir–Vivir Bien approach that includes a policies for democratic participation for implementing Buen Vivir can be further distilled into the first three of six guiding principles for transformative change through the SDGs (Hujo et al. 2016):

1. Re-embed markets in social and ecological norms by making policies and building institutions that make the economy work for society and respect planetary boundaries, rather than the other way around (Buen Vivir principle: SSE);
2. Reverse the existing normative hierarchy to position social and environment priorities above economic ones (Buen Vivir principle: Reciprocity);
3. Promote and enable meaningful political participation and empowerment through inclusive and transparent political processes, access to information and assets, and governance reforms at the national and international levels (Buen Vivir principle: Democratic participation).

Needs and avoiding the materiality trap

On the first guiding principle, implementation of Buen Vivir would shift the focus from economic growth and GDP as a driving indicator of wellbeing to a more socially and environmentally just economic approach through an SSE. The SSE comes under the material dimension of Buen Vivir, and, as discussed in Chapter Four, economic principles under Buen Vivir go beyond material "progress" or accumulation and economic growth and focus on satisfying fundamental needs and achieving the communal vision of sustainability and wellbeing.

The SSE requires ethical consumption, communal wellbeing, redistribution of wealth, and a system that is inclusive and participatory, founded in endogenous self-determination, and usually small in scale and local. Ultimately, the change in productive matrix from a growth model based on the exploitation and exportation of natural resources also requires a cognitive change on behalf of both society and the state.

Linked to the material dimension is the issue of poverty. As identified in Chapter Four, a Buen Vivir approach conceives a different way of looking at poverty than in the current model of development – one which also considers poverty from environmental, cultural, and social wealth and which does not measure economic poverty based solely on externally devised development indicators, but rather on the contextual needs of the community in question. This is not to say that economic poverty is disregarded, but that it is approached differently.

Goal 1 of the SDGs seeks to "eradicate poverty in all its forms," but it still only alludes to material poverty. Moreover, the goals aim to eradicate extreme poverty for everyone, everywhere by 2030, but "eradicating poverty of this magnitude would require more than just weeding around the edges of the problem – it would require changing the rules of the global economy to make it fairer for the world's majority" (Hickel 2015).

Prior to COVID-19, many people were of the view that changing the global economy on a structural level may not be a feasible target in the short-term, but the unintended degrowth of the global economy due to the crisis has left open a door of opportunity to address the roots of the problem, rather than simply continuing with the status quo (Chassagne 2020). The approach to productivity that Buen Vivir takes by diversifying the economy with reciprocity in mind and moving towards post-extractivism promises to help support the necessary changes. Moreover, proposals such as the SSE which are central to Buen Vivir's economic approach can help focus on redistribution on the micro or community level, which can feed back into policy over the long-term. Accordingly, neoliberal arguments which have typically used measures such as GDP would become redundant, as wellbeing under Buen Vivir also takes into account multiple non-economic poverties or wealths.

From a post-developmental point of view, the issue of poverty is problematic and the consequence is that poverty alleviation "slips off the map" (Pieterse 2000), which can have dire consequences for those populations which have been adversely affected by development in the first place. There is no doubt that extreme economic poverty is real and worrisome, and so a denial of poverty will only result in worsening conditions. The SDGs, however, fail to acknowledge the structural causes of the problem owing to extreme wealth accumulation and consumption supported by policies of extractivism and industrial exploitation (Hickel 2015). What is needed in the dialectical debate is an acknowledgement that development's economic-centred notion of poverty is outdated, and there needs to be a focus on the other dimensions of poverty equally, as well as a fundamental change of the root causes of extreme poverty.

"Other" notions of poverty, or "softer" issues of poverty or non-material wealth (e.g. social cohesion and a healthy environment), must be considered and promoted at a policy level and in full consideration of reciprocity through locally identified needs. Otherwise, it risks reverting back to the top-down, growth-centred approach of the current model, which does not consider divergent and contextual realities.

The problem with an exogenous identification of needs is that it seldom results in positive outcomes because it is often economically rooted and does not take into account local context, nor does it consider the other "wealths" of a community. Well-meaning governments and outside organisations often identify needs based on Western indicators for development, akin to the targets promoted by the SDGs, but do not consider the real needs and realities on the ground, the satisfaction of which can often lead to better social and environmental outcomes.

Rodriguez says it's "because each community or city has its own history, and when organisations of government projects come out of political intervention, they come without having anything to do with us. Nothing is adapted to our reality here in any respect." He argues that "our needs have nothing to do with NGOs or public employees. They can be heartfelt and want to do the right thing – but from above, since the government mandate comes already written, says this or that has to be applied – but it's got nothing to do with them."

Laura also states that the exogenous identification and satisfaction of needs is neither effective nor beneficial in a community and often creates a false reality, "What happens in [development] planning and what is often very vertical is that they [the government] come and impose things on you. I have seen it in other places, how they impose their needs to construct something. Instead, they first build you the sewer, [then] they tell you that you have to clean the street."

The fulfilment of "soft" issues and the principles of Buen Vivir cannot be measured by top-down, exogenously identified quantitative methods and therefore can only be captured at the local level, with a focus on qualitative means. As discussed in Chapter Four, needs satisfaction under Buen Vivir must not only cover basic needs related to economic development, but must also include all other types of psychological needs. This is where it is important to ensure that the identification, implementation, and measurement of the principles of Buen Vivir are pursued endogenously. The question for both the practical and policy implications of such an approach then becomes, how do we measure whether these needs are being met? As Valentina also argues, once the political structures are in place for such participation, communities also have a responsibility to participate and become accountable to the process: "We ourselves must manifest, propose needs." Therefore, communities, governments, and organisations all play a role in Buen Vivir, as well as in the measurement, not of linear progress rooted in economics, but rather of the achievement of its principles (and consequently Socio-Eco Wellbeing) through change and the satisfaction of real needs.

The issue of measurement

In every political system there is a requirement to understand whether fundamental needs are being met, at the very minimum. The data related to the measurement of Buen Vivir is somewhat contradictory. At the institutional level Buen Vivir is already measured in terms of statistical values by the national government, in quantitative measurements that allow governments to track progress over time. From an exogenous standpoint, Delgado et al. (2010) assert that "if as external actors we are interested in the construction of Buen Vivir we need to define indicators to better understand it." However, in the Indigenous worldview of Sumak Kawsay, there is no such thing as linear progress; it is in fact antithetic to the attainment of Sumak. That suggests that in the true ethos of Buen Vivir as a translation of the indigenous worldview, it should not be measured. Buen Vivir, however, has undergone a necessary process of co-construction and has evolved, since its original Indigenous conception, so as not to end in a co-optation of Indigenous beliefs. While it may be inappropriate to refer to a Western developmental concept like "progress," in an alternative concept like Buen Vivir going from a state where Buen Vivir does not yet exist, to one where it has been achieved, involves change. Therefore, one must consider the issue of measurement if policy is to play any part of it, and if as a society we can begin to understand that change. Moreover, most key informants, both Indigenous and non-Indigenous, believe that Buen Vivir can and should be measured.

While there is certainly a vital role for the local and national quantitative measurement such as water, energy, emissions, waste, public health, education, sustainability, and climate change, research often belittles the role of qualitative measurement, such as is conducted in social science for example. These sorts of data also have a place in the quantitative measurement of policy on issues that affect Buen Vivir, which in line with the principles for Buen Vivir can better be understood to support a set of aspirational, long-term goals for policy. In that regard there are two roles for measurement: One refers to the quantitative measurement of government targets towards the aspirational Buen Vivir policy that support global and national sustainability and wellbeing commitments, considering the satisfaction of basic needs; the other refers to the qualitative assessment of Vivir Bien to ensure that people's fundamental physical and psychological needs are being met, and that the rights of both society and nature are being upheld.

On the one hand, the key informants generally accepted the role of statistical measurement in understanding issues that impact on Buen Vivir such as education, housing, water sanitation, and decent work. On the other, many believe that most of the principles of Buen Vivir cannot simply be reduced only to statistics and merit a more qualitative understanding. On a policy level, the need for qualitative measurement and assessment of data on behaviours, values, and beliefs in the SDGs has already been identified as a priority policy area for implementation of the goals. Therefore, through qualitative understandings of Buen Vivir assessed locally, governments would be able to easily determine how meeting each of the Buen Vivir principles will be facilitating the attainment of the global SDGs.

On the community level, qualitative measurement would help both drive and guide the process of change through Vivir Bien. Indigenous community leader David sees the value in understanding whether or not a community has advanced against the principles of Buen Vivir through qualitative means, and suggests "a census to find out if they have progressed if they have identified themselves as having Buen Vivir. Then according to that do an analysis depending on the communities, to assess whether they are making progress." Javier argues that there are certain things that affect Buen Vivir that are already measured, but not statistically: "One can measure the distance, the difference, that is the easiest to measure. The gap between reality and what happens, and the application of Buen Vivir. But what is not measurable is the process, that is not possible." Laura also believes that Buen Vivir should be measured qualitatively. She argues, "I think that this issue of measuring Buen Vivir from the institutional part is closely related eco-nomic development. So that's misleading because then everything is money, [but] it is not true. In other words, we can have a good income but these other things that do not allow us to be tranquil and happy also exist."

There is an assumption by organisational and governmental key informants that happiness is often related to economic development or levels of poverty. Talking about the correlation between poverty and happiness, Rafael tells me that it is hard to be happy when one is poor, though he is speaking of the economic dimension of poverty: "It [happiness] is very difficult for a poor person, or someone of extreme poverty, right? Just like it is very difficult for a rich person or someone of extreme wealth to be happy." Javier asks how this translates to daily practices: "In the end, the challenge to Vivir Bien is the universal desire to be happy. So then, how do we measure that?" This highlights the importance of a hybrid practice–policy approach to Buen Vivir because, as Gale (2018) states, "what individuals think and feel is an outcome of the complex biological, social, cognitive and cultural factors and cannot be taken at face value."

The need to move towards a more holistic measurement of wellbeing has long been noted by governments, as well as academics and economists. At the 2012 High Level Meeting on Wellbeing and Happiness: Defining a New Economic Paradigm, the Prime Minister of Bhutan, Jigmi Y Thinley (Royal Government of Bhutan 2012), stated:

The GDP led development model that compels boundless growth on a planet with limited resources no longer makes economic sense. It is the cause of our irresponsible, immoral, and self-destructive actions. Irresponsible, because we extract, produce, consume and waste ever more, even as natural resources are rapidly depleting. Immoral and unethical because having consumed far beyond our share of natural wealth, our reckless profligacy amid unconscion-able inequities comes at the cost of what belongs to generations unborn. Self-destructive, because, aided by technology, we are bringing about the collapse of our ecological life support systems. Having far outlived its usefulness, our fundamentally flawed economic arrangement, has itself, become the cause of all problems. Within its framework, there lies no solution to the economic, ecological, social and security crises that plague the world today and threaten to consume humanity. Mankind is like a meteor, blazing toward self-annihi-lation along with all other innocent life forms. But this course can be changed if we act now.

The same sentiment was echoed widely and strongly amongst the key inform-ants with the opinion that if we carry on with business as usual it will lead to the eventual self-destruction of the current way of doing things. Akin to H.E. Thinley's metaphor of a meteor, Emmanuel likens humankind in the current sys-tem of development to living organisms without the capacity to stop producing: "[In the current system] we do not have the capacity to stop, because [similarly] if the thermophilic bacteria had the capacity to stop they would not manage to transform the compost to 70–80 degrees, but they cannot stop, they produce, and reproduce, that feeds back… it's the self-destruction of the system."

The inclusion of multidimensional aspects of poverty in national planning is a good step in the right direction to including other values other than economic; however, to comprehensively tackle the issue of Buen Vivir these policy measurements must also include the "softer" issues of poverty or non-material wealth – those more socially oriented issues which cannot effectively be measured statistically – such as social cohesion and a healthy environment with full acknowledgement of the cyclical character of the nature–society relationship. These soft issues are arguably imperative to happiness, which in turn is an outcome of Buen Vivir as revealed by the data. For many of the key informants, happiness leads to Socio-Eco Wellbeing; it is part of the outcome, not the end target, for Buen Vivir.

Moreover, "soft" issues cannot be effectively measured quantitatively and therefore can only be captured at the local level. This is where it is important to ensure that the identification, implementation, and qualitative measurement of the principles of Buen Vivir are pursued at the grassroots level. There must be a co-construction of knowledge and a hybrid convergence of policy and practice for Buen Vivir to be achieved. It cannot be solely based on communities acting individually, nor can it be attained by governments acting unilaterally. As Utting (2015) states, "effective co-construction also relies on full commitment by the government, which in turn requires sufficient capacity, coordination and resources in all relevant branches of government at both national and local levels." Therefore, the role governments and organisations play in Buen Vivir measurement – not of linear progress, but rather the achievement of its principles through change and the satisfaction of needs – must be assessed.

Buen Vivir is a contested concept, though, that is tailorable to specific context, unlike other more universal frameworks for measurement such as the Human Development Index (HDI). There is the argument that the priorities reflected in the HDI are no longer appropriate as they do not reflect the "needs and values of the population that affect" (Ruttenberg 2013). To address that gap, Buen Vivir may best be served by "living indicators," measurement that is tailorable to the specific community context, its particular definition of Buen Vivir, and its fundamental needs as related to the core principles. Javier affirms that only this type of measurement can help society understand if Buen Vivir is obtained, "because we also need indicators to see that we are advancing [towards Buen Vivir]. But perhaps [by] *mobile* indicators, *living* indicators." Here he is speaking of the ultimate outcome of Buen Vivir, the utopia, not Vivir Bien. According to the data, this can only be successfully achieved through democratic participatory processes, supported by a socially organised society. What this might look like is further discussed in the next section.

As the data from this study demonstrates, the measurement of Buen Vivir should be centred around community-defined indicators, to empower communities to understand the priority areas for meeting their own needs for Socio-Eco Wellbeing. As Laura says, indicators for Buen Vivir "can be qualitative. But I think they should be indicators that are developed here – in the community – from our reality. So, we are going to measure [it] ourselves or [for example] how *we* are going to define the question of poverty." This type of community-driven assessment is closely intertwined with the practice of Vivir Bien.

Qualitative data can make sense of the aspects of the community which cannot be captured quantitively and make "measures more comprehensible and relevant to respondents, provide contextual information to explain particular outcomes, and, most importantly, ensure that influence measures of human well-being are based on what matters to people" (Camfield 2014). This is important because, as Fernando asserts, "Buen Vivir has to be a strategy to change the way people think in the long run. It has to be sustainable by the same society, it does not have to be sustainable by a political party. Good living has to be transformed into rights but also into obligations."

In sum, Buen Vivir is implemented practically – the process of which is Vivir Bien – and it is managed endogenously, at the community-level, facilitated by governments (particularly local government) and with the support and mediation of organisations. From that perspective, communities must have the tools with which they can start to identify their fundamental needs and implement the principles of Buen Vivir, for both long-term structural and systemic change (Buen Vivir) and daily through behaviour, practice, and attitudes (Vivir Bien). At this juncture, I therefore propose the following framework for Living Well as a community tool, based on the entire findings of this research.

Buen Vivir's pathway to Socio-Eco Wellbeing: A framework for change

This research has identified the need for a framework of 'living indicators' that are in line with the principles of Buen Vivir to provide the community with an effective tool to achieve Buen Vivir and, in the process, satisfy its fundamental needs by its own processes. It requires locally identified needs and a community assessment of the principles of Buen Vivir. The framework in table 8.1 is a proposal for a community tool which allows communities to identify their specific needs under each of the principles of Buen Vivir through a stoplight approach. It is a convergence of both practice and policy, which provides communities with the capacity to identify their fundamental needs and determine, in cooperation with other actors the ways in which to actualise those needs. The community thus defines the indicators under the principles of Buen Vivir, and according to their own fundamental needs through democratic participatory processes. Fundamental to the framework are the three pillars identified in Chapter Two: Social, spiritual, material. The framework puts social and environmental wellbeing at the core and comprises three necessary and interrelated elements: Principles, practices, and fundamental needs satisfaction.

As pointed out in Chapter Four, the HSD approach to fundamental needs, which comprises both basic needs and psychological needs, is the most appropriate in the context of Buen Vivir because: 1) It allows for contextualisation; 2) it is based on self-determination, participation, and a reciprocal relationship between the community and nature; and 3) they include both the tangible basic needs and the intangible psychological needs identified as part of this research. Additionally, HSD takes the approach of fundamental needs and self-reliance as a bottom-up process, where the state facilitates this process rather than drives it (Guillen-Royo 2015). Like Buen Vivir, the economy in HSD has a subsidiary rather than a primary role, supporting the satisfaction of fundamental needs without detriment to the environment. Participation plays a central role in the implementation of the methodology which emphasises the importance of a horizontal relationship between communities and local, regional, national, and global governance (Guillen-Royo 2015). Therefore, through analysis I have adapted Max-Neef's nine axiological needs for Human Scale Development (HSD) to align with the Buen Vivir principles.

HSD still focuses on human needs, whereas fundamental needs in Buen Vivir include both human and environmental needs. So, the principles which encompass environmental needs (reciprocity, healthy environment, food security, holistic rights) can be aligned with the Max-Neef's axiological needs that consider the environment (subsistence, protection, and leisure) to identify ways in which to ensure those needs are being met through the Buen Vivir principles. In adapting the nine axiological needs, I have changed the language slightly for certain needs with more communal connotation and away from individualism, to better reflect the ethos of Buen Vivir:

- Continuance (subsistence) – the process of sustaining life, livelihoods, and the living environment with respect for its cyclicality;
- Protection;
- Affection;
- Understanding;
- Democratic participation (participation) – beyond "participation" as it is used in traditional development;
- Leisure;
- Creation;
- Connection (identity) – encompassing not only self-identity but a deeper connection to oneself, one's community, and one's environment;
- Autonomy (freedom) – referring to increased community capacity, autonomy, and reduced dependence on externalities.

The community identifies its specific fundamental needs based on the 17 core principles of Buen Vivir and classified by Max-Neef's axiological needs, with consideration for its own practices or ways the principles are realised on a daily basis. They do not indicate "linear progress" against traditional development objectives; rather, they base social and environmental wellbeing on the attainment of community defined Buen Vivir through the satisfaction of fundamental needs. Buen Vivir aims for net positive change based on the particular geographical, socio-economic, and cultural context of a community. Moreover, basing a framework on the principles of Buen Vivir drives the consideration of needs in a more biocentric way, respecting both environmental and human needs rather than viewing the environment as a commodity to meet the needs of society.

This tool is to support a community's own processes for defining what Buen Vivir is to its members and what the fundamental needs are of the community and its environment in order to attain Buen Vivir. Nonetheless, as Buen Vivir is plural, its practical implications influence and are influenced by its political implications. Participation is a prerequisite for both the principles and the fundamental needs being actualised. Therefore, it is important to keep in mind the importance of democratic participatory processes in implementing the framework, and in particular in instituting a participatory budget with cooperation between the community and local government. The measurement of the satisfaction of fundamental needs within the community setting can be undertaken by a using the stoplight approach (green, yellow, and red): Green meaning it has been met, yellow meaning it is of concern, and red meaning immediate action required.

The stoplight approach allows a community to decide whether a principle has been met through the satisfaction of locally identified fundamental needs. The indicators are based on community perception of the current state of Buen Vivir and can assist local communities in conjunction with local governments to identify priority areas for action for Buen Vivir for a participatory budget, as well as create an awareness of the priorities for behavioural change under Vivir Bien. A stoplight system can incorporate information in a way where one can easily see whether a principle has been met when statistical indicators are inappropriate, and is recommended for qualitative indicators as the best way to understand if conditions are met (*Wgi's working group on "indicators"* 2016).

The intention is that it can be used by communities and for communities and can be used to support community processes in participatory planning and budgeting in cooperation with local government participatory budgeting. The framework can be used in a two-step process, first to identify which needs are unmet and then to identify ways in which the needs can be satisfied. The stoplight representation can help with prioritising needs to determine the implementation of projects and can further help communities identify which principles have been met through this process. At the same time, it can help communities understand the different roles in satisfying those needs through practices, values, attitudes, actions, organisation, and policy.

The indicators can be further scaled up from the community level to demonstrate how Buen Vivir locally can be complimented to meet national or local governmental requirements. A cross-analysis with table 7.1 in Chapter Seven can assist policy-makers in understanding how each principle allows them to meet the broader SDGs. The stoplight method can also help communities identify their various poverties (factors which are lacking in a community, e.g. environmental, economic) and their wealths (factors which are rich in the community, e.g. cultural, social) to strengthen community solidarity, harmony, and connection (Table 8.1).

Buen Vivir will require rethinking sustainability as an endogenous approach with the support of governments and organisations for its full realisation at the community level and the attainment of Socio-Eco Wellbeing. Implementing Buen

Table 8.1 Framework for Vivir Bien/Living Well

Principles	Fundamental needs								
	Continuance	Protection	Affection	Understanding	Democratic participation	Leisure	Creation	Connection	Autonomy
Equality									
Fundamental rights									
Community									
Solidarity									
Harmony									
SSE									
Decent work									
Leisure									
Good health									
Culture									
Education									
Reciprocity									
Healthy Environment									
Food security									
Self-determination									
Respect									
Participation									

Vivir in this way can help achieve the utopian long-term goals for sustainability and wellbeing with more rapid and genuine effect than current neoliberal approaches.

Nonetheless, its implementation must come from the people on the ground, with a high level of political will and facilitated by organisations who can act as mediators to help prevent the co-optation of local processes for a wider agenda. At the grassroots level, this includes changes that need to be made day-to-day on a practical level to achieve real social and environmental justice and sustainability built around communal practices. At the political level, it refers rather to a political concept anchored in law and policy which provides the structures and processes for communities to pursue their own conception of Buen Vivir through democratic participation.

The proposed framework can help facilitate the convergence of policy and practice. Locally implemented and qualitatively measured living indicators that seek to satisfy community-identified needs would not only help achieve self-determination and real, grassroots-led democratic participation, they would also help influence policy by feeding back into the more quantitative structures of measurement required at a governmental level. This would allow both the achievement of Socio-Eco Wellbeing at a local level through Vivir Bien and government to fulfil its global political responsibilities.

To that end, the proposed framework for Living Well would seek to serve as a tool for communities on the ground to identify fundamental needs through living indicators based on the principles of Buen Vivir and manifested in Vivir Bien. Helping communities meet the principles of Buen Vivir for its full realisation could be a beneficial way of capacitating communities to realise their own conception of Buen Vivir.

References

Camfield, L 2014, 'Qualitative indicators of development', in AC Michalos, ed., *Encyclopedia of quality of life and well-being research*, Springer Netherlands, Dordrecht. doi: 10.1007/978-94-007-0753-5_2338.

Chassagne, N 2020, *Here's what the coronavirus can teach us about tackling climate change*, The Conversation, viewed <https://theconversation.com/heres-what-the-co ronavirus-pandemic-can-teach-us-about-tackling-climate-change-134399>.

Delgado, F, Rist, S & Escobar, C 2010, *El desarrollo endógeno sustentable como interfaz para implementar el vivir bien en la gestión pública boliviana*, Plural, La Paz.

Eversole, R 2014, *Knowledge partnering for community development*, Routledge, London.

Gale, F 2018, *The political economy of sustainability*, Edward Elgar Publishing, Cheltenham.

Guillen-Royo, M 2015, *Sustainability and wellbeing: Human-scale development in practice*, Routledge, London.

Hickel, J 2015, 'The problem with saving the world. The un's new sustainable development goals aim to save the world without transforming it', *Jacobin Magazine*.

Howard, J & Wheeler, J 2015, 'What community development and citizen participation should contribute to the new global framework for sustainable development', *Community Development Journal*, vol. 50, no. 4, pp. 552–70. doi: 10.1093/cdj/bsv033.

Hujo, K, Braumann, H, Esquivel, V, van Griethuysen, P, Krause, D, Utting, P & Yi, I 2016, *Policy innovations for transformative change: Implementing the 2030 agenda for sustainable development*, UNRISD Flagship Report 2016, UNRISD, Geneva, Switerland.

OECD 2016, *Wgi's working group on "indicators"* , CET highlights from Discussion OECD, <http://www.oecd.org/gov/regional-policy/Summary-Webinar-Indicators-15N ov16.pdf>.

Pieterse, JN 2000, 'After post-development', *Third World Quarterly*, vol. 21, no. 2, pp. 175–91. doi: 10.2307/3993415.

Royal Government of Bhutan 2012, *Defining a new economic paradigm: The report of the high level meeting on wellbeing and happiness*, The Permanent Mission of the Kingdom of Bhutan to the United Nations, New York.

Ruttenberg, T 2013, 'Wellbeing economics and buen vivir: Development alternatives for inclusive human security', *Fletcher Journal of Human Security*, vol. XXVIII, pp. 68–93. <https://fletcher.tufts.edu/Praxis/~/media/Fletcher/Microsites/praxis/xxviii/arti cle4_Ruttenberg_BuenVivir.pdf>.

Utting, P 2015, *Social and solidarity economy: Beyond the fringe*, Zed Books, London.

9 New horizons for Socio-Eco Wellbeing
Concluding remarks

Buen Vivir has gone on a conceptual journey from its Indigenous roots. As a concept under co-construction, there has been a lot of uncertainty about what exactly Buen Vivir entails, what its principles are, and how they can offer a concrete path for its practical application. One of the ambiguities lies in its heterogeneity, the fact that it is contested by different groups of actors; which is why in this book I sought to bring together their points of convergence to better understand the concept, while honouring its endogeneity. My aim has been to demonstrate how Buen Vivir could become a viable and practical alternative to Sustainable Development.

Chapter One started with a brief history of development to the emergence of Sustainable Development. Here, it was clear that mainstream Sustainable Development has failed to achieve its aims. It was developed in reaction to the failure of traditional development to consider environmental aspects in development policy and practice, but it is proving in itself to be unsustainable. The main critique of Sustainable Development is twofold: That it is anthropocentric, and that it is still based on the neoliberal idea of progress through economic growth.

I discussed how this model based on unbridled economic growth has been argued in the literature to be at the root of social and environmental problems like climate change, global inequality, and poverty – the lattermost of which certain intellectuals maintain is a modern construct. This failure of development has led post-developmentalists to call for "alternatives to development."

In Chapter Two, I examined the growing legitimacy of the post-development argument for alternatives to development. In Latin America, several progressive countries like Ecuador and Bolivia have been quite vocal in their advocating for a change in paradigm – away from neoliberalism, towards a post-development future. This has spurred Buen Vivir to be argued as a possible alternative to development, though in line with post-development's premises there have been discrepancies between discourse and practice.

Underlying neoliberalism's growth imperative is the push for extractivism, which has long driven development policy in much of Latin America. This has resulted in a nature–society dualism which has led to greater social and environmental issues. In recent times Latin America's more progressive left including Ecuador has changed the focus to neoextractivism, which is just, as Acosta (2013) has pointed out, the other side of the same coin. The only thing that has changed is the role of government. The status quo prevails in all but name.

The literature ascertained that what is now important in the search for alternatives is working towards retrieving, articulating, and identifying the underlying objectives of Sustainable Development, rather than just criticising it. Instead what is needed is "new paradigm thinking", working towards a dialectical solution to achieve transformation and Socio-Eco Wellbeing, rather than a direct attack on Sustainable Development. Heeding the post-developmental call for "alternatives to development," I argue for Buen Vivir as both a practical and viable alternative to Sustainable Development.

Conceptually, however, Buen Vivir as a post-development alternative to development has only resulted in discursive critique and has not offered any concrete and practical solutions. In that light, I continued Chapter Three with a critical conceptual analysis of Buen Vivir, to better understand the concept and work towards a practical way forward.

I examined Buen Vivir's Indigenous origins, but affirmed that, as a plural concept, and one "under construction," the way that it is understood in the literature is as culmination of community, politics, and academia. Nonetheless, the importance of its endogenous approach must be emphasised yet implemented in cooperation with all actors and epistemologies. This chapter identified Buen Vivir as a contested concept, and one which lacks universal definition but contains a set of core common principles – as opposed to Sustainable Development which has a universal definition but is contested by its loose principles. I argued that this point is its greatest strength as it leaves it up to the communities to provide the prescriptive elements, meaning that it is contextual and sensitive to the realities on the ground.

Through an analysis of the literature I identified 15 preliminary conceptual principles of Buen Vivir, demarcated to six dimensions: Social cohesion, sustainability, empowerment, livelihood, equity, and capabilities. This is further classified under three pillars: Social, spiritual, and material. I also argued that rather than being heralded as an offence on Sustainable Development, it can be embraced plurally, because to try to force a sudden and immediate change in the system is unrealistic and will end up in Buen Vivir being largely ignored and a "short-lived discursive enterprise" (Vanhulst & Beling 2014).

This critical review of the literature started to put the pieces of the conceptual puzzle together for a better understanding of what Buen Vivir entails.

A coalescence of the core common principles was a start, but it was missing the empirical evidence: How do communities understand and practice Buen Vivir; and is there scope for measurement? This necessitated empirical research to complete this understanding and work towards a concrete path for implementation, paving the way for my field research in Ecuador, because as Escobar (1995) justified, "The nature of alternatives as a research question and a social practice can be most fruitfully gleaned from the specific manifestations of such alternatives in concrete local settings."

If Buen Vivir is to become a viable alternative, then its application in community practice is the key determinant. To understand this, I conducted ethnographic fieldwork study within Cotacachi County in Ecuador to find out the community understanding and how it might play out in practice. Cotacachi is a region which has a historical battle with extractivist activity, but one where its people also value their ability to live the Good Life, to fight for Buen Vivir. For this reason, we have much to learn from these communities in terms of social and environmental wellbeing.

Chapter Four began Part II of this book, examining my empirical fieldwork findings. To support an endogenous approach to Buen Vivir, I combined fieldwork data with existing literature to develop a final set of core principles delineated under the same three pillars: Social, spiritual, and material. This changes from the three-pronged social, environmental, and economic pillars of Sustainable Development where the latter two are reliant on a market economy with economic growth as its end-goal. These pillars denote a more holistic and biocentric approach to Socio-Eco Wellbeing.

The principles of Buen Vivir that incorporate various epistemologies with practice have resulted in contested meanings and change according to the context in which they are interpreted. This contextuality is one of Buen Vivir's greatest strengths and the factor which maintains it as an alternative that can fill the gaps of a failed one-size-fits-all Sustainable Development approach.

The principles are interrelated and interdependent. If the principles are not applied, then fundamental needs cannot be met and vice-versa. Therefore, an integral approach to needs satisfaction must be taken which includes not just basic needs, but psychological needs too; and not just human needs, but also those of the environment. Importantly, these needs must be identified at the community level, allowing communities to define their own approach to Buen Vivir.

In this chapter, key informants emphasised the importance of meeting fundamental needs, in order to achieve Buen Vivir. In their understanding, fundamental needs include basic needs and psychological needs such as culture, leisure time, community, family, and more spiritual needs such as respect and a sense of reciprocity with the environment. A fundamental needs approach channels the Max-Neef, Elizalde, and Hopenhayn (1991) conception of needs and allows for: 1) Contextualisation; 2) self-determination; and 3) both tangible and intangible needs. Beyond that, it also takes into consideration the needs of the environment.

I found that to meet fundamental needs under Buen Vivir, a new economic model must be adopted. The data and the literature identified the Social and Solidarity Economy (SSE) as the most appropriate economic approach that aligns with the principles under the material pillar. It takes into account other types of "wealth," which also act as capabilities. In terms of non-economic wealth, it is important for policy to include these in poverty measurements, to enable a move away from economic growth as a driver and measure for wellbeing. The idea of using only the natural resources you need to meet fundamental needs, not desires, is central. An SSE can help guide this approach because it means taking a biocentric and local perspective towards meeting needs, rather than a fast, consumer-based economy perspective towards satisfying desires.

While the material pillar of Buen Vivir denounces traditional development's emphasis on growth, economic productivity still plays a crucial role in Buen Vivir, albeit on more just terms. The data found that an SSE approach, supported by local government and implemented by communities, provides an ideal economic model for communities to meet their own needs and determine their own path for Buen Vivir. It changes the paradigm from one promoting growth and wealth accumulation to one based on needs, community, and the sustainable use of resources, ultimately helping to achieve intergenerational social and ecological sustainability. While the social and ecological dimensions are the most important outcomes of Buen Vivir, the unique material pillar is fundamental in understanding Buen Vivir's contribution to both sustainability and wellbeing – Socio-Eco Wellbeing – and ensuring that the approach remains an alternative to traditional development models rather than an alternative within the current model.

Chapter Five demonstrated that it is not enough for society to leave sustainable Socio-Eco Wellbeing to governments, authorities, and institutions; change must also happen at the local level in the attitudes, behaviours, and practices of the people. The local level change is referred to as "Vivir Bien" or "Living Well," and it is how the principles of Buen Vivir are manifested laterally, daily, and in practice. The distinction of Vivir Bien (daily practice) from Buen Vivir (policy) was the most important finding because it highlights the dual practical–political implications of Buen Vivir.

Key informants explained that Vivir Bien translated from the Kichwa term "Ally Kawsay" is not an endpoint, but rather a state of being, as opposed to the political utopia of Buen Vivir. It is the day-to-day changes communities make to their reality. In that respect several examples of this practice were highlighted in this chapter. These practices are manifested by the communities under study and generally involve cooperation with one of more key actors. Although the examples were particular to the context of the field site, they nonetheless exemplify what the principles related to (or which are dimensions of) a healthy environment, reciprocity, education, solidarity, culture, community, decent work, and the SSE can look like on the ground.

As Vivir Bien is coupled with the utopian goal of Buen Vivir, a hybrid approach must be adopted in which policy and practice cooperate through endogenous processes. This hybrid approach ensures that Buen Vivir's plurality is honoured. This does not mean generalising the endogenous framework or reverting to a top-down variation of participation as has been done in the past in development, as this will just risk becoming a part of the status quo. Rather, it means that the power structures must shift to let communities manage their own notion of Buen Vivir as the agents of their own processes; and that communities work with organisations as the mediators between themselves and government, not as agents of Buen Vivir. This partnership with organisations is key to avoiding the co-optation of processes to a wider agenda that has been criticised of occurring in processes of development and its variations.

A hybrid approach where Vivir Bien, as the community practice, and Buen Vivir, as the policy response, converge may seem complex in a development model that is very much top-down-driven, but it is necessary because 1) political will and cooperation need to be present to achieve Buen Vivir; and 2) daily practices at the individual, family, and community levels are what will ultimately bring about real change. In such an approach Vivir Bien is scaled up to achieve the principles of Buen Vivir and influence policy. Buen Vivir policy can be understood as the political condition to facilitate the attainment of Vivir Bien on a practical level, and Vivir Bien can be understood as the endogenous implementation of the principles of Buen Vivir. Both are necessary and equally as important, albeit one at a high level (Buen Vivir) and the other at a practical level (Vivir Bien). Therefore, "new institutional mechanisms capable of reconciling participation with heterogeneity are required on the part of the state" (Max-Neef, Elizalde & Hopenhayn 1994).

In that respect, the data found that applying Buen Vivir as a policy for opening up structures and spaces for endogenous change would result in increasing capacity and capabilities for communities to achieve Socio-Eco Wellbeing. Buen Vivir policy can therefore make it possible to achieve the aims at all levels of society but is nonetheless driven by community practice and decisions regarding needs.

Key informants affirmed that there is thus a vital role for government, especially at the local level to create these structures and processes necessary for achieving Vivir Bien as a practice of Buen Vivir within communities. Taking Cotacachi County as a case study, I found that this can best be achieved through a participatory democracy where participatory budgeting plays a key role in community self-determination. The data stipulated that organisations also play an important role in implementing Buen Vivir through financial and knowledge cooperation, and by acting as "moderators" of a bottom-up approach to prevent political co-optation. Buen Vivir consequently becomes a practical tool for community-led change. Understood in this new way as opposed to a political co-optation, a theoretical paradigm, or a purely Indigenous worldview limited to cultural nuances, Buen Vivir offers real promise as a practical and viable alternative to Sustainable Development that can lead change through concrete practice based on community values and needs.

Nonetheless, the concept itself is at risk of being co-opted for political interests with contradictory policies, which jeopardise it as an unachievable utopia. Yes, broad aspirational political goals can work alongside specific concrete practices, but these must be achieved plurally. In this symbiosis, the concept then takes on dual meaning: Buen Vivir, or Good Living, is the aspirational political ideal, which can be associated to larger, global goals for wellbeing and sustainability such as the SDGs; and Vivir Bien, or Living Well, is the practical tool for communities to achieve wellbeing and sustainability for themselves, within the spirit of endogenously led change, self-determination, and participation.

This analysis brings me back to the plurality of Buen Vivir. In Chapter Five, I also discussed how cooperation is vital to implementing Buen Vivir at the local level, because if communities could do it by themselves, it would already have been achieved. The empirical data found therefore that each group of key actors plays a role. The role of governments at all levels, but particularly local government, is to act as facilitators providing the spaces and structures for communities to identify and implement Buen Vivir for themselves. This includes ensuring genuine participation through a participatory democratic approach. In Cotacachi, this is demonstrated through participatory budgeting. Government also has a role though policy and regulation to lead towards a genuinely post-extractive economy.

This will not happen immediately, but transitions can start immediately starting with policy and supported by consumer and community behaviours and practices. It involves a shift in thinking and doing from society at the centre of the idea of wellbeing, to a more biocentric idea whereby the needs of the environment should also be taken into account. This can be done on the political level through programs, policy, and education, and according to nature rights; and it can also be done at the community level through a shift in values and ways of thinking about the environment and the use of natural resources.

The role of communities is then to fulfil their rights and responsibilities in terms of participation, as well as to follow the principles for Buen Vivir in daily practices in a Vivir Bien approach, changing attitudes and behaviours to reflect that. Finally, the role of organisations is to act as the power brokers or mediators to avoid the co-optation of Buen Vivir for political purposes, help communities find their "voice," and assist with knowledge and resources where appropriately identified by communities.

After developing a solid understanding of what Buen Vivir entails, how it is practiced, and the role of the different key actors, Chapter Six examined several key challenges to achieving Buen Vivir. These challenges referred principally to the implementation of the principles at the local level (Vivir Bien), and included education for Buen Vivir, changing behaviours, beliefs, and attitudes; but they also included more political challenges such as participation and the extractivist economy.

As a viable and practical alternative, Buen Vivir will require a transformation of both society and politics and a swift move towards a post-extractive society, a more sustainable and inclusive one. This last challenge is the most important because ultimately extractivism and Buen Vivir are wholly incompatible because of the social, environmental, and economic impacts. Hence, this was the focus of this chapter.

I started the analysis with a look at the experience of extractivism in Cotacachi. Cotacachi Canton resides in an area with a high degree of biodiversity and endemism of plant and animal species. This natural environment is highly valued, and many communities fear their environment and their values are threatened by the push for extractivism in the name of development and economic growth. These communities also hold the philosophy of Buen Vivir in high esteem.

The Correa government had opted for an extractivist position for achieving Buen Vivir, albeit under a neoextractive model. The neoextractive model claims that extractivism, if managed by the state, can have benefits that can help achieve Buen Vivir in the long run. At the national level, extractivism is argued to create greater wellbeing. However, it ignores the negative social and environmental impacts that large-scale extractivism has proven to have on communities and the environment. This creates a false dichotomy and is problematic for a concept like Buen Vivir, which considers the wellbeing of both the environment and society with equal importance. My research found that this contradiction was at the root of tensions between the government and communities, who originally believed the good intentions of Buen Vivir policy.

In that respect, I examined how the conceptions of environment and nature have different meanings to the key informants than they do in Western society, which is crucial for their particular perspective on natural resource use. The wellbeing of society and that of the environment are integral to one another. One cannot exist without the other. That said, the use of natural resources is necessary, but the scale and way in which we extract and use them needs to change. It requires new ways of thinking and doing based on fundamental needs, rather than desires to move towards transformation and away from the status quo. This analysis helped better understand the impacts and perceived impacts of extractivism on the community's Socio-Eco Wellbeing.

This chapter cemented the fact that a policy of extractivism is incompatible with Buen Vivir – therefore we must move towards a post-extractive society. The opposition to extractivism in Cotacachi has led to local government support for economic alternatives in a bid for post-extractivism. Local government here has been heeding change in more horizontal processes, generating transformation from the people. Ultimately, these changes also require genuine national government support which may be more likely obtained if the political implications of Buen Vivir can be demonstrated.

While Chapters Four to Six were primarily concerned with the practical implications of Buen Vivir, Chapter Seven examined the political implications of Buen Vivir in an era of global Sustainable Development action. In particular, I discussed how an implementation of the principles of Buen Vivir might allow governments to position themselves for their global political responsibilities, specifically in addressing the SDGs.

The reasons for comparing Buen Vivir to the SDGs and not to any of the more nuanced contested definitions of Sustainable Development is because the literature identified Buen Vivir as an alternative to neoliberal development – Sustainable Development's parent concept. I further argue that Buen Vivir is an alternative to Sustainable Development because of its biocentricity, which has the possibility to achieve a greater state of holistic Socio-Eco Wellbeing.

The SDGs are the manifestation of global action for the mainstream neoliberal conception of Sustainable Development. Neoliberal Sustainable Development takes into account environmental factors but remains nonetheless within the realms of neoliberalism. Therefore, any alternative to development with an environmental focus would have to be contrasted against neoliberal Sustainable Development and its gaps. The contextuality of Buen Vivir maintains it as an alternative that can fill the gaps of a failed one-size-fits-all Sustainable Development approach.

The argument against the SDGs is that they seek to reinforce the status quo, rather than promising transformative change. There is, therefore, a real risk that they will fail to achieve sustainability and social wellbeing unless an alternative approach is taken. And given the constant re-evaluation of Sustainable Development and the re-emphasised urgency of the environmental situation, is it wise to continue with the status quo? The global uptake of the SDGs does not mean giving up on alternative avenues for achieving sustainability and wellbeing. Never has the motto "think globally, act locally" been more prevalent than now when thinking about how we can achieve ecological sustainability and wellbeing now and in the long-term.

Both Buen Vivir and Sustainable Development share the same fundamental aims: Guaranteeing social wellbeing and ensuring the intergenerational sustainability of the earth's environment, albeit with vital differences in the processes by which to achieve those aims. One major difference is that mainstream neo-liberal Sustainable Development is universal (yet contested) in how it aims to bring all societies in line with its Eurocentric, modern idea of progress. It is based on the traditional model of development, a "single model... which does not account for cultural diversity and refuses to recognise Mother Earth as a subject of rights" (Samaniego 2012; Vanhulst & Beling 2014). In contrast, Buen Vivir leaves it to the communities themselves to decide what Buen Vivir means to them. Nonetheless, there is one major similarity between Sustainable Development and Buen Vivir, which is that they are both contested concepts – they both mean different things to different people. Translating that into the broad-based universal SDGs, it is a weakness because it has rendered them too ambitious and ambiguous at the same time; however, for a grassroots concept, Buen Vivir's strength lies in its contextuality. Yet local communities do not exist in isolation.

The key for guarding this strength therefore and understanding how Buen Vivir cooperates with a global framework is by looking at local implementation of the principles and seeing how it dialogues with SDGs; not by managing the implementation of the SDGs locally by co-opting Buen Vivir and trying to retrofit its principles to the SDG targets. In other words, bottom-up, not top-down.

On the matter of grassroots change, in Chapter Eight I then examined how Buen Vivir might be implemented at the community level to honour the ethos of endogenous change. I discussed the issue of measurement and found that key informants agree that there is scope for the measurement of Buen Vivir, but that it should be community-driven and focussed on qualitative living indicators that allow for contextuality. To that end, Chapter Eight concludes Part II with a proposed framework which addresses the key informants' concerns for measurement – meaning that living indicators are defined by the community itself based on the principles of Buen Vivir, and implemented through a stoplight framework. This allows for communities to define what Buen Vivir means to them, identifying their own fundamental needs and ways in which these might be satisfied without relegating them to a linear model for "progress." This way of measuring Buen Vivir allows both governments and local communities to visualise where change must be made to meet the community's fundamental needs and fulfil the principles of Buen Vivir.

Ultimately, approaching the implementation in this way would allow a cooperative and plural relationship with government and organisations, whereby governments act as facilitators and organisations act as mediators, while allowing for communities to "take the reins" of their own alternative to development. It also helps address the earlier-mentioned concerns of post-development critique, providing a concrete practical plural pathway to transformative change. Embracing Buen Vivir's plurality and contextuality, this pathway can be pursued in any community, regardless of geographic, size, cultural, or linguistic context.

Applying and implementing Buen Vivir beyond Latin America

While I have reiterated throughout this book that Buen Vivir is contextual and thus can be applied in different community settings, before concluding it is imperative to summarise the most pertinent aspects of Buen Vivir that demonstrate its ability to be applied outside of the Latin American context from which it is derived.

In the introduction, I outlined the definition of community that is most operable for applying Buen Vivir in a cohesive context. With regard to institutions, the most appropriate level of governance is local. Local government in different countries looks different. For example, in Australia the most local level of governance is local councils; in Ecuador, this is the parish government, then the municipality. The idea is that local governments drive the local policy changes that allow the necessary spaces and structures for community-led change.

One of the areas this can work well is in promoting an SSE, which includes cooperatives, social enterprises, or businesses with a social purpose; fair trade, ethical agri-economy, small-scale and rural enterprises; and microcredit institutions. An SSE can change the way we view economics in our daily lives by creating economic opportunities built around "solidarity, reciprocity, and cooperative relations" (Giovannini 2014). As opposed to a capitalist free-market economy driven by individual wealth and competition, an SSE is participatory and inclusive, and works towards the collaborative and communal wellbeing of a community, whereby a community's needs are central.

The COVID-19 crisis has created a "new societal normal" across the globe, built on the principles of respect, reciprocity, and solidarity, of which SSE have played a key role. The pandemic has led society and governments to question whether we want to return to the "old normal" of increasing social inequalities and ecological destruction. There is a growing justification as to why we should not and must not. SSE initiatives are key in times of crisis (*Cooperatives and wider sse enterprises respond to covid-19 disruptions, and government measures are being put in place* 2020), as has been demonstrated during the COVID-19 pandemic with mandatory shutdowns of non-essential businesses and work environments altered indefinitely. With climate change already having intense social and environmental impacts around the world, there will be many more crises to come in the future. What these will look like we do not yet know, but ensuring our communities are strong, capable, and harmonious will help dampen the impacts from future crises, be they related to health, climate, or economics.

During COVID-19, the International Labour Organization found that SSE initiatives were increasing workplace safety and worker protection, protecting food security by small-holder farmers' production, innovating and ensuring access to information, and providing support for community members and the most vulnerable.

In terms of how governments can help provide the structures necessary for Buen Vivir to flourish, support for an SSE can help communities in any geographical, cultural, or linguistic context to start moving towards transformation for Socio-Eco Wellbeing. Faced with the challenges of COVID-19, local and national governments are already starting to integrate SSE into emergency responses (*Cooperatives and wider sse enterprises respond to covid-19 disruptions, and government measures are being put in place* 2020), and there is logical benefit in extending their reach and power into the economic recovery period and beyond, to start to change the economic face of society, albeit plurally and cooperatively.

SSE initiatives can also help ensure that the real needs of local communities aligned with Buen Vivir are addressed, rather than perceived needs pertaining to neoliberal development standards. Satisfying needs by communities and for communities is a vital factor in attaining Socio-Eco Wellbeing. Not least, scaling back consumption to local communities as much as possible through an SSE is undeniably more environmentally sustainable, as is being more socially sustainable by supporting local businesses.

With a renewed focus on communal wellbeing and solidarity post-COVID-19, culture and community are regaining importance. All communities, regardless of their context, manifest a culture specific to that place and the people within it. It is important to maintain this and sustain a thread of community identity in individuals, and thus a loyalty to that community. Culture and community are vital in helping foster education for a healthy environment and citizen responsibility and in investing in care of that environment and the overall wellbeing of the community. This is relevant to any community interested in the wellbeing of its citizens; and again, it comes back to those intangible needs of communities and goes beyond a basic needs approach.

Buen Vivir is community-led, but because of the need to cooperate with all key actors, an organisation can act as an interlocutor between local governments and communities, and local governments can ensure that local needs are addressed through a participatory democracy. Under a Buen Vivir approach, communities' needs are included in local development planning by implementing a participatory budgeting process that involves community members in development policies or projects that are collectively shared and approved by communities. With shared control, communities become empowered to increase their capabilities, along with enhancing their rights and responsibilities (Ondrik n.d.), building stronger communities. With over 3,000 cities now practising participatory budgeting globally (*What is pb?*), it provides a promising way forward for local governments to look at how Buen Vivir can be implemented within their communities.

When it comes to governments' global commitments to sustainability, table 7.1 in Chapter Seven demonstrates ways in which the principles can cooperate with the SDGs. It helps to view change at the local level plurally with the first three guiding principles for the SDGs, namely the need to re-embed markets that work for society and the environment rather than the other way around; to reverse the normative hierarchy and prioritise social and environmental needs above all else; and to promote and enable full democratic participation of the people through inclusive political processes such as a participatory budget (among others).

Reflecting on ways Buen Vivir can be applied in any community regardless of context, I reiterate some of the ways that communities can draw on practices through Vivir Bien to promote the principles outlined in Chapter Eight, including (but by no means limited to):

- Adopting a reciprocal approach to our relationship with nature;
- Public participation and enabling decision-making in a manner that honours that reciprocity;
- Fostering solidarity and harmony through an environment of community;
- Ensuring equity in participation in public decision-making;
- Manifesting a responsibility to participate in decision-making;
- Educating future generations on the principles of Buen Vivir;
- Participating in economic life;
- Understanding their fundamental rights and responsibilities, including those of the environment;
- Exercising and upholding those rights;
- Promoting and protecting cultural values and practices;
- Valuing the role of health in a community.

Conclusion

As an alternative to Sustainable Development, Buen Vivir can help move from status quo to transformation through a bottom-up yet plural approach, which aims to shift the focus from growth for development to Socio-Eco Wellbeing. Valuing the wellbeing of society as equally as that of our environment while reinforcing the importance of biocentrity, it promises to lead us to a more ecologically sustainable and socially just world – towards new horizons for Socio-Eco Wellbeing.

It is in the combination of bottom-up change, contextualisation, and biocentrism that can possibly help us to concretely achieve Buen Vivir through its principles. That said, envisaging Buen Vivir as an alternative to Sustainable Development does not necessarily render it as an offense, or an outright attack, on the current model. Nor does it mean watering it down to become another development alternative.

Buen Vivir as a plural concept and tool for community-led change can be implemented from within the current economic development system leading the status quo on the path to transformation, provided that the structural and political processes are in place to do so. This way of approaching Buen Vivir is important to avoid the co-optation and outright refusal by the power structures, and represents an alternative that could ultimately lead to long-term change, rather than short-term rhetoric. As Escobar argues, this change towards transformation may require moving away from development sciences in particular and a partial, strategic move away from conventional Western modes of knowing in general to make room for other types of knowledge and experience. This transformation demands not only a change in ideas and statements but the formation of nuclei around which new forms of power and knowledge might converge.

(Escobar 1995)

It also requires surmounting certain challenges – particularly extractivism - that block the ability to both achieve the utopian Buen Vivir and implement it in daily practice. Entirely overcoming these challenges, however, requires both the transformation of society and politics. In the meantime, by communities taking a Vivir Bien approach, we are not "waiting for the world to change" to start acting practically on sustainability and wellbeing issues, nor are we assigning great universal, aspirational goals which are destined for failure, but we are enacting change from the people and scaling it up through participation to allow for the momentum to follow.

Grassroots change has profound policy implications, but coming full circle, policy also has the responsibility to allow for that change to happen. As Mander and Goldsmith (2014), assert:

Long-term solutions to today's social and environmental problems require a range of small, local initiatives that are as diverse as the cultures and environments in which they take place… Most importantly, rather than thinking in terms of isolated, scattered efforts, it is helpful to think of institutions that will promote small scale on a large scale.

Pursuing the principles of Buen Vivir at the community level as Vivir Bien allows us to guard the authenticity of Buen Vivir as an endogenous process. It allows for people to take charge of the processes and vie for a world in which their Socio-Eco Wellbeing is safeguarded. And examining these principles against the SDGs allows us to understand how practical, local-level change fits into a global agenda for sustainability and wellbeing, without generalising Buen Vivir and losing its contextualisation. As Howarth (2012) argued, "A sustainable future will emerge if we build institutions that, on a practical level, sustain the natural environment and the social and technological conditions that will empower future generations to define and pursue their own conception of the good life."

It is a two-speed hybrid practical–policy approach incorporating the above-mentioned roles of the different key actors, but one whereby a community can implement it for itself while aiming for change through Vivir Bien, or the daily practice of Buen Vivir principles (addressing the role responsibilities of communities). The boundaries of power and knowledge will have shifted if this is a genuine process. Moreover, the scaling up of Buen Vivir from practice to policy places governments in a position to satisfy their global commitments to sustainability, albeit with a local agenda.

Approaching Buen Vivir in this way does not automatically halt dominant development thinking and practice, but it alters the hegemonic nature of the system "so that the range of existing social experiences that are considered valid and credible alternatives to what exist is significantly enlarged" (Escobar 2010). In that sense, it prioritises the local over the global, the particular over the universal, and the communal over the individual. At the same time, it embraces others' knowledge and experience, rather than refuting it or hierarchising it. It refocuses the debate towards biocentrism over anthropocentricism and focuses on fundamental needs over consumerist desires.

A biocentric approach helps reduces the level of consumption, consumerism, and consequently natural resource use whereby alternative economic models are called for. Under Buen Vivir, alternatives are part of an SSE which limits levels of consumption and encourages a sense of reciprocity with the environment. Sustainable degrowth or "A-growth" becomes an outcome (but not the aim) of a Buen Vivir approach, which would see the more damaging sectors of the economy decline and replaced with smaller, more sustainable local economic alternatives.

Ultimately, for Buen Vivir to become a viable alternative to Sustainable Development, the following conditions will need to be met:

- A transition towards a post-extractive economy: This involves immediate action from both governments and communities;
- Implementation being achieved plurally from the ground up in a participatory democracy: In other words, community-driven change facilitated by governments and mediated by organisations;
- Attitudes, behaviours, and policies reflecting a biocentric approach to wellbeing: This approach aims for Socio-Eco Wellbeing over the primacy of human wellbeing in the satisfaction fundamental needs.

In sum, Buen Vivir is not just a political project, or one applied exogenously by development professionals at the coalface. It is a project for civilisational change with a plural agenda, whereby practice at the community level drives the political agenda and cooperation is required. It is an endogenously led change, which requires a hybrid two-way approach between community and government in a post-extractive economy, to achieve social and environmental wellbeing for current and future generations. In other words, its practical application can help achieve the transformation required through enacting change at the level of the people and scaling it up whilst governments provide the structures and spaces to do so, including a genuine move toward post-extractivism. Approaching it in this manner makes it more operational and practical than a utopian policy idea, and in that way change and transformation is not only possible but within easy reach.

Transformation away from the status quo of development is required by all levels of society. The transformation towards new horizons for the Good Life and Living Well, away from prioritising societal needs with nature as a commodity, and the individual over the collective

May be a slow process, but it may also happen with relative rapidity... The dialectic [in the West] tends to push for another round of solutions. Even if conceived through more radical categories – cultural, ecological political, economic, and so on. This will not do. The empty defence of development must be left to the bureaucrats of development and those who support it... it is up to us, however, to make sure that the life span of the bureaucrats and the experts as producers and enforcers of costly gestures is limited.

(Escobar 1995)

In the pursuit of transformation for Socio-Eco Wellbeing, it is therefore no longer appropriate or desirable to follow the anthropocentric growth-centred path of neo-liberal Sustainable Development. Buen Vivir can lead us to the transformation our society and environment needs. Along the lines of Sachs (2009): "The time is right to write [sustainable] development's obituary." Let us do so with both people and planet equally in mind.

References

Acosta, A 2013, 'Extractivism and neoextractivism: Two sides of the same coin', in M. Lang & D. Mokrani (eds.), *Beyond development: Alternative visions from latin America*, Fundacion Rosa Lumxemburg, Quito, Ecuador.

Cooperatives and wider sse enterprises respond to covid-19 disruptions, and government measures are being put in place, 2020, ILO, viewed 5 May, <https://www.ilo.org/globa l/topics/cooperatives/news/WCMS_740254/lang--en/index.htm>.

Escobar, A 1995, *Encountering development: The making and unmaking of the third world (new in paper)*, Princeton University Press, Princeton, NJ.

Escobar, A 2010, 'Latin America at a crossroads', *Cultural Studies*, vol. 24, no. 1, pp. 1–65. doi: 10.1080/09502380903424208.

Giovannini, M 2014, 'Indigenous community enterprises in chiapas: A vehicle for buen vivir?', *Community Development Journal*, vol. Advanced access, pp. 1–17. doi: 10.1093/cdj/bsu019.

Howarth, RB 2012, 'Sustainability, well-being, and economic growth', *Journal Center for Humans & Nature*, vol. 5, no. 2. pp. 32–9.

Mander, J & Goldsmith, E, eds, 2014, *The case against the global economy. [electronic resource]: And for a turn towards localization*, Routledge, London. doi: 10.4324/9781315071787.

Max-Neef, MA, Elizalde, A & Hopenhayn, M 1991, *Human scale development: Conception, application and further reflections*, Apex Press, New York.

Max-Neef, MA, Elizalde, A & Hopenhayn, M 1994, *Desarrollo a escala humana: Conceptos, aplicaciones y algunas reflexiones*, Icaria Editorial, Barcelona.

Ondrik, RS n.d., *Participatory approaches to national development planning*, Asian Development Bank, Manila, <http://siteresources.worldbank.org/INTEASTASIAPACI FIC/Resources/226262-1143156545724/Brief_ADB.pdf>.

Sachs, W 2009, *The development dictionary*, 2nd new ed., Zed Books, London.

Samaniego, J 2012, '*La sostenibilidad del desarrollo a 20 años de la cumbre para la tierra: Avances, brechas y lineamientos estratégicos para américa latina y el caribe* CEPAL, Santiago.

Vanhulst, J & Beling, AE 2014, 'Buen vivir: Emergent discourse within or beyond sustainable development?', *Ecological Economics*, vol. 101, pp. 54–63. doi: 10.1016/j. ecolecon.2014.02.017.

What is pb? 2019?, Participatory Budgeting Project, viewed 5 May 2020, <https://www .participatorybudgeting.org/what-is-pb/>.

Index

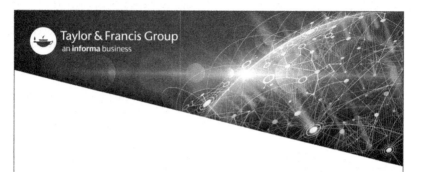

Taylor & Francis eBooks

www.taylorfrancis.com

A single destination for eBooks from Taylor & Francis
with increased functionality and an improved user
experience to meet the needs of our customers.

90,000+ eBooks of award-winning academic content in
Humanities, Social Science, Science, Technology, Engineering,
and Medical written by a global network of editors and authors.

TAYLOR & FRANCIS EBOOKS OFFERS:

A streamlined
experience for
our library
customers

A single point
of discovery
for all of our
eBook content

Improved
search and
discovery of
content at both
book and
chapter level

REQUEST A FREE TRIAL
support@taylorfrancis.com

Printed in the United States
By Bookmasters